The Blind Chick

AUTOBIOGRAPHY BY
SUE-ELLEN LOVETT

CONTENTS

OTHER GREAT ADVENTURES BY SUE-ELLEN LOVETT

Johno & The Blind Chick – Walk in My Shoes

The Blind Chick – Vision is Much More than Seeing
(Autobiography)

Guide Dog Woody, Lola & The Blind Chick – One Step at a Time

Documentary on Sue-Ellen Lovett
– Overcoming Adversity & Moving Forward

*

Stay up to date with Sue-Ellen's adventures via her Facebook:
www.facebook.com/SueEllen.Lovett

*

DEDICATION

I dedicate this book to a
beautiful friend of mine
who is at the moment
fighting for her life.

We have been friends
for many years. We may
speak once a year, we
can speak twice a year.
But we're always best
mates. She has always
been in my corner
looking out for me.

We are all in your corner
beautiful Katie Classon,
praying for your speedy
recovery.

Mudgee, Guide Dog Tara & I

Katie you have more strength and determination than anybody
I know. You rock beautiful lady. Thank you for the love, the joy
and the beauty you bring to my life. You make me smile every
time I think of you.

I love you, always.
Sue-Ellen

*

TRIBUTE FROM A DEAR FRIEND

Sue-Ellen
For Sue my hero, by Bob Cooper

She lives in constant shadows, the darkness of the night,
But strength is her companion in the ever-fading light,
Sue may be blind to others, she is not blind to me,
For I have found her secret, that my friend Sue can see.
Though eyesight may elude her, I have known it from the start,
She doesn't need the eyesight, for Sue sees with her heart.
Her sense of hearing , smell, and touch,
are sharpened by her plight,
Her kind deeds and compassion have kept her from the night.
And no complaints are offered, affliction is her shield,
A knight in shining armour, upon life's battlefield.
We loose our way, we rarely hear the song bird in the tree,
And often we blunder through life with things we will not see.
Her great love for her animals , her courage through each trial,
Her great determination, still leaves me with a smile,
I know that others call her blind, it matters not to me,
For I have found her secret, that my friend Sue can see.

*

THE HORSE

by Sue-Ellen Lovett

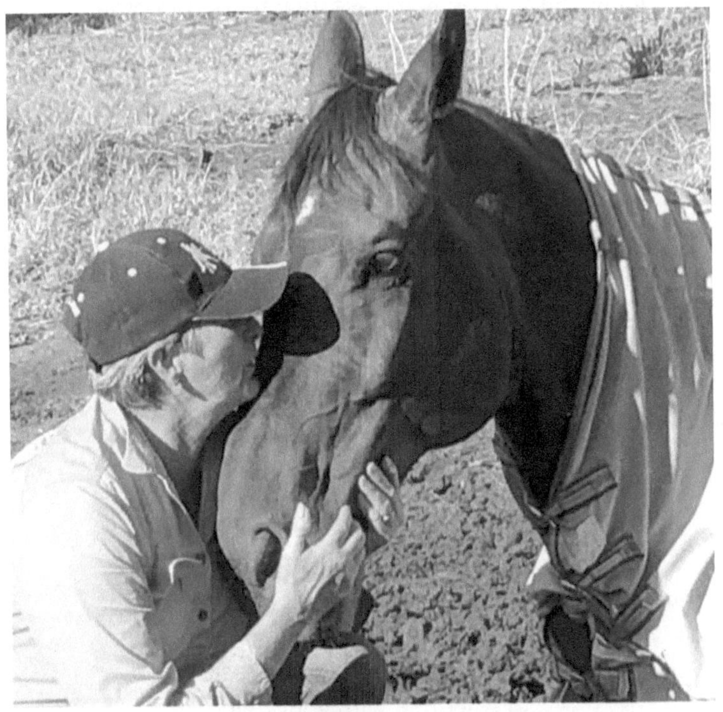

Johno & I

You bring Grace, you bring Beauty.
You bring Love, you bring Assurance.
You love unconditionally, without judgement.

Through your eyes life is Simple, Beautiful,
Uncomplicated and oh so Special.

If we could only see through your eyes,

Accept people for who they are and what they are.

All they need to do is look into your eyes,

For the reflection of themselves.

You bring Unconditional Love and Attainable Dreams.

All we have to do is believe, reach out and dream.

With you the dreams come true.

There are lessons to be learned from you
my beautiful friend, my horse.

Learning not to judge, accepting people for
who they are and what they are,

Bringing us back to life, to love unconditionally.

The unconditional love you bring to my life
allows me to Grow and to Believe.

To use my wings and fly, instead of winging it.

So I can soar in the clouds.

I will listen, I will learn to be present and
I will grow with your help.

I will not listen to the outside influences
that don't know how to listen.

I will learn and do the work, so we can grow and be as one.

I will learn to trust you as you trust me.

I will learn to trust myself.

I will learn to ask and not tell.

I will learn to be present, to listen, to feel
the love and not to question.

Thank you, my beautiful horse, for bringing
unconditional love, trust, and belief to my life.

With your guidance I will endeavour to
be the best person I can be.

Together we shall work on moving forward,
one beautiful step at a time.

Thank you, my beautiful friend, my horse.

*

PREFACE

If you had told me that the person who'd be able to teach me to see, to listen, to enrich my day-to-day life with a joy, a laughter, and an ability to celebrate life, even the suckiest moments, was a Blind Chick... I'd never have believed you.

In the golden chain of friendship, Consider me a link.

P. Yorwood, Dec 1925

I recently discovered these words in an autograph book. That book was nearly 100 years old.

Instantly I knew.

I read these ten simple words again, and again. 'Simple' – no! These words captured the magic and solid gold link that I feel with Sue-Ellen. Our friendship is indeed golden.

To many she may be the almost surreal human that although totally blind and a cancer survivor, raised $3.2 million while sitting on her bum! Who does that?

And if that's not enough, she's in her 60's and still rides her horse at an elite level one day, and bareback the next! Who does that?

Maybe it's because she can't see her own reflection in the mirror, that she hasn't realised... she's not a kid anymore! Kick any talk of wrinkles, fillers and Botox to the curb, this Chick is real!

Sue-Ellen has a rare warmth and an openness that rides alongside incredible courage and a vulnerability that's almost childlike. It would be easier for her to hide away. But no! She continues to push herself to improve, to chase down goals and to face the Itty-Bitty-Shitty Committee in her head that attempts to plunge her confidence in the wrong direction.

Sue-Ellen is NOT like everyone else.

She is a rare gem in this world. She lives in total darkness yet the light she shines on so many lives, every day, is beyond measure. Her eyesight may elude her, but she sees with her heart.

I had NEVER EVER met anyone like her.

Her ability to INSPIRE is off the charts incredible.

Sue-Ellen has changed lives and will continue to do so until the day she dies.

It's who she is, it's in her DNA.

When a Blind Chick tells you to get off your bum and make things happen, and she's got a list of achievements that make even the most enthusiastic Award collector gag, people listen!

Come join me in these pages. You'll soon discover her magic like I and thousands of others have. Without even realising it Sue-Ellen will get into your heart. She'll challenge you, she'll inspire you, she'll support you.

Let her show you what being a link in a golden chain of friendship really means.

WARNING! You'll never be the same again!
WARNING! Don't expect it all to be sunshine and roses.

This Chick is real.

"Vision is much more than seeing" – I now know this to be true. THANK YOU Sue-Ellen.

Jacqueline Thompson
(NSW, Australia)

P.S. It was only when I started looking at all Sue-Ellen's achievements that I got to realise the generosity and magnitude of her 40+ years spent helping others.

This amazing woman is to humble to include such a list in this book. But I couldn't wait to share with you a small snapshot of highlights of her life so far.

And she's not done yet!

Perhaps you'll be lucky enough to join her on her next adventure?

Australian of Year Nomination 1991: Paul Keating, John Newcomb & Sue-Ellen. Sue-Ellen receiving the Australian Achievers Medal

Degree of Difficulty of the Achievement and Sacrifices Made

Sue-Ellen is TOTALLY blind. She doesn't even have shades of black.

- EVERY day Sue-Ellen gets lost trying to navigate around her own back yard
- EVERY day Sue-Ellen gets zapped by one of the properties electric fences
- EVERY day Sue-Ellen walks into something ouch; a wall, a tree, a table, a bucket, a snake!
- EVERY day this amazing person gets out of bed, gives generously to others and changes peoples and companies lives and financial positions with her determination and commitment to Make A Difference and Be A Positive Role Model.

Funds Raised
$3.2 million for various charities raised by doing 10 long-distance horse rides.

Years of Service
40 years of FREE Service. None of Sue-Ellen's four decades of service in Australia have ever been paid for.

Reach

950+	**number of speaking engagements** delivered (fundraising, inspiration, life lessons, showing ability not disability, overcoming adversity, If its going to be – its up to me.
50,000+	**number of people reached via speaking engagements** * Largest speaking gig was at the Melbourne Cricket Ground to a packed crowd, 22,000 in attendance. She was riding her best horse mate Mudgee while presenting!
650+	**number of towns/cities/hamlets** presented to
Thousands	**International and National audience** – Johno & The Blind Chick Facebook Influencer

Magic Moments
- The only totally blind equestrian to ride at Grand Prix level - in the world.
- Representing Australia in the Paralympics – Atlanta (1996) & Sydney (2000)
- Represented Australia at the World Equestrian Games in Denmark (1999) – Bronze Medallist
- Ranked 4th in the world in Dressage at the World Equestrian Games
- Ranked in the Top 10% of Elite Dressage Riders in Australia
- Australian of the Year Finalist (1991)
- Won Young Citizen of the Year Award – Mudgee, twice
- Australian Sport Medal - endorsed by the Queen

- Author of 3 books (2020, 2021, 2022), being sold internationally, 4th in the pipeline
- Competed solely in able bodied competitions since 2000.
- Wife of 20+ years
- Cancer Survivor
- Documentary on her life – due out in 2023

*

INTRODUCTION

Welcome, thank you for choosing my book to read.

I hope you find it enlightening and entertaining in some way, shape or form.

I hope this book encourages you to live your life to the fullest and realise you are never alone.

Sometimes life is crap, it's hard, it's difficult.

But we always have choices with how we deal with these curveballs.

I have tried always to see the positive, even in the darkness.

Happiness is a choice.

Being brave and asking for help is a tough gig for anyone.

But what I want you to feel when you join with me in these pages is, if there isn't a light at the end of the tunnel you can, take my hand and we will walk down and light the bloody thing ourselves.

Together we can make your dreams come true.

You are never alone.

The bravest thing you can ever do is ask for help.

Dare to dream big and endeavour to do something nice for someone else each day. Whether it is a smile or the words "Good morning," it really is that easy to make someone else's day.

This book is fun. It is full of love. I have been privileged to have been touched by so many beautiful people and this is only a small part of my journey. I'm not done yet!

Thank you to all the wonderful people who have believed in my dreams and helped my dreams come true.

WARNING – buckle up! I use real language to describe real life events. I'm sorry, I'm not always politically correct. Welcome to the Real Me.

Sue-Ellen Lovett

*

QUESTIONS MOST PEOPLE AREN'T GAME TO ASK! PT 1

"Happiness is a Choice"
Sue-Ellen Lovett

It's interesting! I've been doing speaking gigs for years and people always have questions but there are many questions people aren't game to ask. So, I thought I'd shed some light on some of those questions you are too afraid to ask or that I've heard murmured in corridors and behind my back.

I hope by sharing these answers with you it helps put a lid on many misconceptions and inaccurate assumptions.

DO YOU KNOW WHAT YOUR HUSBAND MATTHEW LOOKS LIKE?

No!

But we fall in love with what's inside someone, not what they look like.

I met my lovely husband Matthew through my coach Judy Cubitt. I'd gone to Dubbo to train in preparation for hopefully qualifying for the Sydney Paralympic games. We stayed at Matthew's Mum and Dad's property and Matthew was there. I'll touch on what happened next in the book.

WHAT IS ONE OF YOUR MOST EMBARRASSING MOMENTS?

Wow this one is an easy one. I was not just embarrassed, I was mortified.

It was amongst people that I knew. I was doing a speaking engagement for Riding For The Disabled Mudgee New South Wales in my hometown of Mudgee. I was up on stage presenting, I'd been on stage for probably half an hour when I heard a lone giggle, then more giggles!

Then out of the blue a long time friend of mine, Huey Bateman, said to somebody "would someone please go and turn her around so she is facing the crowd, this is really bad and embarrassing for all."

Someone quietly came up to the stage and touched my arm and turned me to face the crowd then explained to me how I'd been standing with my side to the audience that whole time, talking to a wall! I was horrified, I was embarrassed. I don't think I'd ever felt so gutted in my entire life, that someone would let me stand and speak to a wall. Oh my lord, I'd never been so humiliated. But as you do, I made out there was a funny side to it and got on with finishing my presentation. But it wasn't funny, it was humiliating. I had a major meltdown afterwards at the magnitude of the embarrassment. Now every time I do a presentation I hold onto a lectern, and I make sure I'm facing the crowd. I don't ever want to experience that level of embarrassment again.

AREN'T YOU TERRIFIED WHEN YOU RIDE A HORSE, AND YOU CAN'T SEE?

NO – people forget what it's like to be a kid. I'm still connected to that inner child. (I still love my pony.)

COULD YOU IMAGINE YOUR LIFE WITHOUT A HORSE?

That is a definite no! I could never imagine my life without a horse. I could never imagine my life without animals in it. They bring pure magic and love to my life. The horse has two beautiful brown eyes that make up for my eyes that don't see (by the way, my eyes are hazel.)

So definitely, I could not imagine my life without my beautiful horse. The joy I get just going down and feeding my horse, brushing her, spending time with her, going for a walk. It's a simple thing, life for me without a horse is not a life. They bring pure magic to my life, every day. They make my dreams come true. They make it all worthwhile.

HOW MANY GUIDE DOGS HAVE YOU HAD AND WHY DO YOU RETIRE THEM?

Well sometimes you don't have a choice about when you retire your Guide Dog.

My first beautiful Guide Dog was Donna, she was a German Shepherd who died from pancreatic cancer. The rest of my Guide Dogs retired because they got to a stage where they were possibly incontinent, getting a little bit slow and/or a little bit arthritic. You generally get seven maybe eight years, if you're really lucky nine years out of a Guide Dog. My last Guide Dog Armani I retired early because I thought I didn't need a Guide Dog anymore. I wasn't using her at home and I was worried about her being bitten by a snake. But after the last two years without one, I've realised I definitely need a Guide Dog. Bring it on!

Is your Guide Dog also your pet?

No. Absolutely not!

My Guide Dog is my work tool. I give them praise for doing the right thing, I don't have it sitting on my lap or shower it with love to bits, they are very very much a Guide Dog. They have a job to do and to support them doing their job I am very strict about people not interfering with my Guide Dog. Please don't pat the Guide Dog, please don't feed the dog, otherwise the Blind Chick bites, ha ha.

Why do you wear dark glasses if you can't see?

Often when I am doing a presentation, I wear my dark glasses. Sometimes I take them off halfway through, to prove a point.

I think perhaps I hide behind the glasses sometimes. Why? Because my eyes look normal! My retina is the thing that's died, that makes me not see, so if people see my eyes oh my heavens, the first thing they say is "oh she can see! She can see more than she says." I found it very hard in the early stages of going blind to cope with this.

I also wear dark glasses when I'm outside to stop the pain. My left eye is totally black but my right eye is totally white with fog. So if the sun gets on my right eye the pain I get from the glare is enormous, it makes me nauseous ... it's that bad. Hence the dark glasses outside.

Do you ever feel like you're inconveniencing people?

Absolutely! On a daily basis.

There are so many things I can't do. Like something as simple as knowing what's inside a can that I've taken from the pantry; is it cat food, is it dog food, is it pumpkin soup or chicken soup. It's the little things that have to be done on a daily basis like "can you please tell me how many calories are in this" that might annoy people (a lot!). When you live this constant enquiry about simple things day in, day out, I'm sure it gets wearing. But I try to be as independent as I can.

I now have some apps on my phone that read labels to me, so I'm a little more independent.

IS IT HARD ASKING FOR HELP?

I can ask for help for someone else, every hour of the day, if that asking makes a difference to their life, but I truly struggle asking for help myself.

Yes, I feel compromised. It is a really hard one for me to get my head around. I try to be as independent and capable as I can, but sometimes you really do have to be brave and just ask for help.

DO YOU EVER FEEL USED?

Wow, wow and wow! This is a confronting question.

Yes, I find it hard to ask for help.

Having the NDIS has made the world of difference because I can now afford to pay someone to help me. Previously I would often find myself in a situation where I was unable to do things for myself and while people would offer to help, they'd done so because it was cool to help the blind girl, "I'm doing something for the blind girl," "I'm taking the blind girl here."

That often made me feel funny in the tummy, but someone helping you is still someone helping you and I was very grateful. Hence, I've often felt like I was the novelty friend. And invariably, that novelty soon wears off.

*

LET THE FAIRY TALE BEGIN

"Life is good. Life is happy. Life is joy.
Life is pure magic."
Sue-Ellen Lovett

Mum (Mary) & Dad (John)
on their Wedding Day

Mum's Debutante Ball

Born May 1st, 1933.

I'm sure she was born in a manger far, far away.

Her Mum and Dad were Tom and Ivy Welch hard-working God-fearing people who'd travelled all through New South Wales doing shearing, cooking for the shearers, trapping and whatever job needed to be done. Poppy was there doing the harder work while Nanna generally did the cooking for the masses.

They had five children; three boys and two girls. My Mum was one of those get in and do it type kids. She was the one that was up at five in the morning milking the cow, doing whatever needed to be done. Even as a youngster she was never one to sit back and watch everybody else do the work.

She also had a bit of a feisty temper. Mum often tells a story of one day when she was doing the ironing, all the family ironing mind you which sounds like a little bit of a Cinderella story, but her brother Tommy started pestering her and pestering and pestering. So she just quietly put the iron on his back! The iron mind you, had just come off the stove. (Keep in mind this is in the late 30's when irons were heated on the top of a wood stop). Tommy wore the scar of the iron on his back all his life. That certainly taught him not to give my Mum a hard time.

They were definitely not a wealthy family so they all went from farmhouse to farmhouse, wherever Poppy could find work. The cottages they lived in normally had dirt floors.

Mum was an exceptionally good reader and speller. She puts this down to the wallpaper that was on the walls of the cottages they stayed in over the years, they were wallpapered with newspaper. So, every night and every morning when the sun shone through the window, she would lie in bed reading the newspapers. From wall to wall.

My grandparents and family spent a lot of time around Hargraves, Pyramul and Windeyer. Originally these were places in an old gold mining area of central west New South Wales.

Poppy's brother Uncle Ted used to also do some shearing for us. It was very cool and while I do digress, it's an excellent story. Every year from when I could walk, I'd take my little bear, Little Ted, down to Uncle Ted to shear him. This went on for about four or five years and my poor Little Ted by the end of this was quite bald. But Uncle Ted did an excellent job shearing him.

I never ever remember my Poppy and Uncle Ted shearing together. But Mum talks of many years of Poppy shearing and rabbit trapping together with Uncle Ted.

During Mum's teenage years Nana and Pop settled in Mudgee and Poppy built a mud brick house for the family to live in. While this was being built, they lived in a tent. Mum said it was terribly cold in the Mudgee winters. Yet each morning she diligently went out and milked the family cow. I'm not sure why those boys didn't get off their bums and do it, but Mum was one of those girls that just got in and did what needed to be done.

Mum really loved school and I truly think if she was born when I was born, she would've ended up going to university and doing something very special. In my book she is one very clever lady with intelligence laid on. It seems such a waste really. But she did the best with what she could learn.

Where Nana, Poppy and family lived, it backed onto a property called Heaton Lodge owned by the Loneragan family, Mr Tim Loneragan and Kitty Loneragan. Poppy often used to talk with Mr Tim of an afternoon when they were going around checking fences and making sure everything was fine on the farm before it became dark. Often Mr Tim would say to my Pop "we would love Mary to come and work for us and be the Nanny for our children."

This went on for quite a long time until one day Mr Tim really insisted that Poppy ask Mary if she'd be interested in the Nanny job. Keeping in mind, Mum was only 12 or 13 years old at that stage and really worried about other children telling her what to do. He would've picked up by now that my Mum was fairly strong tempered and would not have done well with another child telling her what to do. So Poppy approached my Mum. This is where the fairy tale begins.

Mum worked for the Loneragan family for two years, just going across the paddock and looking after the children. Then one day Kitty Loneragan asked Mum would she like a full-time job looking after the children? What a wonderful but daunting opportunity. She was not sure if she was ready to leave the family home. She was only 14.

Kitty showed my Mum the bedroom that would be hers; it was very spacious with a lovely big double bed covered in beautiful linen, her own bathroom with a bath, and a lovely sunroom.

Kitty suggested my Mum give it a go for a little while, to see how she liked it. Well wow! My Mum totally loved it. The family treated her just like one of their own children. Mum looked after the children when they were home from school and Kitty also organised for Mum to start a TAFE course at the ripe old age of 14. Her first course was dressmaking then she did furniture covering, curtain making and every course imaginable. She even did furniture making. My Mum was very clever and loved learning.

The Loneragan family employed quite a few staff at their Lodge. From gardeners to the guy that looked after the horses, a cook, a couple of maids and then there was my Mum.

Mum loves sitting, listening and learning. She loved all the staff members. She taught all of them to ballroom dance, as Mum also loves dancing.

Wow what a transformation, Mum's going from quite a poor family to living not quite in the lap of luxury, but very comfortably and beautifully looked after. She had everything in front of her to allow her to grow into a beautiful young lady.

Every year the Loneragan family spent at least three months of the year holidaying down at Collaroy in Sydney's northern beaches. During this time Mum continued to go to TAFE and learn.

These times were really special for my Mum, she'd never been to the beach before. The Loneragan's holiday home was right on the beach. You walked out the front door and you were on the beach. Mum said it was incredibly beautiful. She spent many many years there with the Loneragan family. She counts herself very very lucky and very blessed.

She often talks about the time they went down in the 1950's and spent six months at Collaroy. Again, when she was not looking after the children, Mum went to TAFE. Mind you the children were at school a lot, they went away to private boarding schools, but she loved it when they were home. There was always so much love, laughter and joy in the house.

When it got to the age where Mum was old enough to start dating, Kitty was very very strict on when my mother could go out, and who she went out with. One day and I'm not sure how old my Mum was, but probably about 18 years old, a young man asked her out. A young man by the name of John Lovett. Mum had explained to him that she would have to ask Kitty whether she'd be allowed to go to the movies with him.

When Mum asked Kitty, Kitty told Mum definitely not, that Mum knew the rules of no dating during weekdays. As Mum was turning to walk away Kitty asked, "by the way Mary, who has asked you out?" "Johnny Lovett from down the road" replied my Mum.

Kitty's reply surprised my Mum. "Oh well then, let's not make this a common occurrence, but yes, you may go out to the pictures with him." This was the beginning of Mum and Dad starting to date.

When Mum went with the family down to their holiday house in Collaroy, Mr Tim would fly my Dad down to visit with my Mum, then he got Dad to drive a brand-new car back for the car yard. Loneragan's also owned a car yard and a lovely big store in town called .... Loneragan's. Funny that!

They were a totally amazing family. They carried many a farmer through hard times and while farmers waited for their next wool cheque.

In the Loneragan company there were five brothers, all very capable young men. Mr Tim Loneragan was the boss. He was also ex-Air Force. There are many amazing stories about this wonderful man.

Back to my Mum and Dad. They dated for quite a few years and together they did a lot with local groups, like taking the elderly out for picnics. They were very, very community minded.

Time flew by. During these years there are so many other stories I could share with you, enough to make a whole book on their own of my mother's fairy tale.

Mum went to her first official ball when she was 17, she hadn't yet made her debut. Mrs Loneragan had a lovely dress made for her which Mum said was beautiful with lots of lace. I asked Mum if her dance card was full and she said no! She didn't know many people, but she had a lovely time. It was one of the Loneragan balls and she said everybody was so beautiful and elegant.

Mum made her debut when she was 18. She had her dress made by a lovely spinster called Mrs Spees. The dress was full of lace, and she felt very glamorous and grand.

Mum and Dad dated for four years, marrying in 1954.

The wedding was beautiful. Mum was dressed at Heaton Lodge at the Loneragan family home then driven to the church. One thing that made my Mum very sad was that Mr and Mrs Loneragan did not come to the church service, they were devout Catholics and Mum and Dad got married in the Methodist Church. In those days Catholics weren't allowed into a Methodist Church, so the Loneragan's sat outside and watched my Mum walk up the stairs into the Church. They waited outside until Mum and Dad came out. They did go to the wedding breakfast which Mum and Dad loved.

All this time my Dad was also employed by the Loneragan family to deliver groceries or work around the property. He worked for them from the age of about 17 driving the truck out to the outlying farms with the weekly groceries. Often, he had his young sister Jennifer by his side, a little 2 year old full of life and laughter.

When my Mum and Dad married there was a big discussion with Mr and Mrs Loneragan on where they would live, and where my Dad would work. Mr Loneragan offered Dad the job of Kaludabah Property Manager, their property between Mudgee and Gulgong. The latter was the town on the Australian $10 note. This property was actually two properties joined together, the total amounting to 21,000 acres.

My Dad was 24 at this time and really wanted to go and work on Kaludabah but did not want to take the Manager's position. An amazing man called Tony Jensen was the then Manager, Dad did not want to take his job. So, Mr Loneragan put Dad in as the Manager, he and Mum lived in the homestead and Dad worked with Tony as joint Managers until Tony retired.

Another one of the little tid bits which I thought was really quaint was Mrs Loneragan and Mum's regular chats. They were very close. One of the things Mrs Loneragan suggested was that Mum and Dad should be married for five years before they had children, so they could have time together to get to know each other. I was born five years and 10 days after they married. How cool is that!

Mum and Dad's early life at Kaludabah was very busy. Mum often helped Dad on the farm feeding the sheep during the drought or going out mustering. She was quite a handy horse woman. She also spent a lot of time making curtains and flags for a little bit of extra income, she was a very good seamstress.

They also spent a lot of time going out to Yarraman to visit my Nan and Pop who ran the telephone exchange.

When Mum and Dad moved into the homestead at Kaludabah, they moved into only half of the Homestead because it was so massive. It was such a big place, and it was beautiful.

Mum and Dad also used to play cards a lot. With Dad's sister Nancy and her husband Bruce they mainly played a game called Canasta. They played Canasta generally once a week.

The wonderful Tony Jensen was in our lives for many years after he retired, he and Dad were best mates. He was my protector and confidant, but I will tell you more about that later.

Like every young couple Mum and Dad didn't know what their future would bring. They never knew what was just round the corner. They were not to know that my Mum had a degenerative disease called Retinitis Pigmentosa that was going to send her blind.

They certainly didn't know that this disease was hereditary.

*

CURIOSITY

LISTEN WITH CURIOSITY
By Roy T. Bennett

"Listen with curiosity. Speak with honesty.
Act with integrity.

The greatest problem with communication is

we don't listen to understand. We listen to reply.

When we listen with curiosity, we don't listen
with the intent to reply.

We listen for what's behind the words."

*

MY HERO

"Tears fall for a reason - they are your
strength, not your weakness."
Sue-Ellen Lovett

Left to right: Dad's Birthday | Dad & Peter | Dad, Bradley & Daniel | Dad & Mum

For years I've heard people talk of their heroes, which often stars sports people, singers, movie stars and the list goes on. But my hero comes with all these extra things, like being my friend, my confidant, my mate, my Dad, my hero.

From a very, very young age my Dad and I had a special bond. My Mum was very sick and nearly died when she had me, from blood poisoning. So, for the first six months of my life Dad looked after me. Hence our bond was great. We did so much together from way before I can even remember. I went out in the ute with him mustering, I was on the front seat of the ute, dogs in the back seat. From that front seat Dad did the feeding, the nappy changing, all the stuff that goes with being a first-time parent. He was so much more than just a Dad.

Every weekend we would go shooting, gold digging, fishing, or fighting fires. Always together, always doing things as a family. He was also a wonderful stirrer. My heavens! Dad could get you as you jumped in the ute with the electric prod as you slid your bum across a seat. He was always playing practical jokes. If I was out playing skip rope with my sister, Dad would be out there playing skip rope or elastics or seeing who could jump the highest with the rope.

We were so blessed with the fact that Dad and Mum never said, "You can't do that." There were never any excuses why we couldn't try our best at doing something. If we didn't succeed, we were encouraged to try again. That was our attitude and we achieved so much together with this mentality. Whether it was mustering sheep and cattle, having cattle on the road for 10 months, driving 800 head of cattle or just sitting on the riverbank dropping a line to catch a fish for dinner.

My Dad was the Manager of two wonderful properties; Kaludabah and Eugalong, both owned by the Loneragan's. These properties were 21,000 acres. Imagine that, being a kid and having 21,000 acres as your backyard! Yes, it rocked, it was awesome.

As soon as I was up in the morning I was on my pony and out of there as far away as I could get. I was also a bit of a heathen child. I'd be away early on Sundays, so I didn't have to go to church and Sunday school. This didn't impress my mother.

Over the years Dad took us kids to Pony Club, everything was done as a family. I was the one who loved horses, so I was the one that got them ready, washed and I packed the ute. Lizzie, my younger sister, Dad, and I would drive to Pony Club. Pete, my little brother, also rode but he didn't do Pony Club as much as we did. Why? Because we only had a two-horse float. But at home Pete would come riding with us, which was cool fun.

We'd often go riding as a family, but one day my Dad had a really nasty fall in the shearing shed and hurt his back. Well guess what this lucky chickadee inherited? Her Dad's horse Silver! Which was very cool. Silver was a very clever little coloured mare. I taught her many, many tricks, like rearing on command. Much to my Dad's delight, watching us from the backyard, we would jump around my cross-country course with no bridle or saddle. I think Mum came and watched once and never ever came again. It frightened the hell out of her.

As I grew up, I knew Dad was there for guidance, not rules or regulations. He never ever ripped into you if you made a mistake. He was just there to pick up the pieces. When I came home after receiving my first Guide Dog, I remember the evening in the lounge room suggesting to my Dad that I do a long-distance horse ride from Mudgee to Melbourne to raise money for Guide Dogs Australia. Well holy cow, that certainly made him laugh.

He said, "You can't even ride around the lucerne paddock, let alone ride a horse from Mudgee to Melbourne!"

Well, I proved him wrong! We did ride from Mudgee to Melbourne, it was the first of my 10 long distance fundraising rides.

My Dad did every one of my rides bar my last ride. He was there in spirit with us on that one, all the way. Dad passed away in 2010 from aggressive cancers.

So many amazing stories and rides with my Dad. When we did the Cairns to the Gold Coast ride, Dad took all my horses up to Cairns with his best mate Jeff Pitt. My God it was a laugh a minute, those two characters had everybody in stitches.

So many amazing stories with my wonderful stallion Yarrahappini Hectic. My Dad took me to State Championships, Australian Championships, you name it, we went. We'd turn up at the event in my horse truck with the stallion tied to the side, Dad cooking a baked dinner in the truck. Everyone around us could smell those baked dinners and wanted to join us. It was excellent! Nothing was ever a problem with my Dad. He was and will always be a great mediator, a wonderful gentleman.

It never mattered what we did, Dad was always proud of us and made us feel loved and special. I am so very grateful to have had such a great man as my Dad, my hero.

Out of all the things that come and go in your life I miss my Dad the most. I no longer have that wonderful, kind hearted man to talk to. The words of reason and wisdom. I miss my Dad terribly. But at any time, I can close my eyes and chat to him.

There is so much more I could add. So, very much more.

*

LIFE

THE DAYS OF LIFE
By Bob Cooper, Spring 2014

Every time you see the morning or the sunset coming down,
Or a river murmuring softly as it wanders through a town,
Or you see the roaring ocean as it races to the shore,
Or a whisper of a soft wind as it brushes past your door,
You might feel the chill of winter as it moves across your soul,
Feel the heat of raging summer, like a fire sides glowing coal.

Hear the sound of songbirds singing in a treetop far away,
Watch the antics of the wildlife as they venture out to play.
See imagination change the shape of clouds as they move by,
Watch a sombre thunderstorm as it invades a clear blue sky.

Marvel at the changing colours of a mountain far away,
As the sun kisses horizons of another passing day.
See the stars light up a night sky, full of ancient mystery,
Or the moon cast moving shadows on the ever-changing sea.

You may contemplate the making of a single grain of sand,
Wonder at the ancient majesty of forests on the land.

You may touch a single snowflake as it settles on your skin,
Race barefoot in front of waters as a searching tide comes in.

You may revel in the company of a husband or a wife,
Or just dry the tears of children when they cause a little strife.
You may hold a little puppy with its muzzle slippery wet,
Or visit at a grave side of someone you can't forget.

These are things and times that lead us
to our road and destiny,
We are lucky we're Australian, we are lucky we are free.

*

ATTITUDE

I really love this quote about choices. What do you think of it?

ATTITUDE IS A CHOICE
By Roy T. Bennett

Attitude is a choice.

Happiness is a choice.

Optimism is a choice.

Kindness is a choice.

Giving is a choice.

Respect is a choice.

Whatever choice you make, makes you.

Choose wisely.

*

MAGICAL CHILDHOOD

"Fairy Dust, Fairies and Magic – Bring it On!"
Sue-Ellen Lovett

5yo me on Sugar

Things don't get any better. I had my wonderful Dad, and I had my wonderful horses.

From before I was three, I'd be out on my pony riding around the stockyard or going out with the station hands on a lead. It just didn't get any better.

I was surrounded by animals. I had my beautiful cat, Charcoal. Yes he was a gorgeous black cat that had been born and bred in the charcoal box of our local blacksmith's shop. He was such a cool cat, he followed me everywhere. I spent hours playing with Charcoal in the hay shed and in the stables. We were inseparable.

As time went on, I got more independent with my riding and was able to put my little riding pad on old Pentecost, a flea-bitten grey mare. What I thought was pretty cool about her but which no one else did, was that she used to bite everyone! What a mischievous child I was!

Pentecost and I did lots of miles with Poppy trapping rabbits. Every morning we'd set off very early with rabbit traps across the back of the horse and a scrumptious morning tea. The later provided by Nana. They were blissful days being a kid.

I know these days rabbit trapping is not too crash hot, but that's what we did back then. It was free feed for the dogs. We even had the odd bunny for dinner ourselves, which I quite enjoyed. Especially baked and stuffed. Yum!

I waited all year for Christmas to come around because every Christmas the place would buzz! One year around Christmas we were shearing sheep, we'd been at it for over a month. That's what it takes when you have 56,000 sheep! We cut 999 bales of wool, and then the drought hit.

That meant we had sheep on agistment and droving all over New South Wales. They were everywhere. Drought is such a cruel thing.

The other reason I loved shearing time so much was because of my beautiful teddy. I'd had Ted since I was born and every year, I'd take him down to be shorn. Everyone in the shed would stop shearing while the shearing of my bear took place. This little one and a half year-old girl ruled the roost. Apart from my Uncle Ted who shore Ted for me, everyone else stood still. It was so cool.

I would be in the shed all day. When I wasn't helping my Dad pen up with his wonderful sheepdogs, I was up with the Wool Classer talking with him. In fact, I think talking his ear off might be a better phrase.

Then I'd just go and fall asleep in one of the bays that held the wool. It was interesting sitting with the Wool Classer. He taught me about the crimps in the wool (the crimps are the wiggly bits you get in the wool.) As I got older, I got more jobs in the shearing shed. Sometimes I was the Tar Boy, well girl in my case, and used to take the tar and stitching equipment around, ready if a sheep got an injury while being shorn. It totally rocked working in the shed.

Then of course there was smoko! Mrs Riley did the best smoko. She would bring it up to the shed and ring the bell. That sound welcomed everyone to down tools, take a break and sit around. The shearers and the roustabouts would sit drinking black tea and telling jokes and stories, while my Dad and I would sit on a bale of wool enjoying a lovely fresh scone baked by Mrs Riley. Man was that lady a wonderful cook. Dad and I often went there and ate with the shearers for lunch. I just loved it.

Then one year the bell sounded for lunch, we were all sitting at the table when Mr Riley, Mrs Riley's husband who was the cook, said "Come outside Sue, I have something to show you." So, I toddled on out. I was about four at the time and here was this beautiful little golden puppy. Mr Riley informed me that it was a corgi, I instantly named him Mr Riley. He was the coolest little dog. Mr Riley thought he would save my Dad sheepdogs the extra work by getting me my own working dog. Riley proved to be an exceptional sheepdog.

So, I set out to teach my little corgi pup to be a sheepdog. Man was it a keen little worker. He was great in the shearing shed for penning up and putting the sheep in the yards for overnight. Plus he was such a brave little dog, his pintsize little body looked tiny next to great big western merino sheep. How brave!

Before we started penning up though, it was Dad's and my job to count the sheep out that had been shorn for the day. My Dad was so good at this. I got better as time went on, but sometimes the sheep came out so very fast. But it taught me to be a big counter, a quick counter, and generally accurate.

The shearing shed had 12 stands, so we had 12 shearers, generally 6 to 8 roustabouts and a couple of sweepers. Sometimes I got the job of sweeping but being quite little the broom was nearly as big as me. It needed a bit more speed they said. But as I grew up, I became very proficient at sweeping, skirting the wool, and picking up a fleece and throwing it. That was such an exhilarating day when I could throw a fleece. Woohoo! The whole shed stopped and clapped. Mind you, I had been practising for years!

This went on for years. Every time it was shearing time man I hated having to go to school. So I'd have the worst tummy ache until the car that was taking the kids to the bus had gone. Then I had a miraculous recovery and was out on my horse. I'm sure my Mum and Dad knew that I was playing tricks on them, but it was such a fun time and I learnt so much in the shearing shed. Including how to swear!

Being a smart kid, I knew not to swear in front of my parents, especially my mother. I think she would've washed my mouth out with soap and water. But unbeknownst to me I talked in my sleep. Well apparently, the words were choice, my mother was not impressed! So, I was banned from going out with the station hands for a month. It was a killer! I hated every moment of it. All I wanted to do was be back out mustering the sheep and cattle.

At shearing time, we also took the opportunity to put rings on all the little lambs to remove their tails and on the little boy lambs so they couldn't breed. I had the job of putting the Scabby Mouth Vaccine onto each of the lambs. It was quite a production. We would do hundreds of lambs in a day.

For the little lambs that didn't mother up, after they had their tails docked, I'd take them home. So it was nothing for me to have 16 to 20 little lambs to hand feed each morning. My Poppy would milk the cow and then we would feed the group of bleating little babies. It was so cool. I was in my element, and I was still only five! I didn't think things could get any better than this. But then hell came to visit.

It came in the guise of school. Oh man I hated it. I was a square peg in a round hole and didn't enjoy one moment of it. I could be home riding my pony, helping with the mustering, penning up sheep, so many things I could be doing more interesting than listening to Dr Seuss books and how many eggs the chicken had laid! I had real chickens at home, and I could collect real eggs and tell you how many eggs they had. I didn't need some silly book.

Well things didn't go that swimmingly at school. Every morning getting me to the bus was a major drama. Tears, a screaming child, a very unhappy mother who was also exhausted, frustrated and not happy. So, they decided to send me into town to board! Man, oh man was that a disastrous time? Sending me away from my animals and my Dad was .... crap. I was not happy, I was distraught, absolutely devastated. I did not cope with that time of my life.

Mum and Dad had hunted around to find somewhere I could board in town, where I would be safe. I ended up going to a lovely couple called Mr and Mrs Darcy. Now they were very nice people, but I hated being there. It all started to go pear shaped with a couple of things happening. Mrs Darcy and I would go up to the shop every afternoon to collect some bread and milk for dinner that night and for breakfast in the morning. There was a gentleman there halfway along the block who had a lovely kelpie bitch. So Mrs Darcy, I ended up calling her Auntie Mary, and I would stop every day to talk to the guy with the kelpie. His name was Jim. I formed a lovely friendship with his little red kelpie but sorry, I can't for the life of me remember its name. But it was beautiful, and we would rumble and play in the front yard of the house Jim was doing up.

Jim informed Auntie Mary and I that the bitch was having puppies. I was so excited! I couldn't wait! So, every afternoon we would call-in; Mary and Jim would chat while I played and rumbled with the beautiful kelpie, then we'd go home. Then Auntie Mary thought I could possibly go to the shops by myself and get the milk and bread, which was a big thing to be trusted to do that.

Weeks went by and I was doing this very confidently, walking one block, picking up the milk and bread, and coming home. One day Jim came out when I walked past and said the bitch has had her puppies. "Come and see the puppies Sue-Ellen, come and see the puppies, they are lovely," he exclaimed. So, I diligently followed Jim through the house to the back where he had taken off all the wood flooring so there were just bare timbers that the flooring would normally sit on. Then he pulled his pants off and he molested me. I ran away! Holy hell there are some absolute mongrels in the world.

My only way to cope with what had happened to me was to run away. I wanted desperately to go home. I was forced to live just up the road from that hideous man. When they would find me, I would run away again. I started wetting the bed. I started having nightmares. They took me to the doctor. No one knew what was wrong with me. It was unbearable living with these nightmares of that horrible man, who was still there.

Eventually they got it out of me what happened. Straight away my Dad and Mum went to the Police. The Policeman kept telling my Mum and Dad that saying something and filing a report would do me more harm rather than good. The Police convinced Mum and Dad to do nothing, and so this rotten mongrel of a man is still living happily in the Mudgee Valley. Who else has he molested?

So, things really didn't improve that much. I ran away a few more times. I had a wonderful friend Gloria who would come and pick me up on her beautiful white horse and we would ride around the streets of Mudgee. I loved it when Gloria came to visit, and I loved her beautiful white horse too.

Then somewhere along the line, I can't remember in which order all of this happened, but my parents got called up to the school. It was when I was in first class, I do remember that. I was 6 years old. The Principal, Mrs Herman, informed my parents that I had .... an intellectual disability! Holy cow. How far things had gone. Now the fact that the kid couldn't see was the problem, but they had to figure that out. So many specialists and doctors' appointments later they realised I had very, very short sightedness. So, they put me at the front of the class, which really didn't make it any better. I still hated school.

So much happened and I was still so young, only six. Things were not improving at school. After one visit to the doctor, the doctor convinced my Mum to speak to my Dad about me coming home. This is not working, obviously the child is getting sicker and more stressed and anxious. "Take her home," said the doctor.

So I ended up going home. Man, oh man was that an awesome day. But I was still fraught with nightmares. This followed me through all of my life. As far as trusting people, I would never go into town and stay at a girl friend's place. Not even when I was 18. I was still afraid something would go wrong. I needed to be at home with my Dad, in our home, with my animals.

At this stage I still hadn't been diagnosed with Retinitis Pigmentosa. That was yet to come. Before that diagnosis they put the fact that I was constantly running into things, down to me being a 'clumsy child'.

No one could know, what was to follow.

*

Smile – It's Infectious

What a wonderful reason to smile.

Matthew & I on our wedding day

Credit: Debra Lovett

I came across something a bit special today and thought we could start our own special pandemic to make people smile and be happy. Have a read and let me know what you think.

*

SMILE

By Spike Milligan

Smiling is infectious, you catch it like the flu.

When someone smiled at me today, I started smiling too.

I passed around the corner, and someone saw my grin.

When he smiled, I realized, I'd passed it on to him.

I thought about that smile, then I realized its worth.

A single smile, just like mine could travel round the earth.

So, if you feel a smile begin, don't leave it undetected.

Let's start an epidemic quick and get the world infected!

*

Okay everybody, let's be prepared to share, let's make a difference, let's start our own Pandemic. Smiling makes us feel good. Let's together start spreading these good vibes around the world.

*

ME AND COOKING!

"Dinner is done when the smoke alarm goes off!"
Sue-Ellen Lovett

Can I cook?

Absolutely!

I really do love cooking. Especially when I get to cook for someone who appreciates the effort and time you go to, to make a lovely meal.

I'll admit up front that my cooking technique is quite radical. I am definitely not good at measuring anything. Everything I prepare is done in slurps! Except the wine! My cup of wine is always fuller than the cooking pots.

Matthew and I are probably more savoury than sweet people. Which makes it especially good for me if Matthew gets given chocolates as a gift from a student. Guess who he gives that box to? Yes, me! Why? Because chocolate gives him migraines.

I was very fortunate to have a Mum and Dad who were both extremely good cooks. My Grandma also did the best baked dinners, nearly as good as my Dad's.

Interestingly Dad was not-negotiable about one particular thing in the kitchen. That was, he always cooked the meat! Whether that was chicken, lamb, beef or pork, it didn't matter. Mum never cooked the meat. In fact, Dad was the one who cooked most of our dinners, the meat and whatever else was on the menu that night.

Because we lived on the land Dad didn't just cook the meat, he also often butchered it. We always had a big vegie garden, so we were brought up knowing how empowering growing and harvesting your own food is. From a young age we were taught the importance of Paddock to Plate.

I remember one year in particular; my Mum and Dad have gone to a Lions Club conference in Hawaii for two weeks. Guess who was left in charge of my brother and sister? Okay fine, my grandparents were only a kilometre down the road, so they checked in on us each day, but I was in charge.

I decided for one of our meals to make something extra special, something worthy of inviting our grandparents to as well. But first, I had to catch it! We used to trap rabbits; sometimes for dog food and sometimes for our food. It really was Paddock to Plate. So off I went trapping. I came home with a couple of rabbits which I proceeded to skin and gut.

I was mighty proud of my meal. The baked vegetables were delicious, the gravy was yummy and the baked rabbit was pretty darn good. But my Grandfather, well he was hilarious! He was sitting at the dinner table nudging my Grandma, and saying "she hasn't gutted the rabbit, she hasn't gutted the rabbit." Unbeknownst to Poppy I had gutted the rabbit, and I'd made stuffing with onion, breadcrumbs and egg, which was yummy. I'd even used waxed thread to sew up the bunny's tummy hole, so the stuffing wouldn't fall out. But poor Poppy was beside himself thinking I hadn't gutted the bunny. My sewing was so good, he couldn't see where there'd been an opening. So convinced that I hadn't gutted it, he was refusing to eat my beautiful baked rabbit.

When I was quite young one of my cooking exploits involved our families love of caramel. I'd been told that if you put a tin of condensed milk in boiling water and you boil it for one hour, you ended up with lovely caramel! So I did this. But I got distracted while out in the paddock moving some cows from one paddock to another. Nothing ever takes just one hour! I I came home and the two tins of condensed milk that had been in the boiling water had boiled dry and exploded all over the kitchen! There was caramelised condensed milk, hanging from the ceiling. Boy, was I in trouble!

But time goes on. I also love fishing and I love cooking fish. When I first met Matthew, we lived on the Macquarie River and used to go fishing most every day. I would often catch beautiful cat fish and the odd yellow belly. They are both beautiful when cooked on the barbecue.

I would scale and gut the fish then prepare them to be cooked on the barbecue. This was done very simply. I would cut tomato and onion, and then stuff this inside the fish and squeeze lemon liberally over them. I'd then cook them on the barbecue for 10 minutes each side. Oh my heavens, the meat was so soft, tender and delicious.

When my brother-in-law Tone (Anthony) comes up from Sydney he also likes to go fishing. He recently caught a lovely big yellow belly and I cooked it for the family on the barbecue. As is my habit, it was stuffed then sprinkled with lemon juice, wrapped in foil and cooked for 10 minutes each side. Oh heavens, the meat was superb.

We used to do lots of fishing when I was a child. Sometimes in the dam, sometimes on the Cudgegong River. We loved catching yabbies and cooking them up with a little bit of vinegar, pepper and salt. Oh my heavens, yabbies done like that are just mouth-watering.

I particularly love cooking in winter because I love making stews and soups. One of my favourite things to make this past year has been Osso Bucco. To make this delicious main meal I get 10 lovely big Osso Bucco steaks, one litre of beef stock, two cups of red wine, (well it's really three cups but I drink the third cup!!) and then put it all in the slow cooker with a couple of cut up onions and one very large, sweet potato. I cook it for about eight hours. When it's nearly cooked, I add half a cup of pearl barley to help thicken it. Then I make some gravy. This is beautiful served on a bed of white mashed potatoes. Gee whiz, this reminiscing about cooking is making me hungry!

Another one of my favourites for the summer is a salad I make. It's my own recipe. It's called **Suey's Salad** and uses about 13 ingredients. To make it bake up some sweet potato, zucchini and capsicum in the oven for about 3/4 of an hour. They've been cut into small pieces. When they cool, put them on a bed of rocket lettuce, baby spinach, sun-dried tomatoes, olives and bacon that has been cooked up with the asparagus, artichoke hearts and shredded almonds. To finish off drizzle some delicious Chang sauce over the top. This salad feeds a family and there's always some left over. You don't need another salad dish, just Suey's Salad and a lovely scotch fillet steak. Yes, the salad takes a bit of preparation, but it's worth it.

The other dish I love to make in summer is **Suey's Wombok With Extras Salad**. I generally have to count my fingers after I cut the Wombok cabbage up mind you. Once it is cut up and in a bowl, I cut up half a dozen shallots and put them in with the Wombok cabbage. Then I add a punnet of grape tomatoes, six cut up boiled eggs and two avocados that have been cut into cubes. Then I sprinkle it all with slivered almonds and once again drizzle some Chang sauce over it. Then it's time to gently toss it all together. It takes no time at all to throw this one together, and it is totally delicious.

Now to my failures! I have been known to serve my wonderful niece Sarah cremated offerings! I love doing baked vegetables in olive oil, with the vegetables cut into small pieces. It doesn't help when you go and feed the horse and get caught out in the tack shed doing things and... forget about the vegetables. They really were quite cremated! Sarah kept saying to me; "charcoal is good for you Suey."

The other reason I love cooking is because I love using food to share joy with other people. I love taking soups and stews over to my mother-in-law Lee, and father-in-law John. I always get a wonderful message back from Lee saying how much they enjoyed the meal. There is nothing like being appreciated. It's such a lovely thing to do, to cook a meal for your neighbours.

At home I cook all our meals. Once every two weeks or so we get fish and chips, which I love. We have also been known to get takeaway Indian and Thai. Matthew and I love both of these, but I don't think you can beat a home cooked meal.

What is my favourite meal? Easily that'd be roast pork, roast vegetables, and gravy, bring it on! But it's very much a winter meal.

You may ask "do I get many injuries when I'm cooking?" Absolutely! Especially when I use the barbecue, I always get burns. I have to count how many chops I put on the barbecue and how many chops I get off! I've been known to leave a chop or two behind. This is quite hilarious when you find these lone chops next time you go to use the barbecue.

I love, love, love barbecuing. My Dad was an absolute wiz with the barbecue and always cooked chops or steak to perfection.

One of the cooking tools I couldn't do without is a... timer! I time everything. So I don't overcook things or get distracted, I use the timer that's built into my phone. I pride myself on cooking a mighty fine steak, lamb chops and pork chops with crackling thanks to technique and... my timer!

So yes, the Blind Chick loves cooking. I also enjoy eating! I also love entertaining but sadly with Covid we don't do much of that at the moment.

But when I get a chance, I love to have people come for nibbles, drinks and a meal.

The only rule I have while I'm cooking is 'NOBODY comes into the kitchen when I'm cooking.' Why? Because it's not worth... their life!!!

*

QUESTIONS MOST PEOPLE AREN'T GAME TO ASK! PT 2

"Being kind to yourself is one of the greatest kindnesses."
Sue-Ellen Lovett

WHY HAVE YOU BEEN MARRIED THREE TIMES?

Wow, this could be a touchy subject!

I was young when I got married the first time and I was terribly in love with David. We had travelled Australia for many years doing itinerant work, but I think I did this lovely man a disservice by getting married. I ruined a beautiful friendship and I regret to this day not so much the getting married, but for ruining the wonderful friendship.

Now the second one, let's put that down to a learning experience!

The third one! I've now been married happily for 22 years. Yes, there have been ups and downs, no relationship is a bed of roses, it's bloody hard work. Our marriage has lots of compromise and lots of communication which is so critical. It takes hard work, dedication and a lot of love. I am very happy and blessed to be with my wonderful husband Matthew. We have many more years to enjoy each other and get on with life.

WHEN REPRESENTING AUSTRALIA HAVE YOU HAD AN EMBARRASSING MOMENT?

Absolutely!

When I was at the Atlanta Paralympic Games in 1996, Dressage, our horses were provided by the host city. I drew a little redhead out of the box. I can't remember her name but she was chestnut and I had one day to get to know her before I competed.

Drum roll - our first day of competition!

I rode my little red-haired mare the centreline and halted. Then I continued up the centreline then turned left and from the corner start going across the diagonal. Oh my Lord! Halfway along the diagonal the mare started bucking. She bucked and she bucked. Thankfully I stayed on and didn't come off, but I was devastated to find I didn't get a score for riding eight seconds!

Oh my heavens I was not expecting the horse to do what she did.

HAVE YOU EVER THOUGHT OF GIVING UP?

Yes of course, I'm human.

There have been some especially though times like Johno's last year where his degenerative condition so overwhelmed everything else in our life. It was a living nightmare. I've dubbed that year The Year of Magical Thinking because I had to recalibrate how I thought about things, to see the good in even his smallest try, or the slightest improvement in his mental health. It sucked, but I learnt a lot. I'm better for it.

How do you know if a horse is going to be suitable for you?

It's a certainly feeling I get deep in my gut when I first ride them.
It's a feeling of contentment, like I'm home, I'm where I need to be.
I can't explain it any better. It's a feeling.

If you are so blind, why are you looking at me?

This is the question that mortifies teachers. It generally comes from the primary school child or the infant that is up the back of the room and busting to ask a question. The teacher keeps ignoring them till eventually they have to say, "yes Johnny, what's your question" and he comes up with "if you're so blind, how come you're looking at me?"

This is a great question.

I may be blind, but I can still hear, and I can hear the direction your voice is coming from. So I look in the direction of your voice. This is no different to the way that I ride a dressage test. I am called to the markers around the arena by the people standing at those markers. I always look to where the sound is coming from.

Ha ha, the poor teacher is usually mortified, horrified by their student. But it's okay, it's a great question.

How do you cope in crowds of people and join in the conversation?

This one is quite difficult unless someone addresses me personally as it gets my attention and engages me. It is really hard to be in a conversation with many people because I never know when someone is speaking to me unless they address me by name. Then I'm off putting my two bobs worth in. Alternatively, Matthew says "but they're not talking to you."

WHERE YOU FRIGHTENED AS YOU
WENT PROGRESSIVELY BLIND?

Holy hell yeah!

I was cranky, I was sad. Absolutely I was so very scared. I went through the five stages of grieving many, many times. You just have to take the time it takes, one step at a time, and find a way to make things work. Dreams still do come true.

WHAT DID YOU DO TO COPE?

This is a hard one.

I suppose it depended on the day on how I was feeling, how big the shitty committee was in my head. Every day it was about finding something that I could achieve and go do it. Going blind seemed as if everything was being taken away. I was able to do less and less, which was not a good thing. So, I had to find a way to slowly do more, and find things that I could do, that I could achieve.

One thing I've always been able to do is ride a horse! Having a horse has kept me sane, kept me moving forward and feeling loved and feeling love.

*

PONY CLUB

*"Biggest waste of time -
Comparing yourself to others."*
Sue-Ellen Lovett

I love being on my horse. I love being around horses and horse minded people, so when Dad suggested we go to Pony Club, wow that sounded pretty cool! I was so keen for the opportunity to learn.

So, we rolled up to Pony Club, Dad, Lizzie, and I, every second Sunday. It was so cool. Firstly, we would do troop drill, then in the afternoon some jumping and sporting, which I loved. I enjoyed the hacking as well, especially at the shows. But no one looked at our horses at the shows. My horse was called Silver, she was brown and white, very, very pretty. Lizzie's horse was called Sausage, she was brown and white with a bit of black through her. Very beautiful and very talented horses. But our horses got frowned upon in the hack ring!

You would often hear people talking as we rode out of the ring, "if their parents would only buy those children a couple of decent horses, they are not bad riders. Those coloured horses really don't cut the mustard."

Well, the mustard surely got cut because when it came down to the flag racing or bending races, we were hard to beat. We weren't too bad at the barrels either, we always got a second or third. The Best family had the most amazing horses at doing the barrels. But for the flag and bending nothing could beat Silver and I. When it came to show jumping well, I had wings! Silver and I could do anything, jump anything.

In the show jumping they had a course set up and you had to go around the course and jump the jumps in numerical order. For some reason, which was to become obvious to me as I got older, we kept getting lost! Then Mr and Mrs Stevens introduced us to 6 Bar Show Jumping. This is where you jump six jumps in a straight line. Well holy cow! Didn't we love that! It was wonderful and .... I couldn't get lost!

I'm not sure of the year but off we went to the Mudgee Spring Show. At lunchtime in the main arena was one of their big events - the Six Bar Show Jumping competition. Silver and I lined up against a pretty classy field of horses. In the line-up was one particularly special horse, it was called Handy Andy and owned by the Best family. Andy Best used to ride Handy Andy and jump like a flea. He was such a clever horse, and he was such a character. They were always a hoot to be around.

But this particular day Jenelle Chapman was lucky enough to be given a loan of Handy Andy for the jumping. Jenelle and I did clear rounds. What started off with about 12 horses was now left to just Handy Andy and Silver. We drew straws to see who was going to go first and Handy Andy went first. Over the first fence, refusal at the second, over the second fence, refusal and then another refusal and the bell rang. Okay Silver it's up to you and me, no pressure!

Silver and I cleared the first fence, over the second fence, but coming into the third fence Silver baulked, she never baulked, she never stopped! We went back, then cleared the third fence, over the fourth fence, over the fifth and over the sixth! Oh my God! We did it! One refusal, and the height of the last fence was 5 foot 8, which was higher than I was! And Silver was only 14 2 hands high. What a gutsy little mare. A true champion.

The spectators clapped and cheered and carried on! It was lovely. As we rode out of the ring all our friends; the Best family,

Mr and Mrs Richardson, Mr White, Andrew and Nigel, Mr and Mrs Stevens all cheered us on. What a wonderful day. I can still relive the memory; it was such a cool moment in time.

Each year we'd attend the Pony Club Camp which was often held at Lue Station at Mr and Mrs Coombes's place. We stayed in the shearers quarters which was rather wonderful, on camp stretches. Parents cooked up a storm for each of the meals. It was such a fun time. We used to go out trail riding, then some days we'd go to Havilah, the White family's property, and have a run through the cross-country course which was so much fun.

I made lifelong friends through Pony Club. We travelled to Coolah, Dunedoo, Gulgong, Rylstone and Sofala to attend their local shows. Always catching up with the same people and watching beautiful horses perform. My wonderful stallion Yarrahapinni Hectic and I had a lot of fun together. He was so good in the led classes, typically winning Champion or Supreme Champion. Normally he'd also win the ridden stallion classes. He was such a cool horse; beautiful temperament, drop dead handsome, but he didn't really like men that much.

How fortunate was I that my Dad used to take me and my horses around the countryside for competitions, Hectic in particular. State Championships, Nationals, you name it, we did it. In 1988 Yarrahapinni Hectic won Highpoints Horse of Australia. That means he was the best at everything, and it was so cool, and it was wonderful to have had his breeders there, Mr Mike Barton and Mr George Richardson. They were there supporting me and encouraging Hectic and I all the time.

Something extra important that has stuck in my mind for many a year that I'd like to share with you is there was one fellow who was a very, very good, strong competitor, and he made the comment; "you only won because people felt sorry for you, because you can't see."

Wow! I will take that to my grave, it hurt so much. I'd like to think that one day karma has caught up with him because it was a very cruel thing to say. Hectic and I won so many different events on our merits, not because I was a Blind Chick.

For many years we used to go down to Sydney Royal and compete each year with Hectic. I had a couple of wonderful people that would be my Sighted Guides in the ring. We got permission from the Royal Australian Agricultural Society for me to wear earphones and they had a Steward stand beside my Sighted Guide to give me directions.

Mostly my guide was Dave McClellan. After Dave would finish in the ring with me, he used to say, he needed a couple of good strong Scotches to calm his nerves. He said people had no idea what it is like watching for a Blind Chick when she was riding a stallion in a Class of another 12 horses. Sometimes the Class at the Royal had 72 riders, so they broke us up into Classes of 12. He'd often comment: "My nerves are frayed."

We would go in the Led Stockhorse Stallion Class, the Australian Stockhorse Stallion Ridden Class and Working Stockhorse Stallion Class. Generally, we made up the numbers because there were some pretty smart horse and rider combinations. But one year we got 6th out of 72 in the Australian Stock Horse Lady Rider Class. It was a very proud moment.

At the Sydney Royal Easter Show we'd often compete in the Dressage classes. One year my Guide Dog Eccles led me out to the arena, walked me around the arena, then went back to the edge where he waited. I mounted, the judge rang the bell, and I went in and rode my test. Keep in mind, I only had 2% sight in my right eye, and none in my left. So it was really quite difficult. But we did it, and I was so very, very proud of Hectic and I!

Imagine my surprise when I found out that someone had put a protest in because my Guide Dog had led me out to the arena and that meant I'd have gotten sympathy points because of the Guide Dog. What a load of bull crap! There are some sad people in the world.

So, in the next Class I didn't use my Guide Dog to get out to the arena. My coach Judy led me out to the arena, walked me around the arena and then I competed. I thought we did okay in our test.

But again, there was another protest! Why? Because my coach had taken me out. How the hell did they expect me to get into the arena without any assistance? I was bamboozled! Bamboozled and perplexed by people's negativity and cruelty. I still to this day don't know how to cope with it. Still to this day, I cannot tell you how well we scored because all that negativity overshadowed my wonderful horse and his lovely test. What a pity.

My involvement with Pony Clubs continues to this day. On all my 10 long-distance fundraising rides, many Pony Clubs have ridden with us, they've helped us fundraise, hosted us at showgrounds. They are the most amazing, wonderful group of people. I am humbled to have met so many beautiful people through Pony Club and Pony Club Members.

*

MY FIRST JOB

"If it's going to be - it's up to me."
Sue-Ellen Lovett

Now let's get it clear right from the beginning, I hated school. So obviously I don't think I really did that well. I left school at the end of Year 10, my mother insisted I do a Secretarial Course. What a waste of blinking time! But I did it even though it was reasonably difficult with my lack of sight. I hated shorthand, lousy at it. The only thing I enjoyed about the typing was the music, trying to keep in rhythm with the keys. I wasn't that good a typist either. But I can still touch type, in a fashion.

So, I guess something did come out of that course. I can touch type. That year was such a slow year. Definitely I felt like a round peg in a square hole, it wasn't where I wanted to be. It wasn't at all what I wanted to be doing. I wanted to be the kid on the farm. So after I had finished having a taste of doing secretarial school, I worked for a couple of Insurance Agents ringing people up checking on insurance policies etc. Again this didn't tick my boxes. I don't mean to sound like I'm an ungrateful little cow, but it is important to be .... happy!

So I asked the boss at Kaludabah if I could have a job there, the boss of course was my Dad. Yippee! I was hired. I loved my job. It just was the same old, same old. I was out mustering with the station hands, working in the shearing shed, penning up sheep and doing the odd job on the tractor, which was always a little hilarious and scary.

One of my jobs ended up not being so pleasant. The job was going out spraying St John's Wart, which is a terrible weed. It would give the cows terrible yucky breakouts on their nose like warts and make their faces photosynthesise. If they had white around their eyes it was really quite horrible. To eradicate it off the property we sprayed it with a product called Brasque. It's not around now, it was a pretty bloody horrible product. I used to hallucinate all the time from it and my skin would be red, irritated, and seriously itchy. Eventually I ended up in hospital from poisoning from it.

We really need to be more cautious of what chemicals we use and using the proper protective gear. Such things were never spoken about or known about when I was a kid. The other way of killing St John's Wart was with Coarse Salt. So off I'd go on my horse out around the hills looking for St John's Wart plants and give them a sprinkle of coarse salt. After a shower of rain this would eventually kill the St John's Wart.

Things were going along swimmingly there for ages, loving my job. Then Kaludabah started up an Embryo Transplant Centre and I was moved to work for the fellow up there. My Dad was his boss, but he was my boss. I think he thought I was a bit of a cocky little piece of goods. But I had been there for a long time and I did things like my Dad did. Which in my eyes was the right way.

I loved my job working at the Transplant Centre though. I learnt so much with the amazing Dr James Loneragan who was the Head Vet, he did all the embryo transplanting. It was also very cool as a lot of the new breeds that were coming into Australia came to Kaludabah and it was also a Quarantine Station.

We had wonderful breeds like the Marchigiana, Maine-Anjou, Charolais and Simmental. It was such an exciting time and a very big growth time for the Australian beef industry and embryo transplanting.

I had numerous jobs there, from helping Vet Dr Peter Howe prepare the recipient, tubing the cattle for the anaesthetic and monitoring the anaesthetic machine. After all the operations were finished my job was to sterilise all the operating equipment, which I took great pride in. I also did a little bit of work in the laboratory with James and his wife Liz. It was Liz who took responsibility for separating the fertilised eggs to be transplanted into the recipient cows. It was a very interesting job and at the time quite cutting edge. It was all done surgically which is unlike today, it is totally nonsurgical. Look how far we've come.

Another interesting job I helped with was calving down. When the Loneragan's brought their first mob of recipients from Queensland, a couple of things happened. They were all Herefords, and before they came down to us they were all supposed to have been tested for Brucellosis, a bacterial disease. So, we tested them again, only to discover 30 cattle tested positive. These cows had to be brought out of the mob and euthanised, which meant men from the Department of Primary Industries came out and shot them, one at a time.

It was bedlam. I had to be the one to be there as they needed a witness. It was just too much. The man couldn't shoot the side of a barn if he was standing right Infront of it! I left in tears, wanting to find my Dad and for him to remedy the situation. This was so cruel, so unnecessary. My Dad did come down, it was he who finished the job shooting the 30 cattle. They were then dragged down to the tip and burnt. It was such a waste and so very, very sad. But we could not afford for the rest of the mob to get Brucellosis.

Aside from that, the mob settled into their new home well. We put two sidewinders which are bulls that have had their penis's operated on, so it comes out the side of their sheath instead of out the front of the sheath. This is so they cannot inseminate a cow. They also wore a harness with a little paint ball on it, so when they mounted a cow that was in season, to try and impregnant her, it marked the cows back with paint.

So every morning and every night we'd go out and check what cows were in season so we could schedule their receiving of a donor egg. We needed the recipient to be ovulating when the transplanting was happening.

So we would bring in 16 to 18 cows that were ovulating, to be transplanted. Each of these cows were sedated, put on a trolley, and connected to an anaesthetic machine. Then they were opened up just in front of their udder and the egg was implanted into their uterus. Once they were stitched up, they went into a recovery area.

After our first lot of transplanting, it became obvious that the Hereford cows were not big enough for these big Charolais and Simmental calves. So Dad and I took 800 head of recipients on the road, because the drought meant there was not a lot of feed around. Droving them 'on the road' means we followed the cattle as they ate the grass beside public roads. We'd generally travelled about 6 miles each day between each Travelling Stock Reserve.

We had the cattle on the road for 10 months, travelling all around the district. It was wonderful. We had lots of fun. Just before we left, I broke in one of the horses we took droving with us, his name was Derringo. By the time we returned home with the cattle, I could have put him in the front of any semi-trailer, and he could have driven it.

We had a couple of odd experiences while we were on the road with the cattle. Down the Lue Road we had an RSPCA Representative turn up. My Dad welcomed him, asking how he was going and everything. Quickly the RSPCA Rep got to the reason why he'd stopped by. "We've had a complaint that there is a cow with its guts hanging out."

My Dad took the RSPCA Rep out and showed him the cow in question. They were not guts hanging out, it was simply a little bit of afterbirth she hadn't passed yet. That cow had recently delivered a healthy calf. So, Dad rectified the afterbirth, and the RSPCA gentleman went away happy. It is sad when people make complaints about something they know nothing about.

After that 10 months of the cattle being on the road they were all sold. Our recipients were replaced by Friesian cows which were beautiful big roomie cows to breed beautiful big calves.

Plus they were also great milk producers and hence exceptional mothers. This worked really, really well and was super successful. One year the success rate of each transplant was over 86%, which was massive!

Now, let me tell you how I got sacked!

The boss fellow and I were down drafting some cattle and I just happened to suggest to him that there was a better way of doing it. He really didn't like my suggestion. I said, "well that's the way my Dad and I would've done it." So, on the spot he sacked me for being a smart arse.

That afternoon instead of being at work I was at home going down to get some grain for the horses. As I was coming back in the Suzuki Dad arrived home from his fishing trip to Bourke. He asked me "what are you doing home for work?"

"I got the sack" I said. As soon as I told Dad why, he was off in the Suzuki down to the Embryo Transplant Centre to have a chat with my ex-boss. Funny enough I was back at work the very next day.

Now I'm definitely not an upstart or a smart Alec, but I have been taught by the best how to be efficient and fast, my Dad. I knew what I was doing. So guess what? Low and behold only a few weeks later a situation arose again, and I suggested politely there was a quicker and easier way to do what was required, otherwise we would still be here on dark. Once again, I was sacked. This time I didn't go back.

I tend to think the boss didn't like me very much. I had a wonderful working relationship with everybody in the Embryo Transplant Centre. James was just such an amazing gentleman to work with. He explained everything well, as did his lovely wife Liz. I spent a lot of time with their beautiful children as they were growing up. I'm still very good mates with their daughter Amelia.

*

PETER – PURE COURAGE AND EVER SO BRAVE

"Never give up, never stop believing in yourself."
Sue-Ellen Lovett

Left to right: Peter | Peter holding Bradley |
Peter's middle son - Bradley & daughter McKenzie Rose

Pete was a small framed, cheeky, good, curious, beautiful child. Everybody loved Pete. He was the sort of lad that would help the old lady across the road with her groceries or he would make sure the table was set for dinner when Mum and Dad came home. He was one of those kids that knew the right thing to do at the right time. He was so much fun and always made people laugh. Peter is my brother.

As children sitting around the dinner table, I can remember Peter shredding his banana so it looked like an octopus. He'd pretend he was Mr Snuffle from Sesame Street. He would make Mr Snuffleupagus sounds, always leaving everyone in stitches.

But my Dad was a stickler. When you were sitting at the table you were there to eat and eat only. You could not laugh or play at the dinner table. So we were always in trouble for laughing and giggling at the table. Also when we got fed spinach! Peter would take his from his plate and feed Mum's favourite plant in the corner of the room his spinach, he hated spinach. He was always such a laugh. Such a gorgeous, gorgeous young lad.

When we lived at the homestead, I remember one particular day. Pete and I were out getting firewood, that was one of my jobs. Pete was always up for helping. He was about three and a half or four years old at the time. We'd loaded up the billy cart. I was pulling it and Pete insisted on carrying a piece of wood. Well on the way to the house Pete tripped on the concrete and the piece of wood he'd been holding nearly severed his thumb. Then came the rush into hospital to have surgery to reattach it. Thankfully the surgery went well, he's had full use of it ever since.

Pete used to come horse riding with us until he found ... motorbikes! Motorbikes are the love of his life. The faster the better. Up and down the roads at Kaludabah he'd go with his best mate Stephen. Pete and Stephen used to be inseparable, always off somewhere on their motorbikes. Sometimes they used to come and help us mustering, but mostly they were just off playing around like lads do.

Then Mum and Dad purchased a property called Carlisle Park, on the Cudgegong River on the Sydney side of Mudgee, so we moved. Pete continued to love his motorbikes. He and Lizzie would catch the school bus to school. One day when Pete was 14 and in High School, Mum and Dad got a call from the school. They were to come quick, there had been a really bad accident. A brick wall had fallen on Peter!

Apparently, a fight had broken out in the girls' toilets. Around the girl's toilet block was an L-shaped Besser block wall. Lots of boys had tried to jump up on the wall to see what was happening. Peter was one of those boys. Being smaller meant he was underneath when the top of the wall fell loose from everyone jumping and pulling on it. All that activity pulled the wall down! If it hadn't been for a young friend of Peter's, John, who grabbed Pete by the collar and dragged him out, the wall would have kept falling on him. We could have lost Peter that day!

Instead, the brick wall fell on both his legs and crushed them. Pete was rushed to Dubbo Hospital, closely followed by Mum and Dad. This was a devastating situation. Poor Pete. My heart broke.

I was in Melbourne at the time, training with a new Guide Dog, away from the family and not able to do anything to help. After Pete had been in hospital for a couple of weeks and was allowed to have visitors, I travelled by bus from Melbourne to Dubbo to visit him. He was in a ward with no one else because they were so worried about infection. They couldn't put a cast on his legs because they had been so crushed by the Besser blocks. They were just sitting there open; you could smell the rotting meat on his legs.

Not long after I left to return to Melbourne, the surgeon told Mum and Dad that Peter needed to have his left leg amputated. Gangrene had set in. Mum and Dad had no idea what to say, or what to do. But the Doctor in his great wisdom told them "This is not your decision, this is Peter's decision. He has to live with this, he is old enough to make the decision himself." The Doctor went and spoke with Peter. He explained to him the situation he was in, and that if he did not have the operation, given how aggressive gangrene is, that within 24 hours Peter would be dead.

So, they amputated Pete's left leg. He then had to endure 17 surgeries! Why? Because the Surgeon did such an appalling job. Pete had to keep going back because one of the bones in his leg kept growing and pushing through the bottom of his stump. Then he got Golden Staph, an appalling bacterial infection you can get in hospital. But that's another story.

Yet though all the time with this drama going on, not once did Pete say; "why me" or "this is unfair." He just got on with it. He met a couple of elderly gentlemen in the hospital where he learnt to do leatherwork. Sadly, one of those men passed away but Pete continued to do some lovely leatherwork. Pete was in Dubbo Hospital for about eight months, with one complication or another while his legs healed. His right leg down to his ankle got totally fused. With just crushed bones they couldn't do anything else with it. And it is still like that to this day. Most people don't know that Pete has a prosthetic leg. He is quite amazing.

When Pete came home from hospital, he got a waterbed to make it more comfortable for his amputated limb, or lack of. Sorry, I'm not quite sure how to put that. Mum and Dad bought him a small pool table, because it was important that he got up and used his other ankle as much as possible. Every day he had to go out and sun his stump to make sure that it dried out. And he still had the Golden Staph! So two things happened here.

The first was Pete ringing my Dad to say, "Dad there's a snake underneath my daybed!"

Dad's reply was, "well shoot it!"

Pete said, "with what?"

Dad told him where the key to the gun cabinet was, so Pete went and got the rifle, the 22. By this stage, the snake had made its way from under the daybed onto the veranda. So, Pete didn't bother opening the door, a good move considering he was only on one leg. Pete shot through the window and when Dad came home that afternoon there was a flute on the veranda! The snake of many holes.

Pete did a great job dispatching the snake, keeping in mind he could've been bitten. Guess how he found out there was a snake under the daybed? He'd been patting Whooshka, the cat, when suddenly its hair stood up and it started hissing. So, Pete knew there was something wrong. Thank heavens for Whooshka who saved him from being bitten by the snake.

Then came the next dilemma with Pete's leg. When I returned home from Melbourne, Pete still had Golden Staph in his stump. I tried horse liniment oil, I tried this, I tried that, but nothing worked. Then one day Pete asked me to mix up a brew of washing soda and if I could "please soak my leg in it before you fly back to Melbourne."

I said no problem and proceeded to put a couple of cups of washing soda into a dish, boiled some water, let it get to room temperature so it wouldn't burn his skin and soaked Pete's stump in it. Well everything was going swimmingly, it seemed to do a good job of medicating his stump. Then Mum and Dad dropped me at the airport.

Ooops! Unbeknownst to me when they returned home they had to take Peter straight to the hospital. I'd given his stump third degree burns! Apparently, I'd put too much washing soda in the water. But guess what? I cured the Golden Staph. The Doctor later told Peter that he would never ever have recommended this cure for anybody, but it worked. So note to Sue-Ellen, get someone to read you the instructions before you go treating somebody.

While all this was happening the plans for my first long distance fundraising ride from Mudgee to Melbourne to raise money for the Guide Dog Association were well underway. Then it was time to start the ride. But I know Dad set off with a very heavy heart, leaving Mum and Pete at home to look after the farm, and Pete to recuperate. It was very hard for Dad. I felt so bad taking him away when Mum and Pete really needed him. But as always, my Dad being the man he was, when he made a commitment, he always kept it. So along with my wonderful crew, we started our 1984 ride from Mudgee to Melbourne.

Every stride of that ride warming my heart was that beautiful little brother of mine who never shed a tear, never said it wasn't fair. He just got on with living, and he still is doing just that. Every day he is getting on with living and making the best of things. I'm so very proud of my little brother.

*

DEALING WITH NEW CHALLENGES

Together we can make a difference.

So, my challenge to everyone is - let's make a difference today!
Let people close to you know you care. Let those you love know,
you love them. Believe me, such words do make a difference.

"One of the most spiritual things you
can do is embrace your humanity.

Connect with those around you today.

Say, "I love you", "I'm sorry", "I appreciate you",

"I'm proud of you". Whatever you're feeling.

Send random texts, write a cute note,
embrace your truth and share it.

Cause a smile today for someone else.

And give plenty of hugs."

By Steve Maraboli

*

MAGIC, DREAMS & BELIEVING

"VISION is much more than seeing."
Sue-Ellen Lovett

Our magnificent stallion at Kaludabah with his herd

Wow this is going to be interesting! I've toyed with whether to share what has been happening in my life since I was a wee girl, or not.

I worried that sometimes I was going silly and not understanding the absolute magic we are surrounded by, and the amazing gifts we have all been given.

This magic started when I was a wee little girl. I'd go and sit in the paddock with our station horses, generally 20 to 30 of them, and many of the horses would come over and talk to me. How low their heads hung, and their big sighs told me how comfortable they were to be so close to me. Some would come closer and nuzzle my arm or my hair. There was no expectation, we were just present. I did this every chance I could. I'd just go and hang out with the horses.

I would jump on my little palomino mare Blondie, guiding her with just a piece of string around her neck, and ride through the horses and down to the river. It never in the world occurred to me to wonder why I didn't need a bridle or a saddle. We just were as one.

I suppose one of the reasons I was drawn to the horses, unbeknown to me at the time, was the fact that I couldn't see very well. Horses have two beautiful brown eyes and they always looked out for me, they looked after me.

On school holidays or before I was old enough to go to school, as soon as the sun was up, I was off on my horse. I'd go far away from the Homestead and just be with my horse. It was perfect, we'd spend the day meandering through the hills, sitting by a dam listening to the ducks, lying in the soft grass around the dam, just hanging out together. It was so perfect, and such amazing beauty. You would not believe the beauty until you take the time to just sit and feel and listen to it.

I had this feel and could listen in abundance when I was a little girl. I didn't realise it at the time, that this amazing affinity I have with them is a pure connection. I could tell if they were in pain, I was drawn to particular animals that were sick, or when they needed help.

Let me share a few occasions to show you how amazing this beautiful gift of being present and feeling is all about. I hadn't been up to check on our mob of station horses for quite a while. This mob were the ones that the boys would bring in every now and again and pull a few youngsters off and break them in.

Something magical happened. I had to go up and check on the mob, there was something drawing me up there. I meandered through the mob, being careful to stay clear of the stallion but ….. he came quite close to me and oh my Lord, he had the most horrific wound on his leg, there was lots of blood and he was very lame.

I knew I couldn't go and let my Dad know about the stallion's plight because he would've shot him. That's what they did in those days. Plus, because the stallion was wild, having someone treat him "would've been out of the question" is what my Dad would have said.

But I must say the universe was looking out for this beautiful stallion and I this particular day. I went back down to the Homestead and opened all the gates all the way to the stockyards. I proceeded to muster 50 maybe 60 horses; including stallions and foals, all the way down to the Homestead, which would've been about 4 km away.

For a little while it was like mustering cats because there was only me and the horses were here, they were there, they were everywhere! Then they got the gist of staying in a mob and were rather lovely. Interestingly the mob kept the stallion very protected because he was slow, and very sore.

Eventually I got all the horses down to the stockyards, but they were very restless, they didn't know what was happening. Very rarely did they get taken down to the stockyards for anything other than for a couple of youngsters to be separated out to be broken in.

So, I quietly broke the mob up into a few different yards, trying to get less and less horses around the stallion. They were so particular about trying to protect him as they knew he wasn't well, and he was in so much pain.

Eventually I got it down to two horses, the stallion, and a lovely old piebald mare. I was then able to quietly split the mare away from the stallion.

When I first went down and opened the gates to bring the

horses down, I also went to the laboratory and got some antiseptic lotion, fresh water and cottonwool bandages. What the heck I was planning to do with all this who knew? But this is how it played out.

I quietly opened the gate into the race and the stallion walked in and stood very quietly. I didn't put a bar in front of him or a bar behind him, I just went and stood with him and reassured him that it was okay. Keep in mild mind you that he was a wild stallion, he'd never had any handling by man at all.

When I'm around horses' things just sort of happen. Next thing I am in the race in front of his chest kneeling down, dressing his leg. He stood patiently, he stood quietly. Oh, my heavens! When I reflect on how dangerous that situation was and what could have happened. It could potentially have gotten even more dangerous because when my father came home from town and drove past and saw me underneath the stallion. But he had the good mind to keep driving and not stop. I will be forever grateful for that because he would've ruined the magic spell that was over the yards that day. Plus, his presence could have made the stallion behave very differently.

There was a fair bit of proud flesh around the wound and while I didn't know what to do with that, I cleaned it the best I could. I wrapped it in a lovely clean bandage and then just sat there for a little while, with my hand on his injured leg. While I sat there with my hands on his leg, I talked to him and explained it would be okay, but he was to take it easy.

I then quietly got myself out of the race, opened the side gate so he could get out and off he walked, slowly, to join his mares. I cleaned up all the things I'd used to dress his leg and thought it'd be best to leave them in the yard for an hour or so to settle before we went on our trip back to their paddock. I wanted to give the stallion a little time to recover from his treatment.

Well, about then my Dad arrived and oh my heavens I was given quite a sermon on how dangerous it was to do what I did, let alone bring 50 to 60 horses down into the stockyards by myself.

My father was horrified. But it was okay, I wasn't hurt, and the stallion was treated, and he was okay.

After my discussion with Dad, I got back on Silver, opened the gates and the horses slowly made their way back to their paddock, stopping and grazing around the dam banks and in the hollows where there was some lovely fresh pick. It had been such a magical day.

I really believe it is all about listening and feeling and being present. The listening is especially important because nature is always reaching out to us. This special relationship we have with our horses gets better when we listen more. They are trying to connect with us all the time. Sadly, we are generally trying to tell them what to do, we don't listen to them enough.

Some of the other wild and magical things that have happened include the number of birds that just come to me. I often get two cockatoos come to me, it's generally the very old cockatoos. One particular cockatoo brought his mate for me to look after while he died. This has happened countless times since I've been living in Dubbo. It's quite amazing. I sit and just nurse the old cockatoos, sometimes I put them in a cage overnight with feed and water. The next morning when I come out there will be two cockatoos in the cage, the partner has let himself in to be with his best mate. Yet with all of this I have never been bitten. It's more of the same magic about animals and being present.

While I'm trying to keep this story short, I'm also just so badly wanting to awaken you to this amazing magic that we are all born with. All you have to do, is take the time to listen and be present with what is happening around you. With your animals, whether they be your cat, bird, dog or horse, you have the ability to listen to them all.

I think animals are attracted to me because all I offer is just pure love, nothing more, nothing less. That pure love is the secret, that's the magic, that's what makes things happen.

On another of these amazing days I was riding my stallion Hectic down to the front gate to give him some exercise. I did this routine every day before I went into the arena. It was one kilometre down to the gate and one kilometre back. Being pretty much a straight line made it really quite safe me for me to ride on a horse that was sensible.

One particular week on each of the days I rode to the front gate one of the horses in the paddock beside the driveway was telling me they were in so much pain. I could feel their muscles were swollen, their feet were sore, and they were feeling very poorly. This went on for three days, so I let the people who owned the horse know it wasn't well, but I think they thought I was a bit of a fruit loop. That week went by and then into the next week the pain got worse. Eventually I was able to convince them to bring the horse down to the stables.

What had happened was their mare had a toxicity reaction to clover and all of her muscles had swollen up and had caused her to founder from the pain. They proceeded to put her in a yard and start treating her. But it was too late. I so wish they had listened because seven days later I was holding that beautiful mare for the vet while she was euthanised. We need to listen. It breaks my heart when we don't listen enough when it matters.

I spend a lot of time listening to podcasts when I go for walks or instead of listening to the TV. It is really interesting how many of these podcasts talk about going down rabbit holes and all of a sudden realising what they can feel from a horse or learn from the horse. This eureka moment is not new for people like me who have been listening, feeling and being present with their horses their whole life. You can do it. You just have to be open enough to feel and to listen to what the universe is sharing with you.

What I think is extra amazing, especially as we get older, is that all of those beautiful things we had as children or that we believed in as children like; Mummy kissing your knee after you fall and that kiss making your knee better, are still so true. It was the love that made you feel better. This is such a special message. It's not hocus-pocus. Love really does have the ability to heal everything.

You may notice in all of my Johno & The Blind Chick Facebook posts that I send loads of love and hugs. I think the world needs more of it. We need to start a pandemic of love and hugs and make people feel better.

But back to these people going down rabbit holes and having all of these courses you can do to learn how to connect. These are courses you pay a lot of money for. What I'm suggesting is that before you pay for that course, explore within yourself if you already have what you're seeking. Can you ...

be present? Can you be open? Can you listen? Are you able to give love?

Giving love is such a beautiful gift, we don't need to pay to learn how to love. You don't need to say mantras or have a talisman, you've got this already. You are enough. Your beauty and your love are enough already.

I was speaking with a beautiful friend in Wales recently. I am so grateful to Kathy Price for listening and convincing me to share some of my stories about this. There are many more, but I thought I'd share the ones that are extra special. Get ready .... I've left the most magical one to last.

I was on my long-distance ride from Cairns to the Gold Coast with my amazing team. Generally, we have two horses on the road each day and we generally do 60, maybe 70 kilometres, depending how far it is between each town.

A lovely young lad who used to work for Riding For The Disabled in Kellyville had won a week to ride with us. He was to ride as one of my Sighted Guides. It was hard to work out what horse to put him on. The quietest and most reliable horse was my beautiful mare Mudgee. So off we started that day, down highway heading south, putting in the miles. Along the way we had to go over a culvert, so we were in single file. Next thing the young lad calls out "Stop, Stop." Mudgee had gone down a hole in the culvert and had punched a hole in her offside kneecap.

Oh no, she could hardly put her foot on the ground, I was devastated. The ride stops, nothing is happening. What are we going to do? We have a horse float with us at all times in case of an accident, so Mudgee is loaded straight away and taken to the nearest town vet, which is two hours away! After the vet looked at Mudgee they announced "this is not good. Your horse won't be going back on the ride." My heart broke. I didn't feel I could continue the ride without Mudgee. She was my everything.

The vet did x-rays which confirmed that Mudgee had punctured her kneecap and her joint fluid was leaking out. He explained that she needed stable rest, that she wouldn't be going back on the road for a while. We took her back to the town to where were going to be staying that night. Well, that night .....

We dressed Mudgee's leg and I sat with her for about an hour with my hands on her leg giving her as much love and healing as I could. I don't like using that word, healing, because it wasn't that that made things work, it was my love that did the magic.

We left a horse with Mudgee to keep her company and finished the days ride into the next town. Every moment I got I went and sat in the stable with her, just cupping her knee in my hands and giving her love. Oh, my heavens, I gave her so much love, and it was so easy.

The next day I didn't do what the vet said, instead we put Mudgee on the float behind us. It travelled along at a very steady pace as our backup vehicle. Every hour I dismounted and spent some time sitting in the float with Mudgee, my hands on her leg, sending her love and healing energy. This routine is what became of those next few days.

We are now Day Three after the accident and Mudgee is moving much better, but still not happy. Every hour I'm in the float giving that horse so much love. We get to Day Four and we're now back in the town where the vet was that we first took Mudgee to.

By Day Four, believe it or not, Mudgee was walking really well. We took her to the vet, she backed off the float perfectly and after the vet looked at her leg he couldn't believe it, he said "You haven't brought me the same horse. This isn't the horse I treated the other day!" But it was.

On Day Five Mudgee was back on the road doing the ride, with me on her back. I never let anyone else except myself ride her from then on. I couldn't bare her having another accident. Not to say an accident wouldn't happen with me on her back, and me being blind, but if that was to happen it would be my fault, no one else's.

Mudgee did her last long-distance ride at the age of 28, from Melbourne to Sydney in 1998. It was a fundraising and awareness ride for the Sydney 2000 Paralympic Games. My last ride, Dubbo in 2018, was done without Mudgee, she had passed away. She was so missed. Oh, my heavens she was just such a magical horse, there was so much trust between us.

She would follow me and my Guide Dog anywhere. She even went in a lift into Sydney Town Hall, stepped out onto the balcony and into a dining room full of 460 seated guests. She walked into Parliament House! She would go anywhere with me, such trust, and love.

But you know the beauty of this is we all can have this level of trust, love and connection. It is at our fingertips. We just need to listen, be present, be open and give love. There are no mantras or talismans that make this happen, it comes from within you. It is the love you have in you. That love is pure energy. That energy can create magical moments, daily.

Okay! By this stage you're probably thinking I'm a bit of a fruit loop. I appreciate that believing love and sending healing energy can be so powerful is a huge stretch for some people. For some even talking about being present or really listening is never going to happen. And that's ok. We all have different fears and blockers to our courage. I just hope that your courage in choosing to read my book can stretch a little more to being open to the magic you already have inside you. It really is there. It's ready when you are.

I'm happy in the skin I'm in. I am so blessed to have the connection I have with my horses. It has not always been easy. Listening to beautiful Johno when he channelled through me and I felt his pain, his discomfort, his frustration, was tough.

Another of those magical moments was particularly sad, but also quite liberating. It was the day Johno was euthanised. After he was gone, the most amazing weight lifted from my chest, my head became clear, I could think again! I'd been picking up everything Johno was putting down, I felt his sadness and his frustration, all of it. How amazing for a horse to share all of that with me! I learnt so very much from Johno and because of that, I am much more present now with beautiful Lola.

With so much love and energy being giving to her, Lola is no longer such a wound-up rubber band. She's like a lovely piece of soft al dente spaghetti, she's relaxed, happy and attentive. I'll keep working on this with her because it's important that I put only beautiful calm, relaxing experiences, no tension, into her memories. I think now when I ride her that she's smiling. When I first started riding her, she was tense and anxious, definitely not smiling. I am loving how she feels now after our first months together, I'm just so grateful. But it's not been easy. I've taken the time she's needed; I've listened, and I've been present.

With the conversation I had with beautiful Kathy, I'd told her I'd keep looking for other people to invite into our lives, to help with Lola's healing, but my insides keep telling me no, I'm enough, I can do it. So, I'm not looking any more. I'm dedicated to doing the best I can and to being present and to listening to her and to continuing along the track we're on where there is so much love, happiness, and joy.

When I think of her, the smile comes from deep inside me.

I am so blessed. Magic and Dreams do come true.

*

SOME OF THE AMAZING PEOPLE WHO INFLUENCED MY LIFE

"Surround yourself with positive people."
Sue-Ellen Lovett

The main influence in my life was my Dad. He was always there, never in judgement, always with a kind word, always with a wise word. He never told me you can't do that. He encouraged the three of us children to take the bit in our teeth and have a go at anything that came in front of us, which we all have done. Still to this day my Dad has left an amazing legacy with his three children – strength, courage, determination, bloody-minded and stubborn.

A wonderful gentleman Mr George Richardson, Mentor and Supporter, has been my go-to man helping me coordinate and organise things. He is an ideas person and is always encouraging. George is a big believer in the saying, "build up, don't destroy a great man in his own right." He was one of the people involved in starting up The Australian Stockhorse Society. He has ridden some of the most beautiful Stock Horses in Australia. Mr Richardson has always encouraged me every step of the way to be the best I can be.

Judy Cubitt, a super coach extraordinaire, best mate, larrikin and amazing lady. For many years Judy was my coach and my best mate. We used to have the best fun together. She loved thumbing her nose at authority. If it said to go down the right lane, Jude would go down the left lane, just to prove she could. Judy took my wonderful campdrafting stallion Hectic and I through to the Grand Prix in a very, very short time with her wonderful coaching and encouragement. The first time we met was when Judy had come to fix the music for my freestyle test. I was riding a horse called Vision which Judy thought was hilarious. We did miles together, travelling and talking.

There's a show on TV called Funniest Home Videos, well I think it was Jude's favourite show. She would ring me when it was on, and sit giggling and laughing into the phone, telling me what was happening. We would both be in our separate lounge rooms on the phone, rolling on the floor with laughter. She loved sharing and making a difference to people's lives. She judged dressage at the Atlanta Paralympics and was Chef d'Equipe as well as Team Manager for the Sydney Paralympic Games. Judy was truly an amazing lady and made everybody feel good and happy.

In 1997 when raising funds for the Sydney Paralympic team, doing the long-distance ride from Melbourne to Sydney, Eccles was my Guide-Dog. He and Judy were there at every stop. The ride finished at the Sydney Town Hall. It was Judy who guided my mare Mudgee, Eccles and I up in the lift and onto the balcony to see the crowd.

When Eccles retired from guiding it was only fitting that he became Judy's constant companion.

Judy loved to laugh and loved to have the last word. In her barely conscious final hours, her nephew leaned over and asked quietly "Can you hear me?" With her eyes shut, she answered, "No".

Sadly, Jude passed away in 2012. Suitably for such a colourful lady her coffin was decorated with images of her and her horses and arrived at the church with her coffin attached like a side car, on a roaring Harley Davidson motorcycle. Judy loved to celebrate life and make people smile.

Caroline Lieutenant is an amazing dressage coach and rider. Most people were scared of Caroline. She was a lady that ruled with an iron fist, but she had a heart of marshmallow. She was the best dressage rider in Australia for many years on her beautiful horse Temuchin. She was everything in one small package, a super talented lady, coach and rider.

It was not unusual for me to be in blubbering tears at the end of a lesson with me saying, "do you think I'm not trying?" Caroline would reply to me, "do you think I don't want the best for you?" She was one hell of a coach, one very determined lady, she made miracles come true. She could turn an average rider into a dressage rider. While I can't say she has accomplished that with me, she gave it a fair go and I do so love dressage.

Moira Kelly first saw me ride at a competition at Bradgate Park in Orange. After I finished the dressage test Moira was waiting outside the arena to greet my horse Ko-Olina, my Sighted Guide Mel and I. We had a lovely chat and she was very complimentary. Then she proceeded to say that she wanted to be part of our journey! So off we went to have a couple of glasses of bubbles and the next day when we caught up with Moira, she offered to sponsor Ko-Olina and I. Wow! This was so greatly appreciated, as it is financially hard getting to competitions on a blind pension. Moira's sponsorship made such an enormous difference, as I'd been struggling with entry fees and fuel.

Moira sponsored us for two amazing years, firstly with Ko-Olina and then the beautiful Cascador. Moira was even there when I trialled for the London Paralympic Games with Cascador in 2012, but it was not to be. He was a bit of a bugger. He knew when he had me by the short and curleys. He warmed up beautifully, but when we got into the dressage arena after about our third movement, he decided he'd had enough of doing it my way and started doing it his way! His way included some leaping and not ideal elevating. It was not very pleasant for me. I was in tears, even some judges were in tears. As soon as I retired from even trying to finish the dressage test and exited the arena, I decided to sell him.

Moira was my first ever Dressage Sponsor. I am forever grateful that she believed in me and provided the financial support we needed. It made a world of difference. Thank you, lovely lady.

Dr John Grant worked at the Royal Northshore Hospital, in Sydney. He was an amazing neurosurgeon and phenomenal gentleman. I met him in his role as Chairman of the Australian Paralympic Board of which we were both members. Dr Grant and the Honourable Michael Knight, Minister for the Sydney Olympics and Paralympics, invited me to join. Dr Grant also came to one of the awards nights where I received an award. What a gracious, beautiful man, and a terrific leader. The Sydney 2000 Paralympics were very, very lucky to have such an amazing gentleman at the helm. He lead by example and although he was quietly spoken he was very effective. He made things happen. I am so grateful for the time I got to spend with this incredible person and all the things I learnt from him. What an amazing community leader, mentor and all-round gentleman.

The next amazing gentleman that has made such an impact on my life is a package deal! Mr Terry Snow and his wonderful wife Janett and family. Terry has vision as I have seen in no other. He is humble, he is gracious, he is generous to a fault with his time and making people's dreams come true as he did for me.

Meeting Terry came about because one of my lovely friends, Kathy Williams, sent Terry an email mentioning her blind friend needed Sponsorship to achieve her goal of riding at Grand Prix level. Well, I didn't give it a thought when Kathy told me she'd sent Terry such an email. Then, out of the blue one day, I received a phone call from Terry Snow!

We chatted for ages, it was lovely. The more we chatted, the more excited I got. Maybe, possibly, my dream could come true. I might get to ride at Grand Prix! Terry then offered to Sponsor me, which was just amazing.

We would go to Terry's amazing property Willinga Park in Bawley Point on the south coast of NSW and train with Brett Parbery, one of our world-class riders. It was just such a blast! Oh my heavens, the facilities are something dreams are made of. To be able to have my horse at this wonderful facility and train in the beautiful undercover arena with a world-class coach is the stuff little girls' dreams are made of! And this little girl was living her dream.

I am so very blessed and so grateful to the Snow Family. Terry sponsored me for four years. Yes we reached our goal, yes I did ride Desiderata at Grand Prix. But along the road there were many highlights. We got to do three displays of me riding dressage at Willinga Park at International Dressage Competitions. The Blind Chick and her amazing Living Markers and her beautiful Guide Dog, it was just such an amazing journey.

I don't think I could have dreamt something that was just so amazing! Each time we finished doing a display, or competing, Terry's wife Janett and their daughters Georgie and Scarlett, would be there encouraging me, giving me so much confidence, making me feel so very, very special. There are no words to describe what this wonderful family brought to my life! What a journey! There aren't big enough words – but thank you from the bottom of my heart to the Snow Family.

We would travel down to Terry's every four to six weeks for lessons with Brett, staying at the family's beach house. This was such a treat for me, a country kid, oh my heavens. We'd take my Guide Dog walking on the beach each morning, and of an evening when we fell asleep you could hear the water lapping on the beach below and the waves crashing just like a fairy tale. I still pinch myself that all of these wonderful things happened. My dream was fulfilled when I did a Grand Prix demonstration ride at Willinga Park on the 19th of February 2019. What a blast. It was absolutely wonderful!

Have you ever had someone you didn't know reach out to you and help make your life better? I am lucky enough to have experienced what it's like to have such a real-life Angel.

My beautiful Johno had just had yet another bout of colic. My life was overwhelmed by living the nightmare of trying to navigate and care for his Degenerative Neurological Condition called Equine Shivers, plus all its secondary issues. Like extreme stress reactions and propensity to have a colicky episode.

Until meeting Linda Lord, I didn't know that managing stress was so connected with gut health. Linda is the owner and founder of Poseidon Equine; her approach and products are all about holistic horse care.

Linda didn't just educate me about gut health, she provided Johno with her Stress Paste, Digestive EQ and Digestive VM products and oh my Lord. Johno improved straight away. So I improved, I got to have the best sleeps I'd had for months.

So, don't stop believing in Miracles, Magic, and Angels! They are out there. There are beautiful Angels out there watching over you all the time. Our Angel came in the guise of a beautiful lady called Linda, to whom we are so very very grateful.

Finally, the amazing, wonderful gentleman called Jamie Manning. Jamie's gorgeous wife Karen helped me most days with Johno. I have had the privilege of spending quite a bit of time socially with Jamie. I never use that word hero lightly, as my Dad is my hero, but Jamie is inspirational. He is filled with determination and an incredible zest for life. He is one of my heroes.

Take the time to read Jamie's story. He was in a car accident. He got caught in the car and lost his left arm from the elbow down and his left leg, they were burnt off. This amazing, courageous gentleman has done a long-distance ride on horseback since then, he is on the speaking circuit as well as running his own business. Jamie blows me away!

When the eye specialist told me I was to never ride again, Jamie sent me a great message. He said doctors had told him a lot of things he would never be able to do again but look at him now! So, I take a leaf out of Jamie's book on a daily basis – I just get on with it.

*

HOW ARE CHARITY RIDES ORGANISED?

"There's no point talking about it –
it's ACTION that counts."
Sue-Ellen Lovett

Melb-Syd Paralympic Ride - Narelle Haywood & I with a Police escort

Horses, shoes, truck, sited guides, PR people, stabling, fuel... the list goes on.

First and foremost, there needs to be a reason for a ride. Whether it be to say thank you to Guide Dogs Australia, to raise money for cancer research or to raise much needed funds for Riding For The Disabled. I managed to find ten reasons. But it didn't just happen overnight.

Firstly, you need to work out where you would like to go. To maximise the publicity, fundraising and awareness, we typically rode through highly populated areas. In particular, you have to line it up so that each night you arrive at an appropriate location to hold a fundraising event. As well as a town that can accommodate six horses, and all the riders and helpers, you need a place for everyone to stay, something like a showground with a shower block. You need this every night.

Then you approach a registered charity. For my first ride I approached my Dad's local Lions Club in Mudgee to help. They have continued to help with all the rides since. All ten of them! They are quite an amazing group of ladies and gentlemen.

Running a fundraiser under the banner of a charity group makes the project easier. You get to run it under the one umbrella and the tax dollars that come in the form of Donations are deductible. So, once you've secured yourself a partner for your long-distance ride you then have to start thinking of the logistics of the ride. Where are you riding to? What towns will you pass through? Luckily most towns have a Lions Club which has been hugely beneficial for my rides. Those Clubs have helped us with our fundraising and often organised the showgrounds and locations for the fundraisers.

You need to form a little committee, small is better than large, then start delegating the jobs that need to be done. In the past years, each town's Lions Club organised accommodation, showers at the showground and stables or yards for our horses. Typically, we stayed at showgrounds and on the odd occasion we have stayed at people's private properties.

We approached the Lions Club and the Pony Club in each town to organise a fundraising barbecue or pub crawl. Pubs are wonderful places to sell raffle tickets and fundraise. I have seen the inside of most pubs in New South Wales, Queensland, and Victoria! I've done lots of fundraising and public speaking in these places.

Next you need to work out how many horses you will need on the ride. Normally we took six horses. Contact people who are willing to assist by lending you their horse/s. I always had one horse to contribute, typically my little brown mare, Mudgee. Apart from my first ride and my last ride, all the horses were accessed through the Australian Stockhorse Society. Mr George Richardson organised that for me, which was greatly appreciated.

On the first ride, from Mudgee to Melbourne, we used two or three Arabian horses and one or two Stockhorses. The Arabs were supplied by Kelkette Arabians down near Albury. They were great for the ride. Then you must organise a truck that can take six horses or a truck and a horse float with four horses in the truck, two on the float. Although there are typically only four horses being transported between towns and two are being ridden, it's critical to have transport for all six horses in case you need to get horses safely back somewhere. Generally, while the two horses were ridden between towns, the other four were on the truck going to the showground where they were then fed and watered. The truck driver was then pretty much finished for the day, unless a horse threw a shoe or something.

We typically had a caravan to sleep in. Some people chose to sleep outside in their swags, some slept in the caravan. When we did the Melbourne to Sydney ride in 1998, Winnebago Sponsored us with an amazing Winnebago they'd set up specifically for the ride. It had six bunk beds and one double bed over the driver's seat. I slept in that double bed. It was awesome! We were very much self-contained.

You generally spend anything from 5 to 13 hours in the saddle and ride up to 100 kilometres a day. Most days though are around 60 kilometres, which gets you from town to town and works well for the fundraising.

Then you need to organise the horse feed you are going to use. Usually, I tried to get stock feed stores to Sponsor the ride. Prydes Stockfeed sponsored feed for eight of my rides and Barrastock Stockfeed sponsored two of my rides. This was greatly appreciated! To ensure the horses have a balanced diet you need to organise some lucerne hay. Unless you have a very large truck you can't carry all the feed, so you need to organise drop off points for the feed, especially the hay. You can pick up extra bags of feed as you go through towns. This can work really efficiently.

Then you need to organise Sighted Guides, truckdrivers, a PR person and sometimes just general dogsbodies to help with whatever needs doing.

On all our rides, except the last one, I only ever used one Sighted Guide. The last ride was quite different though. By then I was totally blind, so we needed to know all our bases were covered where safety was concerned. So, I used two Sighted Guides.

To give you an idea and put things into perspective, when we did the Cairns to the Gold Coast ride, 2400 kilometres and 54 days in the saddle, I had eight different Sighted Guides at different times being ferried up and down the coast by bus. We had six truck drivers. The role of being a Sighted Guide is the one that turned over the most, because it is such a high-pressure job. They must watch where they are going, while watching their horse, themselves, the Blind Chick's horse, and the Blind Chick. It is a very stressful and demanding job.

Getting Fuel Sponsors is critical as this is such a big-ticket item. In some towns they donated the fuel, but overall it's better to try and be self-sufficient, so all the money raised goes into the funds raised for whatever charity you are riding for.

You need to organise a raffle and have tickets being sold in all the Pubs and Clubs you go to, and at all the functions. Generally, we sold the raffle tickets for $2 each. That price makes it affordable for everyone. Everyone can buy at least one ticket and feel involved. The pubs are the best place for selling raffle tickets. People are so generous.

Ideally organise it so you have a selection of auction items that you can pull out and auction at each town. This has always been met with great enthusiasm from the locals, and there is generally a Stock and Station Agent somewhere in the crowd that can do you proud by auctioning your items. We have had many such wonderful functions on all the rides. One time at Gunnedah, at the end of their local show, we auctioned off two little plastic Care Bears. Some of the locals got so enthusiastic they syndicated and paid $1,200 for these two little plastic bears that stood about 2 inches high. One had a red coat and one with the blue coat. It was a hoot!

Organise sponsors for all the basics that get consumed along the ride, including cereals, coffee, tea, milk, bread etc. For lunches we generally did a wrap or a sandwich and a piece of fruit. Often lollies go down well, or a cheeky chocolate bar. Sometimes the later gets donated, other times we just put in and buy it. We don't generally have to worry about the evening meal, as that is typically a barbecue with the local Lions Club or Pony Club.

It is a great idea to plan in a couple of non-riding days, so the horses get a spell and the human team get a couple of days break out of the saddle. I found this really important as people burn out very quickly. Such rides can be very intense and very long hours. We typically ate breakfast at 4:30am and were in the saddle by 7am. Of an afternoon, we were feeding and bedding down the horses by 4:30pm, which then allowed everyone to be showered and out fundraising for the evening. In amongst that routine, we also visited schools and did talks, explaining whatever charity we were doing the ride for.

It is also important to have a good working relationship with the local Police and liaise with them before the ride starts. They need to know when you are coming through their area and when you think you might need an escort into town, out of town, or through an area that is a little bit dangerous for the horses.

Over the years the Police have been wonderful to us, we're so grateful for their support. Even down to riding across Sydney Harbour Bridge! We had four Mounted Police, two in front and two behind, as well as three Police cars. We also had a vehicle in front of us putting big rubber mats down over the drain grates on the Bridge so the horses would be more confident going over them. It was pretty cool!

All these little things you have to think of, and plan for. It's no good thinking about them once you get on the ride as things are just too busy then! So make yourself a checklist - right down to how many buckets, feed bins, bridles, saddles, halters, lead ropes, all of it, everything that you need. On that list make sure you have spares of everything because things get left behind, lost or sadly, stolen.

The other thing that is really important is a comprehensive First Aid Kit for the horses. You need to be ready for anything. Absolutely anything can happen on these rides, and you need to be prepared to be able to look after the situation on the spot.

Also, a comprehensive First Aid Kit for people is critical. Generally smaller ones in each vehicle and the main big one stays with the riders in the two support vehicles, one in front, one behind us.

You need signage on each of your vehicles. Signage on the support vehicle and signage on the horse truck. Additionally on the Support Vehicle you need a SLOW VEHICLE SIGN to alert fellow road users to be patient. The signage should include advertising of Sponsors and most importantly, the Charity you are riding for.

Flyers! It's important to have flyers to hand out to people which inform them about the ride. Well designed flyers become something they can look at when they're having a cuppa or talking to their mates, they can pass them on. On these flyers remember to include the Bank Account details where donations can be deposited so you make it as easy as possible for people to donate. Plus, a link to any website or Facebook page you've set up for the ride.

The other thing you need to work out straight away is how much money you will need for the ride (a budget) and where that money is going to come from.

Probably for seven of these rides, maybe eight, I have provided all the funds required. I floated the budget. And often you don't recoup your money. That's ok, that's part of the giving and part of the making a difference. But you need to plan to have money available for the expected purchases AND the unexpected purchases. At the drop of a hat the weather can unseasonably change and there's no way you could have predicted or planned for it. Then suddenly you need wet weather rugs for six horses, so they stay comfortable and ready to face the next day.

When I was doing my first series of rides years ago, there wasn't as much red tape, such as getting approvals for where you wished to ride. Now, it's critical before you commence a ride that all the necessary Local Councils, towns, Police, RMS and Showgrounds are contacted and have approved your route for your ride. One of the safety requests by the Police was that we were off the road by 4:30pm each day.

A lovely thing to plan for having at the end of each day was for all the Team to sit and chat about the day we'd had over a beer or some bubbles with cheese and bickies. Then off we'd got to have a shower and go out fundraising.

*

MUDGEE TO MELBOURNE RAISING FUNDS FOR GUIDE DOGS AUSTRALIA – OUR FIRST OF MANY RIDES

*"Be bold, be game and be willing to put
yourself out there sometimes."*
Sue-Ellen Lovett

Mudgee, Goolma, Wellington, Manildra, Canowindra, Cowra, Young, Cootamundra, Wagga Wagga, Holbrook, Albury, Wodonga, Wangaratta, Benalla, Seymour, Kilmore, finishing at Moonee Valley Racecourse, Melbourne.

Ride Participants included:
My beautiful Guide Dog Donna, my Dad John Lovett, Dad's best mate Jeffrey Pitt (known as Pitty), Bill Benson, Trevor Parks (nickname Road Runner), Terry McDonald (Macca), Leo Robinson (alias Our Vet), Helen Parks, the Sheik (Owner of Goolma Pub), Padre and Betty Low, Nick Willoughby, John Dent, Teddy Mahon, Willie Singleton, Gordon Nichols and the amazing Carlo Dwyer (he Sponsored all the horseshoes for the ride).

* * * * *

There was a wonderful vibe as we left Mudgee. I think the star of the show was the wonderful Terry Mac on his grey horse and his bookie bag in hand going up to people in the street and into shops collecting money. Everyone was cheering him on as we rode out of town, the bag had filled up very quickly.

We had a little send-off by the local Mayor Mr Turner, then the ride began. Quite a few riders from the Mudgee Pony Club and other mates came along for the ride through the town or all the way to Goolma.

Jeffrey Pitt had the ominous job of picking up the horse poo as we rode through town. But he made great use of these golden nuggets by auctioning each pile of nuggets off to avid gardeners to put on their garden as Lucky Poo.

As we proceeded out of town there were people cheering; "good luck, keep safe, have a great ride!" It was so lovely to be surrounded by so many beautiful friends and be farewelled by your hometown. It touched my heart deep down.

Towards the edge of town, we were joined by riders from the Mudgee Pony Club. We also had the privilege of having Mrs Best ride with us all the way to Goolma, she was 80 odd years old! And the wonderful Leo Robinson, who always introduced himself as Our Vet, yet he wasn't, all in good fun. He rode with us, which he did on quite a lot of our rides. He was an amazing gentleman.

Many of the Pony Club members were those I'd been through Pony Club with: Louise Best, Mary Best, Joe Best and Johnny Prince. We had a great group of mates to chat with as we rode. But beside me all the way was my wonderful friend Helen Parks; she was my Sighted Guide.

All the horses we used on this ride were from Kelkette Park Arabian Stud down near Albury, in New South Wales. They were kindly donated by the Barn family which was so greatly appreciated. The only horse on the ride that was not an Arabian Derivative was my little Mudgee.

Terry Mac continued to be such a super star on our way out of town along the road to Goolma. With his Bookie Bag he rode up to trucks, pulling them up on the highway. I think there were two or three buses and numerous trucks, lots of people travelling to Dubbo for their kids sport on the Saturday, the day our ride started. It was so cool, and Terry's Bookie Bag was getting heavier by the minute. And then there was the Sheik, he rode out from Goolma to meet us dressed in Arab regalia on his Arab stallion. It was all such fun as we headed out on the ride with all our local friends. Lots of jokes and laughter.

Then we arrived at Goolma. The Goolma fundraising night was terrific. We had an awesome host, the Sheik. Things were auctioned off left, right and centre. The wonderful little town of Goolma really got behind the cause. People came out in numbers to support the ride and raise money for Guide Dogs Australia. Such an amazing little town and what an amazing night. I tend to think now there may have been just a few hangovers the next morning, not owning up as one of course.

Goolma was just totally amazing; the hospitality and generosity of this gorgeous little town just blew us away. I think there are five houses in Goolma and the pub was busting at the seams with people inside and outside: partying and dancing. This was amazing country hospitality at its best.

We had 20 riders leave with us to ride through to Wellington the next day, bright eyed and bushy tailed.

As we rode out of Goolma from behind us there was a whole heap of noise, bashing and crashing in the horse truck! One of the horses had gone down and had hurt itself. Luckily it only had minor injuries, but they were still enough to stop it riding any further. We left that horse behind and one of the Pony Club lads dropped it back at Mudgee to be cared for while we borrowed a wonderful little horse from Barney Whale. She was a lovely little coloured Stockhorse who fitted in quite well. Although she was very unfit and very fat, we brought her onto the ride very slowly and she did the job perfectly.

Our next stopover was Wellington, where we were hosted by the Wellington Lions Club. A great night was had by all, and more funds were raised. Possibly a few blurry eyes and a few little fuzzy heads the next morning. Sounds like a bit of a pub crawl, doesn't it?

The next day we were on the road again on the Mitchell highway towards Molong where more fundraising, more talks and lots of country yarns were shared. Just outside Molong, at a fork in the road, we were greeted by three riders, all from the Munge family, who guided us through to Manildra. We had a wonderful time staying at the Munge family farm. We swam in the creek with the horses, such a refreshing afternoon after a very hot and long day.

That night the Lions Club hosted a barbecue at Matilda Park in Manildra. Again, there were lots of fundraising, talks, a few drinks and a wonderful night had by all. I'm still really good friends with the Munge family, Philip and Christine Munge and the two children I met Kathleen and Christian.

One thing that I learnt on this ride, being my first ride, was the generosity and the heartfelt kindness showed by these wonderful country people doing it tough, yet here they were bringing us food to eat, hay for the horses, a bunch of flowers, it was just so lovely. People's generosity and kindness and their donations to Guide Dogs Australia was quite heart-warming.

Then things changed a little. The next day we rode to Canowindra, it was cold and wet. Not only had it been absolutely bucketing down, but the place we'd organised to keep the horses for the night fell through! So instead, the horses were put in the yards behind the Police Station. We thought that was quite funny. Not so funny was trying to get the horses from our original place where we were keeping them up to the Police yards. A couple of our helpers wearing gumboots slushing through the mud, with a couple of horses in tow. It was a little stressful getting six horses to the yards but after it was done it was a unanimous decision not to eat at the camp site that night. Let's go to the pub!

Now is a perfect time to help you understand the magnitude of how many pubs I've been into in Australia. For every little town we rode through, there was typically three pubs, sometimes more in the bigger towns, and we sold raffle tickets and fundraised in ALL of them.

Once again, we are on the fundraising trail, Pitty was selling raffle tickets and doing a little bit of public speaking promoting

Guide Dogs, auctioning off items. As per usual an amazing time was had by all. Again, the generosity of the country people is just amazing!

Well, the day riding to Cowra wasn't much better than the day before. It absolutely bucketed down! The rain felt like it was falling parallel to the ground, it was being driven by such a fierce wind. We arrived at Cowra absolutely saturated. And they say the Driza-Bone is supposed to keep you as Dry as a Bone. Well, we were as Wet as a Shag. We were drenched to the skin and freezing. As soon as the horses were bedded down for the night, we went looking for a lovely hot shower.

It is days like these that you often have amazing magical things happen. Like people stopping their amazing big truck that's fully loaded, step out into the rain and fold a $50 note into your hand and say, "Good on you sweetheart, you're doing a good job!"

This happened often! The truckies looked after us while we were on the road. Via their CB radios, they talked about us all the time, letting oncoming trucks know that we were coming and the ones coming up behind. They nursed us to make sure no idiots caused any accidents. The truck drivers kept us safe, they were our guardian angels. Thank you guys! You did a great job! We really appreciated their support. I was told quite a few times by truckers that they called me "The Angel on Horseback." I think that was a little too kind. To me they were the angels looking after us.

But there were some things our Truckie Angels couldn't help us with. Like the ridiculous rain that continued bucketing down.

After we'd trudged on for about four hours, our horses and riders getting pounded by the rain and winds, Dad arrived with the horse truck and yelled out "we're loading up! This is too unsafe! You need to get these horses into the Showground and get you guys dry." He was not happy.

I was not happy! "No Dad! Our RIDE is from Mudgee to Melbourne, so from Mudgee to Melbourne we will RIDE! We will not be putting the horses on the horse truck and cheating! We will be riding every bit of the way."

With that Dad wound his window up, settled the truck in behind our escort vehicle and followed us into town, just in case of any mishap. But we were safe, all was good. We were just very wet and cold.

At this stage of the ride everyone was getting a little tired of having barbecues every meal. We were hanging for some fish and chips, or a baked dinner. But once again, another barbecue! I don't mean to sound ungrateful, we weren't, but a change would've been lovely.

Once again, the next day we were riding, and the steady drenching rain continued. There was no avoiding it.

As we rode though, there was not a lot of traffic. I think the wet weather had kept people in doors. But that quiet time suddenly changed when next thing a vehicle behind us started tooting its horn and flashing its lights. Oh my God, what's wrong?

Next thing that car pulls over beside us. Surprise, surprise, I recognise the voice calling from the car window through the rain! It's my big sister Lizzie, "what are you guys up to?" she asks! Then my brother Pete jumps out of the car with his one leg and his crutches, he hops around the car! I jump off Mudgee and give him a big hug, yes, it's still raining! Helen holds Mudgee for me while I continue to embrace my little brother. I am so proud; I love him so much. He has been through so much, yet he comes and visits me on the ride. I am blown away! Mum is with them, but as per usual, it was Lizzie the strong one in the family, who made this happen for everyone.

Oh my heaven, what an amazing, amazing thing to do! My brother was still recovering from his leg being amputated, yet he was still so keen to come and join us on the ride. He even joked; "I've come to be your Sighted Guide Suey! I'm going to ride with you." Mum nearly choked; I nearly fell over! And Pete, in his usual fashion calmly said, "I'm just joking Mum."

Well, guess what? Pete wasn't joking! He got someone to hoist him up onto Helen's horse, and he finished that day's ride with me with one leg, a smile from ear to ear and .... drenching wet! I am so proud of my little brother. It was an amazing day. While we talked a bit, we also rode in silence. The silence probably said a lot more words than the words did. It was amazing. I love my little brother to the moon and back. He is so brave, amazingly brave, and so courageous.

At Cootamundra it was Helens turn for a family reunion. Her Dad Trevor Parks joined us. He is more affectionately known as Road Runner. Trevor was such an amazing asset to the ride. He spent so much time up the road, down the road, organising this, organising that, picking up money, dropping off money, making sure we were on time. He is such a well-oiled machine. Trevor Parks was to be my father-in-law, he was an amazing man.

Trevor was a Professor at Duntroon RAFF training base in Canberra. He took time off to help us with the ride which was so greatly appreciated. Plus, it was lovely for Helen to catch up with her Dad.

The next day we entered the amazing city of Wagga Wagga. Police met us just out of town and escorted us in. We rode over the old wooden bridge that rattled and shook as we clip clopped across it. Big metal bolts held the pieces of wood together. It was quite a unique sound underneath the horses' hooves.

Riding through Wagga Wagga was amazing, all of the Team were collecting money, especially our resident Road Runner, Jeffrey. Boy oh boy though was it hot! It was such a nice change from after all the rain.

We rode out to the local Riding For The Disabled Centre where we were hosted by the amazing Willie Singleton and his wife Sheila. It was my first experience with Riding For The Disabled, well was I impressed! Now you will understand as you read further, why I revisit this special place and spend a lot of time with Willie and Sheila. My Guide Dog Donna and I helped the riders at the Centre. This is a place where miracles do happen.

Willie was born in South Africa, Rhodesia to be precise. And his story is absolutely mind blowing. We are so fortunate that he chose Australia to call home.

What an amazing complex their RDA is. We spent a lot of time with Willie or Sheila explaining to us what they did. They provide horse related activities to people with disabilities, in order to enhance and develop those people's skills. Their riders were so diverse: cerebral palsy, people with brain injuries, epilepsy, amputees, blind riders ..... you name it, they have worked with it. They made a difference to so many lives.

Firstly, they put a smile on each person's face. Secondly, the therapeutic value of horse riding is immeasurable, I totally back that philosophy. Plus, it brings such joy and happiness to your mind, body and spirit when you ride a horse.

Well, we weren't prepared for the next hiccup. The Roads and Traffic Authority, RTA as it was then, RMS as it is now, refused to allow us to ride along the next part of the Hume Highway! We'd banked on being able to raise possibly another $2,000 or more along that route. So very quickly, an alternative had to be found.

But the secret is - gifts are found in many places! Whether it be an alternative or another way of doing that same thing. Our detour ended up still being very profitable, plus we met many beautiful people.

So our route took us through Mangoplah and Cookardinia. Two towns we hadn't planned on visiting but ended up being wonderful. We raised quite a bit of extra money.

On our way to Holbrook, we called in at Woomargama for lunch and caught up with a few old friends.

Even though we were not permitted to ride along the Hume Highway, as we rode the back ways from Wagga Wagga to Holbrook to Albury, we still had to cross it many times. Being diverted from our original route ended up being a blessing in disguise. We got to meet so many beautiful people and visited lots of lovely little towns.

Riding into Albury we were greeted by a wonderful group of local Pony Club riders. This beautiful welcome had been organised by the President of the Albury PC, a local Police Detective. Our Team of horses, riders and support crew then took a much appreciated two days off.

The beautiful Jenny Beechey gave us a painting as a major raffle prize and so off went the wonderful local clergymen, he helped us sell raffle tickets. But quickly his pockets were brimming with the sales money. "We need something bigger like a blanket, a horse rug maybe!" So we grabbed a clean horse rug out of the truck and off we went. Money just poured into that rug. "Pennies from Heaven" he called it. They were indeed.

The next day was an absolute highlight. We got to stay with Kevin Bohm and his family their Arabian Stud Kelkette Park. They'd supplied three of the horses for our ride. Oh my heavens, what a shindig. It was amazing. I had never seen an indoor arena in my life, or such an amazing complex.

While we were staying at Kelkette Park there happened to be a Quarter Horse Association function at the local Showgrounds. They sent a blanket around to collect money. Thank you for your generosity, it was so greatly appreciated. Everybody was so generous, and the community was so welcoming. It was such a lovely time.

The next day off we rode to Wodonga. It was such a lovely ride and guess what? Not a normal barbecue! We had cod fish on the barbie instead, fresh out of the Murray River. It was so delicious many went back for seconds.

Off we continued, meandering from one side of the Hume Highway to the other, visiting all the little towns and hamlets along the way. Now raising money is no small feat. Yet we met so many wonderful giving Australians and generally even though they were doing it tough themselves, they always found some coin to put in the blanket to make a difference to Guide Dogs.

The ride clip clopped along through the countryside, then we found Dad pulled up on the side of the road chatting to some chap. Helen's description was: "very baggy pants, very big T-shirt and thongs that flipped and flopped when he walked." It sounded like a local lad!

Well gee-whiz, guess what? He wasn't.

He was the local Policeman! He had come to welcome us and

give us directions on how to get to town. His directions were: "ride straight through town and you'll come to the racecourse. Pull in there and we will look after the rest." So that's what we did.

The gent with the big shorts was there waiting for us. What he did next was a total surprise. He proceeded to take my and Helen's horses and walk off. So Helen and I followed with their night feeds behind the gent with the very big baggy shorts. He stops. We quickly unsaddled the horses, put a halter on them and brushed them off. Then we put a couple of rugs on them to keep them warm, as it was going to be a bit of a cool night. Then we were all standing, bamboozled. What's happening tonight? What are we doing? We were all very much in the dark. It was Leah Robinson who asked the question of Mr Baggy Shorts. "What's happening tonight?"

And he just pointed!

There were car lights as far as you could see, all wandering their way into the racecourse. The rest is history.

Wow what a night! Baggy Pants told many a yarn about his days as a Highway Cop. Pitty jumped in with a few good yarns of his own. It was such fun. We made lots of friends and a good time was had by all.

The next day were back in the saddle, on the way to Wangaratta. Thankfully the weather wasn't so bad. The next day we got an amazing surprise. Three gentlemen in a car pulled us over. They'd come from Albury where the local Paper Mill had done a fundraiser for us, that we didn't even know about. It was so kind of them, especially as they'd spent the last two days travelling around trying to find us. They knew we were somewhere in the area!

The closer we came to our destination town, the more the talk amongst the Team about "what's for dinner?" Everyone was a bit worried about another .... barbecue. I don't mean to sound ungrateful, but three weeks of barbecues had us hungry for a change of menu. We'd only had a couple of nights without BBQ's. Once was that lovely Murray Cod, the other was a night at the Cootamundra Pub.

You can imagine our excitement when as we rode into Wangaratta and one of the local restaurants invited us all in for dinner. It was a .... Chinese Restaurant!!! YAH! Everybody was super excited!

The next day we headed off to Glenrowan, the home of Ned Kelly. It was a lovely ride there. Once we arrived, we visited the Glenrowan School and Donna my beautiful Guide Dog showed her progress in working and guiding me around. The children were very impressed. We were suitably impressed by the gold coin donations they'd collected and gave to us. Their donation towards the ride was greatly appreciated.

Then through to Violet Town and Benalla we went, visiting schools, riding up the main street, fundraising each night and going around to the pubs selling raffle tickets. So many people bought raffle tickets and put them in my name, it was quite embarrassing! But anything for a dollar!

Schools are another thing altogether. The students, and teachers, loved watching Donna work and listening to me tell stories about Guide Dogs and how they are trained. It was such a wonderful time to be sharing such a journey with these youngsters.

Staying in the Imperial Hotel was such a lovely change from being in the caravan. It felt so luxurious to have a shower; a clean, warm shower and lovely crisp sheets to sleep on for the night.

There were quite a few riders that rode out to greet us as we rode into the next town, including riders from that local Riding For The Disabled. There were a couple of blind riders in this group, which was really cool. The Police joined us as well as Mayor Seymour. It was a wonderful town to visit. The pride they showed, and the hospitality they gave us was amazing. Such a big-hearted town, such beautiful people.

We were getting closer to our goal, Melbourne, mile by mile, it got closer. Kilmore was our next destination. This is the place where a wonderful sponsor Carlo Dwyer lives. Carlo had generously supplied all our rides horseshoes. He is amazing, he trains farriers plus his company makes a huge range of different types of shoes for many different types of horses.

This was an especially interesting time for me as I'd never seen a horse being 'Hot Shod' before. As we paused in Kilmore, my beautiful mare Mudgee got hot shod. It was amazing. I think poor old Mudgee must have thought her feet were on fire when the shoes were being seared to her hoof. But it really truly was an experience I will never forget.

Okay, 140 kilometres to go. We are nearly there. Wow how this time has flown. It's been amazing.

Four days later it was over. We'd arrived in Melbourne to the Mooney Valley Racecourse. Helen and I were being escorted down the street at Moonee Valley by the Mounted Police. It was such a buzz! We rode across the finishing line and halted our horses. Our ride really was over!

Our Team took the horses away, gave them a bath and rugged them. Mudgee was a star. She had done such an amazing job on such a long ride.

Then right when I needed it, my beautiful Guide Dog came into her own. She guided me up through the crowd to where we were to receive our Official Welcome. The crowd was clapping, I was so proud.

We were met by the Guide Dog Australia head honchos. They welcomed us home and thanked us for our fundraising effort. We had raised $40,000. At that time, it cost approximately $6,000 to train a Guide Dog, so six Guide Dogs would be trained from the money we'd raised. I found this incredibly heart-warming. I knew the difference that my beautiful Guide Dogs had made to my life, independence, and mobility. They gave me a life of my own and choices ... just like it should be.

This ride did much more than raise funds and meet lots of beautiful people. It lit the flame deep inside me to make a difference and to help others. I had found a way to do that - on horseback, riding long distances and having a fantastic time.

The goal of my ride was massive, to help others. That is what it's all about, making a difference. I am so very grateful to all the supportive people that helped make this happen, and so very, very grateful to my Dad's Lions Club and eternally grateful for him believing in a Blind Chick and her dreams.

How absolutely incredible is the dedication of this Lions Club. They go on to do nine more rides with me. We believe in making a difference and making dreams come true. I am so very grateful to them.

*

FIRST LOVE

*"Life is full of challenges.
Nothing is definite."*
Sue-Ellen Lovett

Well, I know I had many crashes while growing up. Being a teenage girl is not an easy thing. The expectations, hormones, the whole bit ... stinks! I think it would've been much easier to be born male.

With being a teenager of course came romantic crushes. That's how one day ... something changed!

While I was at home at Carlisle Park, I decided to go and visit my friends Jan and Allan. Jan is my cousin, I thought I would go and have a couple of nights with them. Well, the only way this chickie babe was going to visit anybody was on her pony. So, after telling Mum and Dad where I was going, I saddled up my horse, put a bag of clothes in a backpack and off I went. I wish I could remember the horse's name because we had a lovely ride out on the road, down Melrose Lane and passed the beautiful mountain.

For those that know Mudgee well, we went up around the back of Mudgee behind Burrundulla, past the Burrundulla Homestead, down past the local radio station 2MG and out along the Gulgong Road, mainly trotting and cantering. We rode the many miles in no time at all. In fact, I arrived just in time for afternoon tea, which was lovely. The ride was beautiful. At that stage there was still a verge strip on the side of the road so you didn't need to go on the actual road where the cars drove, you could just trot and canter along the edge quite safely. Unlike today, the tar is from one side to the other, so no riding horses down the side of the road these days.

We didn't go over McDonald's bridge, just before the Columbine Reserve. We went down under it, so I gave my horse a drink and a little bit of a swim. After hitting the road again, another few miles, we were at the Kaludabah turn off. Three more miles to the Homestead. Yay it was like coming home! I so love the property. It is so in my veins. The beautiful hills as you enter on the left-hand side full of gold. They say it was a very big gold-digging area and in the paddocks on the right-hand side were hills created by the diggers from when they had been digging in the gold rush. It is such beautiful country.

I arrived at Jan and Allan's and after putting my horse in the paddock I gave it a biscuit of hay, a brush and some water. Then off inside to see my cousins I went. It was lovely to catch up. They even had a couple of cold beers set up on the veranda. While we chatted, we watched Allan with his sheep dog. What a master at working sheep! He trains his dogs on chooks first. I was absolutely mesmerised sitting, watching and learning,

I stayed that night; we had a lovely roast dinner. Jan is notoriously known for her wonderful baked dinners. The next day she suggested I go and meet the Jackaroos, all five of them. So off we tootled over to the cottage to meet the Jackaroos in the yard.

The first thing we came across was an old VH Holden ute. All the front and one side had been pulled off it. Looking down we noticed legs dangling out from underneath it, along with a fair bit of swearing as well. I went over and knocked on the side of the ute;

"Anybody there?"

"Yes" came the reply.

I said, "are you having a few troubles?"

"Yes," came the voice as a skinny grease covered lad slithered from underneath the old car. He stood up and offered me his greasy hand.

"Hi, my name is David." I declined the greasy hand.

I said "seems like you're having a bit of trouble there. Anything I can do to help you?"

He was having trouble attaching the brake line that carries the fluid to the brakes. Having done a fair bit of work with cars with my Dad, I offered to help. Well in no time at all we had the brake line hooked up nice and snug, and tight. Ready to go!

"Oh my God where the hell did you come from?" asked David. I explained how my Dad had been Manager of Kaludabah and that while he'd retired a few years ago, I still kept in contact with everyone. Plus, I'd done lots of work with cars with my Dad over the years, so I had a reasonable idea of how things worked.

After chatting with the guys for a while, I headed off back to Jan. David walked me to the gate and said, "would you like to go to the movies on the weekend?" "Yeah okay." Why not, I thought. So, the next day I jumped back on my horse and rode home to Mum and Dads. I had a lovely visit catching up with Jan, Allan, and everyone.

Well, it was rather lovely going to the movies, and things progressed from there. I told David about my condition and that I had very little time to see all the things I would like to see. I explained to him about the tunnel vision and how it slowly closed in and that I was already legally blind and how I'd never held a car driving license. He understood then why I went everywhere on horseback. I explained how upsetting it was when people called me a fraud and said I could see more than I could see. I thought the fact that I could see a little bit at all was a blessing. But there were lots of people who sat in judgement, and I was very self-conscious and not coping with the fact that I was losing my sight. But I made the best of every day.

David ended up being a great mate and helped me through a lot of very difficult times. I think even David didn't understand sometimes how you could see one minute and not see at all the next. I could see a little bit during the day, but I had absolutely no night vision. It was like looking down the barrel of a rifle. That's what tunnel vision is like. And if you're looking with the right light, at the right place, then yes you might get to see it. But if you're not looking with the right light, at the right place, you'll miss it.

David loved life on the land and soon got bored with being a Jackaroo. He was a very clever young man. So, when I heard my cousin Tony was looking for a Station Hand out at Nyngan on a property called Moonagee, David went for an interview and got the job! He worked out there for quite a while. I'd go visit on weekends or he'd drive back to Mudgee for a visit. There's nothing good about long distance relationships! They're difficult.

Every now and then I'd go up to Moonagee to help Tony out. When their cook Sylvia went on holidays I'd cook for the Jackaroos and the boss, which was always lots of fun. The boys would go shooting of a night and I'd sit at home, watch telly, and wait till they returned. Then I'd make them all a cuppa before everyone headed off to bed.

David worked at Moonagee for quite a while. He developed lots of really good skills, did lots of horse riding and lots of mustering on the large acreage. It was quite an amazing experience, but this long-distance relationship thing wasn't working. So, David started looking in the Land newspaper for job opportunities where we could both go somewhere and live. We applied for a job in Forbes working at a chicken farm ... and got it! It was predominantly caged chickens, called battery hens but they also had quite a few pigs, crossbred sheep and they bred fat lambs. It was a very pretty little place.

It was lovely setting up house with David. The cottage was quaint, very old and the job wasn't hard but it required consistency, seven days a week. It was a matter of collecting the eggs in the morning and packing them. Then of an afternoon, we had to check if any chooks were sick. David had the ominous job of gathering the sick chooks and feeding them to the pigs. Nothing got wasted. Even if there was a sheep that died lambing, that sheep got thrown to the pigs. From which there was nothing left of the carcass after two days. I still find that fact quite frightening!

The reason that no dead livestock was left lying around was to discourage wild dogs or foxes from the property. We didn't want to lose any new lambs.

Feeding the pigs was always an interesting experience. After you've seen them demolish sheep and chickens the thought of ever falling over in their pen was frightening. But it was a cool place to work. I had my horse Zoe there and used to play with her every day. She was a beautiful little Anglo Arab filly by Mr McCander's beautiful Arab stallion called Grey Diamond. I had such fun on her. We'd go out mustering with David, he on the motor bike and I on Zoe.

The people who owned the property, Mr and Mrs Green, used to take me up to visit his Mum and Dad up the road. They were an elderly couple who I'd enjoy having afternoon tea with at least once a week. They were such a beautiful family.

While we were working at Forbes something was more and more on my mind... my sight was getting worse! David and I spoke at length about what we could do about this and what we could do for the future. We decided to travel! So, we set the ute up with a rooftop tent and off we went around Australia for 18 months.

We went north first, heading up to Queensland where the adverts describe it as 'Beautiful one day, Perfect the next.' Well, they were not wrong, we loved Queensland. It was spectacular country. We stayed on a beautiful little farm near Nambour where we did strawberry picking and farm work. I taught the daughter Phoebe to ride. We had a such a lovely time. We stayed in touch with this family and would farm sit for them when they went sailing their yacht around the Whitsundays. We'd go and work, then come back to farm sit while they went up on the yacht. Then off we'd go travelling again, finding more itinerant work along the way.

We spent some lovely time at Airlie Beach, a gorgeous spot in the Whitsunday Region of Queensland. There are beautiful islands out from Airlie, so we went and stayed on deserted islands. At the end of each day, we'd walk along the beach. It was lovely and we met such wonderful people while we were travelling.

Then we headed up to Bowen, it was time to make some more money. So, we went tomato picking. You've heard of Bowen tomatoes?

Well holy cow! I certainly wasn't cut out for tomato picking. But we did it for a while. Then one of the guys said, "hey Lovie would you like a job in the shed sorting tomatoes?" I said that would be awesome, plus it was an air-conditioned job! My new job was simply a matter of picking the green ones out from the red ones. But keep in mind I had tunnel vision! So how many tomatoes did I see at a time? Not many! So then came calls from the boss lady at the front – "Hey, there are too many green tomatoes coming through!" Oops! Someone was missing lots of green ones. So sadly, the cushy job with the air con didn't last long.

While at Bowen we stayed at a lovely caravan park where we befriended the owner. So, at night we'd sit in the spa with the park owner and drank champagne or beer. We had a great time in spectacular countryside, with spectacular people.

While we drove, David would point out things to me that were worth looking at. We'd stop to have a closer look whenever we could. I was always blown away when he was describing things to me! Once he described a guy riding in front of a Brahman herd, the herd following, with a guy riding along behind. I thought that was rather amazing. But apparently that's how Brahman's work, they follow. Very clever!

Another thing I learned is that cows love pumpkins! At Bowen property, as well as tomatoes they also grew commercial crops of pumpkins. If one had a hole in it or something was not quite right or a little rotten, they would feed it to the cattle. The cattle love pumpkins!

We then headed back down towards Nambour. We did a bit

of farm sitting there, as well as a bit more strawberry picking. We used to go around to a lot of the restaurants selling the strawberries, which was pretty cool. I had my 21st birthday up there at a wonderful restaurant that the family we worked for took me to. It was called the Kondalilla Falls, it was just beautiful! I had a magnificent birthday.

When we would go and stay up at Ken and Margaret's place and farm sit for them when they were away sailing, they wouldn't let us stay in our tent. We stayed in the old bus they had set up for accommodation for their itinerant workers. Wow, it was so lovely and comfortable. Plus, it was positioned underneath a most magnificent mango tree. But... there's something else that loves living amongst mango trees. Something I don't like. Big hairy spiders! Or rather – MASSIVE hairy spiders! Every time you picked something up, a hairy spider ran up your arm or up your leg. Oh my heavens, I was on edge all the time! I am definitely not a spider lover.

Two or three nights a week we would be invited up to the main house to dine, which was lovely. We'd often be sitting in the loungeroom and get to watch the most magnificent lightshow of lightning and thunder. The home was on a hill behind Nambour, it was absolutely spectacular!

Our journey continued. We headed back down south, stopping it at different places and checking out the countryside. We popped into Mudgee and stayed at home for a few weeks to freshen up. Then we headed down south towards Mildura, for some grape picking. We were still living in a little blue tent and a white Holden ute. Gosh we did some miles in that ute.

Well I got myself a job grape picking. They were sultana grapes and being Mildura in summer you started picking very early, up at daybreak, because of the pounding head. We'd have brekkie then off we went on the back of the tractor. You had to fill bins with the grapes and then the grapes were taken down and put on paper racks. The racks were spread out with grapes all over them to dry. Then the paper racks were rolled with the grapes in them and packaged. This left you with the sultanas. It was a very cool process. It took about three to four or even sometimes five days for the grapes to dry out enough to wrap them, then they were sent off for processing. It was very simple, easy work.

But man, oh man did I have a problem with those big hairy spiders! So, I went from picking grapes to working on the racks spreading grapes and raking out the stalks. This suited me down to the ground as there were no... spiders!

Well, all good things must come to an end!

The time had come for our travelling to finish. After the grape picking, we went back to Mudgee for a while. From Mudgee David went into the Air Force. He was a very clever young man and was wasted just travelling around the countryside with a Blind Chick. He went to Edinburgh Air Force Base in South Australia where he spent many months training. Then he was transferred to Laverton in Victoria where we met a wonderful family Mick and Fay Craig who I worked for, looking after their show horses. I absolutely adored them. They had a daughter called Fiona and sons Andrew and Darryl. Great family, great fun.

Unbeknownst to me when we were working on the property in Holbrook, David was doing something he knew I wouldn't approve of. He was having a fling with the property Manager's daughter! She and I had become great mates, so I didn't hesitate to invite her to join David and I when we went out to Mick and Fay's for dinner one night. Keeping in mind that I am totally night blind and I had only a little bit of sight in my right eye, imagine my surprise when going home, our young friend sitting between us, I looked across as we were going under a street light and here they were holding hands! I was devastated, absolutely gutted beyond belief. Needless to say, she was on the next bus out.

I really didn't know what to do, or what to think. So, I went to Mudgee for a short while before returning home to Werribee.

Then David did the unexpected. He asked me to marry him!

The question of to marry him or not scooted through my mind, backward and forward, backward and forward. David was such a lovely man, but did I want to marry him?

In my heart of hearts, I believe making a commitment to someone for the rest of your life is a big decision, huge! Was I ready to make that magnitude of a commitment?

So of course, I discussed it with my parents. My Mother was adamant about what she thought I should do. She considered me fortunate to have anyone who'd want to marry me given I was on track to going totally blind. She called it me being stupid, to turn such a man down.

Dad on the other hand was just so Dad. His only concern, as always, was would I be happy, if I married David?

So, what did I do?

I got married! Albeit only for a very short time.

To this day I am so sorry for what I did to David. Getting married ruined a very, very good friendship. We shouldn't have married. I didn't love him enough to make that level of commitment. I shouldn't have listened to my mother. I should have listened to my heart.

But we had a hell of a time while it lasted. We have lots of very fond memories of our amazing travels around Australia together.

Interestingly, David asked me to marry him soon after I did the 1984 long-distance ride. He wasn't a fan of how totally overwhelming the organising, preparing for, promoting of, doing, and after effect, the ride was. So, much to my surprise, after that ride finished, instead of complimenting the Team and I for our successful fundraising and fantastic adventure, he said, "if you do another one, that's it."

So, what did I do?

I did another one the following year, in 1985! I'm not good at being bullied.

Yes, I have been told many times, that my attributes include bloody mindedness and stubbornness!

*

LOVE WHO YOU ARE

Godolphin ex-racehorse Vashka, Amani & I

Look what I stumbled across this in my travels. I thought it was definitely worth sharing. You might like to share it to.

*

"In order to love who you are,

You cannot hate the experiences you've had that shaped you."

I'm wishing you a wonderful day. Be kind to yourself and to others. Smile good morning, it doesn't take much to make a difference.

Sending you loads of love and hugs, Sue-Ellen.

*

QUESTIONS MOST PEOPLE AREN'T GAME TO ASK! PT 3

"It's okay to be vulnerable."
Sue-Ellen Lovett

WHY DID YOU GIVE UP HAVING A GUIDE DOG?

I've given this question a heck of a lot of thought. I think it really had to do with the NDIS starting a program which allowed me to employ somebody to take me shopping. It's so much easier going shopping with somebody who communicates. I hold their arm and they guide me around. Yes, maybe I don't have quite the independence and mobility I would have with a Guide Dog, but it's a lovely interaction and friendship when you go shopping with a mate. Also I don't have to thank people all the time because I'm now able to pay for their service, for them to look after me.

The past two years have I missed having a Guide Dog?

No I haven't. But I have missed my mobility and independence around our farm. While I use my white cane I still get lost in the garden on a daily basis and I hit the electric fence at least twice a week with my white cane, which is not a good look. Apparently Johno used to think it was hilarious. I'm sure Lola gets many laughs as well.

WHAT IS ONE OF THE SPECIAL THINGS THAT HAPPENS ON EACH OF YOUR LONG DISTANCE RIDES?

This is a tough question to answer, there are so many special things, especially meeting our objective of that ride, raising much needed funds for a good cause.

But something very personal, very special to me, is the amazing poetry that my friend Bob Cooper would create for each of the rides.

This is the amazing poem this amazing gentleman created for our Ride to Save Life fundraiser, from Mudgee to Mudgee, 700 km's meandering through local towns and hamlets. The money we raised funded putting in three helipads, complete with fuel dumps and lights, at each of the Mudgee, Rylstone and Gulgong hospitals.

What do you think of Bob's handy work?

THE RIDE FOR THE SKY ANGEL
By Bob Cooper

The tearful anguished cry of pain, a child is almost lost,
And all who hold the small ones dear, can never count the
cost.
This child could be a future King or Queen or Head of State,
This child may be an artist or just one who's always late.
It doesn't matter if this child is poor, or steeped in wealth,
For sickness knocks on any door, in misery and stealth.
But in the darkest night it comes or in the brightest day.
The whirring beat of Angels Wings to take the child away.
The Care Flight Helicopter will find that specialist aid,
To give these kids a fighting chance and leave them less afraid.
Sue-Ellen knows the cost of fear, and has seen the darker side,
She knows when death knocks on your door,
its not a time to hide.
It is a time to face the world and with an outstretched hand.
Fight back, and give, to help these souls
less fortunate in our land.
So with her horses and her dog she does what she does best,
That's raising money for a cause, none better than the rest.
And this one's for a Helipad I'm sure you understand,
There's no point having Angels, if
there's no damn place to land.
Sue-Ellen rides this ride for life, so some pour soul may live.
And you can all be angels, if you dig down deep, and give.

"THE MARE STARTED F***ING, SHE BARKED AND BARKED!" WHY DID YOU GO TO WRITE THAT FOR A POST ON FACEBOOK?

I didn't mean to. To write a post or send an email or message I dictate into my phone, and it converts the audio to text. Because the conversion often ends up with hilarious or rude words being written I always listen to the text being played back to me before I send it.

As an example, this is what I wanted to post on my Johno & the Blind Chick Facebook group about my challenging ride in the Atlanta Paralympics:

"I drew a little red-head mare out of the box to ride . As we went across the centreline, the mare started f***ing, she barked and barked. Oh my Lord, thankfully I stayed on."

Lucky I listened to it before posting it so I knew it needed to be sent to my wonderful friend Jacqueline, so she could fix the barking.

WHAT DO YOU DO WHEN LIFE GETS TOO MUCH?

Always when things get a bit overwhelming, I try and find something positive in it. Typically, there is something to learn from that shitty situation, albeit it doesn't feel like it at the time.

And yes, finding something positive to focus on is not always easy. But when you look hard enough, you do find a silver lining.

Do you cook?

Oh absolutely! I love cooking.

I love cooking for my mother-in-law Lee and father-in-law John because they appreciate my cooking. I have to admit, I'm probably not very adventurous with cooking but I do a mean baked dinner.

Have you had an accident when you are cooking?

Absolutely!

The latest thing I've done was the simple thing of making myself a cup of coffee. You'll get a hoot out what happened. We use long life milk which comes in the same shaped container as some other things. I'd made myself what should have been a gorgeous cup of coffee with milk, but instead it was a totally disgusting cup of coffee with beef stock! It was gross. I nearly threw up. Out over the veranda that cup of yuck went and I made a new one with .... milk!

Any embarrassing moments when you were a kid?

Yes, I think this one is a ripper.

I was probably about 17 or 18 and working at Kaludabah with my Dad. I was working at the Embryo Transplant Centre. Now Dad went up north to Burke fishing for the week. When he left I was employed. When he returned, I was sacked.

Why? Because I tried to explain to the guy that was doing the drafting of the cattle that there was an easier way to do it, and this is how my Dad does it. Oops, he sacked me on the spot. I still giggle about this. My Dad was understandably furious, and I was back at work the next day.

HAVE YOU ALWAYS HAD AN AFFINITY
WITH HORSES AND ANIMALS?

Absolutely.

It is a blessing. I am so grateful for the bond I have with horses, with nature and all the beautiful birds. It is cool how things happen if you just allow it, it's magic. Let it come into your life and live it.

*

LIZZIE

"Not all Angels have wings"
Sue-Ellen Lovett

Lizzie's daughter Sarah &
Sarah's daughter Paisley

Lizzie & son Jack

How blessed am I to have a wonderful sister like Lizzie? I know I didn't think like this as a child, but I've grown up, thank heavens.

I have to admit that when my sister Elizabeth was born, I thought they should have bundled her back up and put her back where she came from! I went from being the apple of my Dad's eye to being not so important. There was a new kid on the block.

Growing up was interesting. As a first child Mum and Dad spent a lot of time teaching me to talk and everything, hence I spoke at nine months and I'm still chattering now! So when Lizzie was born they decided not to teach her anything, because they thought she would learn it all from me.

Lizzie is a very beautiful soul, the apple of my Nana and Poppy's eye. They spent many an hour together. I can remember going out trapping bunnies with Poppy and Lizzie. Lizzie was riding Pentecost and falling asleep. Pentecost was just walking along while Lizzie was sound asleep, not falling off.

We had loads of adventures growing up. Even though Lizzie was not as into horses as I was, we weren't allowed to do Pony Club unless we did it as a family, so I used to wash Lizzie's horse, even work Lizzie's horse, so we could go to Pony Club. I so loved doing things with horses.

When you look at things today, they haven't changed much have they?

But Lizzie was the one at the Shows that would get the blue ribbon for Girl Rider. I was not a pretty rider. I was an affective rider. But Lizzie was a very pretty rider and so she won many, many, ribbons.

Lizzie and I both worked at the local Dairy when we moved from Kaludabah to Carlisle Park. We both had wonderful times with Jack and Jean Cover, going down enjoying cheese and bickies, and a beer! This was always great fun, albeit the later was of course frowned upon by our Mum.

Lizzie also went to Sydney where she did a June Dally-Watkins Personal Development Course. She was very, very beautiful and even competed in the Miss Australia contest. She did us proud.

But there is something really special about our Lizzie. She has an inner strength; she is there for everybody. She is like the hub of a wheel; she carries everybody's weight. She always puts everyone else first. She is such a beautiful person.

When Lizzie grew up, she moved away and had many different jobs, but the highlight I think is Lizzie's two beautiful children

Sarah and Jack. Oh my heavens they are just so gorgeous. They were the apple of Dad's eye. In fact, I'm sure we had Dad at least two maybe three years longer, because of these two beautiful children.

When my Dad was really sick, Lizzie would take him off to the doctors. Dad would tell one story and Lizzie would tell the true story. Dad always made out everything was okay, when it wasn't. So it was Lizzie who would let the Doctor's know, in no uncertain terms, what was happening.

My beautiful sister has an inner strength. Lizzie is like the Angel you would like beside you all the time. She is kind, she listens, she makes out she's tough but she's not quite so. I am very blessed to have such a beautiful sister.

Growing up we fought like Killkenny cats. But we are best of friends now. In fact, she's probably my best friend! We talk once or twice a week and while we don't get to catch up nearly enough, she rings my husband Matthew and speaks to him about when they are coming over to visit because I get so excited. Their last visit was when Lizzie and Sarah came over and stayed the night. Oh my heavens, I was like a kid the day before Christmas! It was just so lovely to be surrounded by my family. Even though they are only an hour and a half away, I don't get to see them nearly enough.

Lizzie even has a job working with people. She is such a humanitarian, such a gorgeous caring girl. I am so very blessed to have you as my sister Lizzie. I don't think you know how very special you are.

I love you; I treasure you, and I thank you for just being you.

*

A Beautiful Little Brown Mare called… Mudgee

"I have magical moments in my day, every day."
Sue-Ellen Lovett

Whilst still living at Werribee I'm desperately wanting a horse. I was riding a fine mix of horses. But there is nothing like having your own horse. Fay and Mick, owners of the property I worked for looking after their show horses, said if I got my own horse, I could keep it there. So I kept my eye out.

I worked out a budget and asked David to take me out to the Dandenong horse sales. David said "you know what your Dad says, not to buy horses from the sales. You never know it's history, what it's been through and what it's capable of." I kept saying "I know, I know, I've heard it all before. I'm just looking ok!"

So we entered the saleyards. All the horses were standing on cement, some saddled, some not saddled, some with their bums to us looked like they would kick our teeth in. Some looked like they'd like to bite your head off, others just wanted a pat and a cuddle. Then we got to this little brown mare! She was about 14.2 hands high and man, oh man was she fat. She was standing quietly with a western saddle on and, a clubbed front foot.

"Well" said David. "She'll barely do. She has a club foot and is so fat you'll never be able to get a saddle on her." I said, "well she has one on now and I'm sure she can lose some weight. but we'll see what price she goes for."

Waiting for this little mare to come up in the sale was like waiting for the jug to boil. Never seemed to be happening. Horses kept coming through, and no little brown mare. I was about to give up, I thought they pulled her out of the sale and then guess who appears, this little brown mare with this massive, big western saddle on her with a guy that just rode around, turn left, and right, made her back up. I don't think she could try anything on, she was too fat. The bidding started and David kept saying no and I kept bidding, and guess what – I came home with a little brown mare with a club foot.

I named her Mudgee, after my hometown. She was an absolute beauty. Very pretty little thing. So, to get started I put her in slow work and worked on her losing some weight.

I had Mudgee at Fay and Mick's for a little while. Then we got on with planning my ride from Mudgee to Melbourne. It was a cracker of a distance, 1,200km! So I needed to find another five horses to put in work alongside Mudgee, to train up so they'd be fit and ready for that long distance.

This was the start of an amazing journey between a little brown mare called Mudgee and a Blind Chick.

I will quickly go through the rides and try to get them in numerical order date wise:

Mudgee to Melbourne
1,200km in 1984 – charity: Guide Dogs.
We raised $36,000 (at that stage a Guide Dog cost $6,000 to train, so we raised enough to train six Guide Dogs.)

Brisbane to Sydney
1,200km in 1985 – charity: Riding For The Disabled NSW

Cairns to Gold Coast
2,400km in 1988 – charity: Riding For The Disabled Australia. This ride was 54 days in the saddle and one hell of a distance.

Then in 1989 I was diagnosed with Cancer! The best way for me to cope when things go pear shaped is to get on a horse. So, I approached Camperdown Children's Hospital and then... we did the next two rides.

Mudgee to Mudgee
1990 We started in Mudgee then travelled out through Central West NSW, Tamworth, Warialda, Moree, Bourke, Cobar, Dubbo and back to Mudgee a distance of 1800km, raising money for the Camperdown Children's Hospital.

Mudgee to Sydney
1991. We went out via Bathurst, Orange, West Wylong, Mount Kosciuszko, Cooma, Canberra, Batemans Bay, Nowra, Wollongong, Sydney finishing at the Camperdown Children's hospital. A distance of 1,800km and 36 days in the saddle.

The next rides were:

MUDGEE TO MUDGEE
A ride in 1994 called 'A Ride to Save Life' was to thank the

local area for all their support. It funded putting in three helipads, each with landing lights and a fuel dump. One each for Mudgee, Rylstone and Gulgong hospitals.

Mudgee to Newcastle
1995. We rode up through the Central West of NSW for 1,200km. We called it the 'Ride To Save Sight', a fundraiser for the Lions Club of NSW.

Melbourne to Sydney
1997. 1,200km promoting and fundraising for the Sydney 2000 Paralympics.

Brisbane to Sydney
1998. Another 1,200km ride promoting and fundraising for the Sydney 2000 Paralympics. 36 days in the saddle. We raised over $1.1 million dollars across both Paralympic rides.

Dubbo to Dubbo
2018. This 700km ride was called 'Ride Against Cancer' and raised money for the Oncology Unit at Dubbo Base Hospital. The only horses we used were Australian off the track thoroughbreds.

* Keep in mind the preparation for each of these rides is massive. The six horses used are in training for six weeks prior to the start of each ride. They need to be fit and healthy – that's critical. Each horse's management is meticulous – they are wormed and have special rubber pads put on their feet under their shoes to prevent any stone bruises.

* To help you put perspective on the huge number of miles we travelled, each set of horseshoes only lasted about 10 days.

The beautiful little horse Mudgee has done all these rides bar the last one. She passed away at the age of 35 due to a severe bout of colic. Yet two weeks before that tragic day, she had carried some of my young students on her back, competing in the local dressage competition. And winning her dressage class. I didn't let the kids canter her then, it was just walk and trot, she was spectacular till the day she died. Just such a pretty little girl.

There are so many amazing memories with Mudgee. We have done so many awesome things together. From the long distance rides to teaching hundreds of kids to ride this beautiful little mare was made to make people smile and be happy. She brought joy to everybody.

My two nephews Bradley and Daniel learnt to ride on Mudgee. They'd be on her, trotting down the road, with one of them just about bouncing off her. Mudgee would slow down until they got themselves sorted and just plod along keeping them safe. Mudgee always remedied the situation.

I used to ride her bareback, all the time. I love riding bareback, and she had the most beautiful back to sit on. In every pace whether it be walk, trot or canter, you could carry a glass of wine and not spill a drop. She was so smooth.

One of my friends, a gentleman who has since passed away called Bobby Cooper, wrote many a beautiful poem about Mudgee. One of them was about a club foot which was quite funny.

On our special ride Brisbane to Sydney, we had the privilege of swimming on the beach at the Gold Coast. Now not many horses get to do this, but Mudgee did. Narelle Hayward riding Steve Cumberland's horse Rocky, we swam at the beach then we rode down 7 Mile Beach and came out somewhere down at Tweed Heads. It was so cool. Followed by the camera man all the time and ducking in for a swim every now and again. Mudgee was not so keen on the white on the waves but once she figured out they weren't going to hurt her we were body surfing. How cool!

Then when we did Cairns to the Gold Coast it was amazing, we left Mudgee in the middle of winter all 6 horses were triple rugged. It was so cold and frosty and the further north we went a rug would come off, by the time we had got to Cairns all the rugs were off and the clippers came out so all the horses got clipped. Boy they looked absolutely spectacular from having their woolly coats on.

In the Cairns to the Cold Coast ride we went up three weeks early so the horses could get acclimatised. The humidity was massive even in winter for our southern horses. But they acclimatised well. We would go out on rides doing 25km a day. Generally riding one, leading another two horses, just depending how many riders we had with us at a time. On that particular ride it was massive organisation and coordination.

It took us three days to drive up, horse truck with four horses on it plus a horse float with 2 horses on it. All the men in the truck were such fun. On this ride we only used Australian Stockhorses. It was amazing, such resilient and tough animals with an awesome temperament.

Before the ride started, we did lots of sightseeing which was amazing. We also went and did presentations to Pony Clubs, talks at local Rotary, Lions and Pony Clubs, attended dinners that doubled as fundraisers for the ride which was for Riding For The Disabled Mudgee. Then the ride started, 2400km, 54 days in the saddle on this ride. I went through 8 Sighted Guides, 8 truck drivers and the only person that was with us all the way was the PR lady Jo, who needed an award. Such a long way to be with the same team!

So, we had the team being transported by bus, up and down the coast for 54 days. Changing drivers, changing Sighted Guides and... and... and. It took a lot of coordinating and organising.

Do you need a break??
Time to grab cuppa??
If so, see you back here ready for the rest of this journey with Mudgee!

THE UNSEEN RIDER
By Bob Cooper

Dust and heat on the western plain and rarely a tree for shade.

Dry and parched by the north west wind and
blurred by the dust it made.

Few would venture to ride this way, for
drought is the master here.

And those that ride on these western plains,
ride with a soulmate – fear!

But the girl pushed on past the empty miles,
her heart as big as the land.

Sightless since her teenage years, but her
guide was the unknown hand.

Pushed by a need not quite understood by
those that supported her ride.

A promise of hope for the ill and maimed,
and a comfort for those that have died.

And in time she too will ride through the gates,
where the great stable lets her abide.

But their too they will know of her unselfish deeds,
and especially Sue-Ellen's rides.

On this ride my beautiful Mudgee did most of the miles. She was a horse you could just pull out at any time if another horse threw a shoe or needed a break. I can remember doing many miles down the highway bareback on days it was raining, I hated the idea of my stock saddle getting wet. My Sighted Guides always rode in a saddle. I was so lucky that all my Sighted Guides came from my hometown of Mudgee. Terry McDonald stock and station agent, Mike Cox a land owner and Richard Woolly a local lad.

On this ride Mudgee was a true champion. She was never ever a problem, until a particular day during the Cairns to Gold Coast ride. We'd run a competition for whoever raised the most money, it had to be a rider under the age of 18. The winner got to spend a week with us on the ride. Well a lovely young lad came to spend a week with us. He used to volunteer at the Kellyville Riding For The Disabled. Mudgee knew him for quite a while, from our work at Kellyville. Lovely young man, lovely rider. So, we thought it'd be best to put him on the safest horse, Mudgee. However, catastrophe hit about 20km into their time together.

He didn't see the hole in the road until it was too late. Mudgee went down a culvert, piercing a piece of steel into her knee. Instantly all hell broke loose. I couldn't believe my beautiful Mudgee had been injured and was out of the ride. The ride stopped there and then, we put Mudgee on the float, took the horses back to the showground and drove to the closest vet.

When we got there, Mudgee still on the horse float and only able to stand on three legs, the vet said, "it's not looking good." He x-rayed her knee and said, "she needs total stable rest for at least three weeks, and I don't think she'll be able to be ridden ever again."

I was so devastated, but I also believe in miracles.

We got her off the float and put her in a stable at the showgrounds of the town we were in. First thing each morning, we floated Mudgee and a stable buddy to that nights designation, and put her in the stable there. This was her box rest as ordered.

But that wasn't sitting well or working for me. I needed her with me. So, we picked her up and brought her back to the Team and every hour I got in the float with her, and I healed her leg.

I could not bear the thought of her not being with me and not being on the ride. This hourly routine of my healing went on for six days. Then we took her back to the vet for a check-up. The vet said, "why are you back here, I told you she needed full stable rest for three weeks." I said, "she's walking fine, she's not irregular, there's no heat in her leg anymore and the swelling has gone down." The vet was very dubious and not impressed, but he proceeded to x-ray her leg and scan her knee again. He could not believe her tragic knee injury had totally healed in... six days! Totally perplexed he turned to me and asked "what the hell did you do? She's fine, there is no scarring, there is no mark, there's nothing!"

I really truly didn't have an answer other than "love and positive healing energy."

The next day Mudgee hit the road again. She was hilarious, quite adamant about being last on the truck! She'd learnt that if she was loaded last onto the horse truck, that meant she was first off. She'd hated the days she'd had the floating boots on, because she knew they were the days she wouldn't be worked.

She was soooo happy to be back on the road, and I was so relieved to have her back on the Team. I would have struggled to continue the ride without Mudgee. She was my safety blanket, my best mate, hence why it was Mudgee and I that rode into all the towns and cities together.

Again, we finished a ride with a swim at the beach at the Gold Coast. It was such cool fun. Mudgee loved it.

All the other rides were quite uneventful as far as Mudgee's safety went. She just did the miles day in, day out and loved it. We had such a strong, solid bond. I could depend on her at any time.

When we did the rides for the Paralympics (Melbourne to Sydney ride and Brisbane to Sydney ride) we also did lots of cool things and lots of PR and promotional things. Which Mudgee got to join in with. She took me inside the Menzies Hotel in Sydney where I booked her into a room. She received carrots and apples on silver platters. The Japanese tourists were blown away by the horse in the lobby. She went to Parliament House in Sydney, another very cool experience. She'd already been to Parliament House in Canberra numerous times and even ridden up the lawn of Parliament House and New Parliament House.

When we finished the ride from Melbourne to Sydney in 1997 the then Lord Mayor of Sydney, Frank Sartor, put on a special Mayoral dinner celebrating the end of the ride and fundraising for the Paralympics.

For that ride, when we were on the final stretch riding into Sydney, we rode straight down Paramatta Road. Well, WOW! I know why they call it road rage. We got told to get off the road quite a bit, in colorful language and no uncertain terms. But there was equally as many people congratulating, tooting their horn and wishing us good luck.

We finished the ride at Sydney Town Hall and proceeded to put all the horses away, except Mudgee. She walked through the bowels of Sydney Town Hall and out onto the balcony. It was truly amazing. Frank Sartor presented me with a beautiful big bunch of flowers, which Mudgee tried to eat! It was an awesome experience.

But it gets better! That night Frank Sartor's dinner had 460 people seated in Sydney's magnificent Town Hall. Then, drum roll... up in the lift, through the bowels of the hall again and down the red-carpet rode Mudgee and I. Down the red carpet she went, with seated guests on either side of her, and Bruce Richardson and Robbie Aitkin on each side of us making sure she stayed on the carpet and didn't step on the delicate parquetry flooring. She was just amazing.

This magnificent mare just took everything in her stride.

At various times I'd thought how lovely it would be to breed a foal from Mudgee. So that did happen. She had one foal with no problems, which was just gorgeous. This beautiful little foal was by Mr Richardson's Australian Stock Horse stallion, Chablis.

Inspired by the success of that pairing I was excited to join Mudgee with my own stallion Yarrahapinni Hectic. The pregnancy went along fine. I was away camp drafting when Mudgee went into labour and things went pear-shaped. I am so very grateful to my Mum and her sister Kathy, plus Caroline and Wiggy Washington for nursing and loving Mudgee back to good health. To the wonderful vets from Ray Gooley, especially the surgeon who performed a caesarean birth on Mudgee, THANK YOU.

Sadly though, the foal had a condition called Big Head. Hence it could not be born naturally. For some reason, the fluid did not drain from the foal's head, and it got bigger and bigger. Although the foal did not survive, thankfully we were so very fortunate with the love and care of Caroline, Wiggy, Mum, Cathy and Jeffery Pitt, that this beautiful little mare pulled through.

I believe that because she was so loved, that contributed big time, to her getting better. She was absolutely loved better. It's amazing what that amazing thing called love does! It can heal lots of things. Mudgee went on to do many more rides after this horrific operation. But I never joined her too Hectic again.

Mudgee was also a star in the dressage arena. She could also jump, and sport. I leant her to many young friends to do Pony Club and dressage. She was such a star in the dressage arena. She carried herself so beautifully and was quite striking to look at.

She did many shows. She won many champion ribbons. I remember at the Mudgee Show one year, Katie Nethery won the led class and the riding class on Mudgee. They also won the Champion Australian Stock horse class. By then Mudgee was 33 years old and her collection of ribbons certainly caused a lot of noses out of joint. When people found out how old Mudgee was, they couldn't believe it. She looked like a 12 year old.

One of the highlights on the ride we did for the Paralympics, the Mudgee to Melbourne, was I challenged The Honourable Michael Knight to come and ride with us as one of my Sighted

Guides. Michael was the then Minister for the Olympics. He took up the challenge which was very cool and very brave.

Bruce Richardson, Michael Knight & I

At that time Campbeltown was Michael's local area. As we rode through his area typically Michael rode on one side of me and Bruce Richardson was on my other side. Everyone rode Australian Stock horses, my own of course was Mudgee. Michael was riding a big horse called Jed who suited him down to the ground as Michael was a very tall gentleman.

We even made the front page of the Sydney Morning Herald. Michael, Bruce and I absolutely in stitches of laughter because only 3-4 minutes ago with 2 Sighted Guides, Mudgee and I cleaned up a camera man. It was very funny. So glad the camera man was ok though.

I used to take Mudgee when we rode through a town to the schools, and we would do a talk about whatever I was doing the fundraiser for. Mudgee and my Guide Dog were always a hit with the school kids.

Mudgee was 35 when things started going pear-shaped. One evening she had a severe bout of colic. Automatically I'd rung Dr Gordon Bentley, our local vet. Gordon came out and gave her some drugs for the pain and we walked for hours until she settled. The next morning, she had another episode of colic. Gordon came back at 8am, Mudgee's gut still wasn't working properly. When Gordon arrived, Mudgee and I were laying together, Mudgee's head in my lap.

Gordon walked to Mudgee, he knelt and gave her a pat. When he looked into her eyes, he said words I'll never forget. "Oh my God Sue, she's blind! She has cataracts in both eyes." "Oh, my heavens," I said. Two weeks prior at the at Dubbo Orana Equestrian Club competition, she had won her dressage class with one of my young riders.

What a legend of a horse. She would do whatever I asked. Our trust in each other had no boundaries.

Gordon continued to try and hear for healthy gut sounds, but there weren't any. He then explained to me that these bouts of colic were going to get more frequent and more severe. He asked me to make a decision.

Sometimes being an adult sucks!

I knew it was not fair to keep Mudgee alive and in pain just to make me feel ok. I did what she needed me to do. I made the decision to let her rest.

This day remains one of the saddest days of my life. I still miss her. I still think about her. She left such a hole in my heart. But I have all those beautiful memories locked safe, deep in my heart. She may be gone, but I will never forget her.

Thank you to my friend the wonderful Bob Cooper for helping keep Mudgee's dream alive.

MULLAMUDDY MUDGEE

By Bob Cooper

The steady beat of the old mare's feet,
on a gravel road out west.

With her head held high in the dawn's grey sky,
she still gives out her best.

She has seen the droughts on the great stock routes,
where the crows and dust prevail.

She has felt the tropical humid heat,
The burning tar of a city street,
And a broken stony trail where the
icy snow with a freezing blow,
Sings on the highland plain.

She's the only one, a rip tearing gun, a heroine under rein,
When the swamps are full on the watercourse,
And the rivers are gorged with flood,
The old mare will tackle them in her stride.

For there is courage in her blood,
But you might reply or just ask why?

This mare should be kept in mind,
Well, I'll tell you true, and I've told a few,
She carries a girl that's blind.

She was bought out of a sale yard,
Where unwanted rejects go.
A mare to old, a horse too bold or a racehorse much too slow.
But a girl's love was her saviour.

You know how the story goes,
The more the seed is watered, the bigger the tree that grows.

Together they worked for each needy cause,
No gain or rich reward.

They rode the trails for charity,
With charity their sword.

10,000 hard kilometres, the mare with her stubborn mind,
She carried with fierce protection her companion almost blind.

There are many great horses mentioned
in the annals of history,
The Olympics have great stories of how good a horse can be.

They have carried mighty generals,
in the wars of days gone by,
They are told of in Greek mythology,
having wings on which to fly.

They have raced for Kings and carried Queens,
They've been film stars in their day.

But few who have worked for charity have ever had their say.
But at last there's recognition and let all who know her cheer.

For Mllamuddy Mudgee has been named –
Horse of the Year.

And now in her autumn ageing, when the trails of the tasks
long gone,
Are but lines in a poem unwritten,
Or words in an unsung song.

There are those who live and those who grow,
A chance through a worthy cause.
Spurred on by the selfless efforts
Of a blind girl and her horse.

*

Restoring the Old Cottage

"Life is full of beautiful magical moments -
take time to notice them."
Sue-Ellen Lovett

The old cottage was snuggled in the Cudgegong Valley, on the side of a hill. In Mudgee, on Mum and Dad's property, barely stood this beautiful old cottage, dilapidated and falling down. The cows took shelter in what was once the kitchen.

She would have been a beauty, once upon a time. The cottage has beautiful old cedar doors, cedar walls, high ceilings and a beautiful bullnose veranda. It just needs some love, attention, and restoration.

My brother Pete left school early to start a Building Apprenticeship and go to TAFE. He and Dad had this great idea of doing the cottage up for me. So that is what happened.

Pete built me a lovely brand-new kitchen, keeping it quite old and authentic to fit in with the style of the cottage. In the bathroom he built something nice, simple and easy. Then it came to painting the walls, we kept them a lovely soft cream color. I bought second hand carpet from my sister-in-law's parents for the flooring.

After Pete had done the inside, we clad the outside in a cream board. We put green shutters on the sides of the windows and built a beautiful bull nose veranda along the front. Everything was done in cream and heritage green. Then I started on the gardens. I planted garden beds everywhere, including a veggie garden.

To furnish the inside with lovely old furniture I bought tables and chairs for the kitchen and my wonderful brother built me a lovely Oregon four poster bed which I dressed in cream lace. My Mum, who is also totally blind, made the curtains and the bedspread for the room.

It was like everything in my life. Everything is a team effort. Including my beautiful cottage and me being able to live there.

I had a lovely open fireplace where I would sit and drink wine and eat cheese in winter. In summer I would sit on the front veranda with my wine and cheese of an afternoon and enjoy the beautiful Cudgegong Valley, listening to the birds and sitting quietly with my Guide Dog Eccles.

It was a beautiful time in my life. It gave me the time and a chance to find myself and be the person I wanted to be, without any structure around me. I loved it. I loved my cottage. I loved my freedom. My horse was in the backyard, so everything was perfect. And I did so love my beautiful cottage. I would burn candles and incense of an evening in the lounge room. I didn't watch a lot of TV, but I would sit and listen to a lot of music. I love the pan flute.

As time went on, the garden grew, and I had beautiful roses and a lovely veggie garden. It was as if it was meant to be, just for me. My perfect little cottage nestled in the hills of the Mudgee Valley. It was perfect.

*

ANOTHER RIDE -
BRISBANE TO SYDNEY, 1985

"Happiness is a choice. Kindness is a choice.
I choose to be kind, to love and to laugh."
Sue-Ellen Lovett

Donna & I

28th of July 1985 to 24 August 1985

1200 km, 28 days in the saddle!

Brisbane, Beenleigh, Southport, Coolangatta, Tweed Heads, Murwillumbah, Byron Bay, Ballina, Woodburn, Maclean, Grafton, Woolgoolga, Coffs Harbour, Macksville, Campsie, Port Macquarie, Johns River, Taree, Foster, Raymond Terrace, Newcastle, Dawson, Gosford, Wisemans Ferry, Richmond then Luddenham Showground.

Our main sponsor was Ansett Pioneer, an Australian long distance coach operator. They provided all the transportation for our Team on this ride.

The charity we did the fundraising on this ride for was Riding for the Disabled NSW. The reason why I chose them came about after my ride in 1984 from Mudgee to Melbourne. It was on that ride that I meet Willie Singleton. Willie was the then Manager of the Wagga Wagga Riding for the Disabled Centre.

It was amazing the difference that the RDA horses and my beautiful Guide Dog Donna and I made. Many of the RDA riders looked at me and thought "well if she can, I can." They tried so very hard. Donna and I assisted in many lessons, and I led many ponies.

This was such a growing period for me. I learnt how much horses can positively impact on people's lives, able-bodied and disabled.

I just couldn't leave it there though, assisting, and leading. I needed to make a difference and bring Riding For The Disabled to the forefront. I didn't want to just raise money for them, I also wanted to bring to light how much of a difference horse riding makes to people with a disability. It is totally mind blowing.

There are miracles that happened on a daily basis at Riding For The Disabled Centres around the world.

After spending quite a lot of time with Riding For The Disabled

Wagga Wagga, I was determined to find somewhere I could fit in to this amazing organisation. Enter an amazing lady in my life, Mrs Pearl Bachelor. Pearl was the Head of the Riding For The Disabled Kellyville.

I applied for a job at the Kellyville RDA as a Secretary and to Assist with the riders. They applied for a government grant to employ me. It was an amazing experience. I loved my time at Kellyville with the wonderful riders and the amazing coach Francis Tsyklas. Alongside Pearl, Francis was my boss.

Keep in mind I had done a Secretarial Course and... I wasn't a very good secretary.

The Riding For The Disabled volunteers were another thing altogether. The amazing ladies and gentlemen that gave up their time to make things happen for those beautiful riders of various ages, sizes and personalities, was mind blowing.

As we got the feel of how things were run, Donna and I participated in many lessons. Donna guided me and the RDA horse around the arena with a rider on top, and two people assisting on either side. It was wonderful the elation and the happiness it brought to the rider's life.

I couldn't help it; my mind was buzzing. I kept thinking, "it cannot be just left at this. I need to do more. I need to make a difference." This kept ringing through my ears every day, it was like a record on repeat. Then it became clear what I had to do. The only way I knew how to make a difference was on a horse, riding long distances and fundraising along the way. With this thought off I went, keen to see where this idea would lead us.

One of my pet things at the RDA was my Blind Rider Group. I taught all of them to ride bareback as I believe it's critical for a rider to learn to feel the horse's movement underneath them. The movement of the horse warms the riders' muscles and gently massages their body which increases the suppleness of their body and aids relaxation. All the riders responded amazingly to riding bareback. It was so cool.

There needs to be more, I need to make a difference, I need to let people know how essential using horses as a therapy animal is for children and adults with a disability. What horses can teach us is totally mind blowing. It's not just about the physical aspect of sitting atop a horse and how that can dramatically change a person's understanding of their own capabilities; horses can improve our mental heath, build our confidence, improve our motor skills and co-ordination. The list is long. Not surprising many stories abound recounting the incredible success RDA has had. Young adults who have been mute since birth speak their first word during that first RDA ride. The severely autistic child who has never shown any affection hugs the horse, often!

The totally blind rider who is clumsy and lacks confidence navigating around their own bedroom but who canters bareback on her own because she borrows the horses' beautiful big brown eyes as her own.

That rider is me!

At this stage David and I had moved to Richmond, a suburb on the western side of Sydney. He was working at the RAFF Base there, and I was working at Kellyville RDA.

At the same time, the question of to marry or not kept scooting through my mind, backward and forward, backward, and forward. David was such a lovely man, but I did not want to marry him. But my mother convinced me that I was fortunate to have someone who wanted to get married to somebody who is going blind, that I'd be stupid to turn that down. In hindsight that wasn't the right reason to get married. I should not have listened to my mother; I should have listened to my heart. If I had, I wouldn't have hurt David in the process.

My Dad was so cool, he said; "you know it's not too late, you don't have to marry David if you don't want to." But Mum had convinced me that no one would want someone who is going blind, and I was lucky enough to have David who did want me. Hindsight is wonderful.

I did get married. That night I got bitten by a White-tail spider, I wonder if that was an omen...

We were married in Uncle Bruce and Auntie Nancy's garden, which was absolutely beautiful. On our way back to Richmond we found a young lass broken down on the highway and we stopped to give her a hand. Well, Narelle Haywood ended up becoming one of my long-term best mates. Narelle accompanied me on many of my long-distance rides and is an all round great friend.

This friendship is still strong to this day. Narelle lives just up the road at a small town called Warren with her beautiful daughter Sarah and grandchildren who she is very proud of.

Things were busy at Kellyville RDA, and I was enjoying every minute of it. While I was so not the best secretary in the world, I loved working with the horses and the beautiful riders that came to ride at Kellyville RDA.

There was also such fun on weekends. I had joined the local Bythorn Hunt Club which everyone at the RDA thought was a bit of a hoot. The Blind Chick was doing fox hunting! I must say I enjoyed sharing in the Stirrup Cup tradition. It was wonderful. Everyone is invited to have some hot mulled wine served in a goblet before the ride.

Extra cool was how this Hunt Club was so very supportive. They wanted to help raise money for Riding For The Disabled, NSW.

So we organised quite a few fundraisers to raise money for our RDA and RDA NSW with the ride from Brisbane to Sydney. We got some extra great publicity when one of the fundraisers was covered by the Ray Martin Show. Their people came out and filmed us. Lots of other media also came. Apparently everyone thought it was a little unusual - a Blind Chick fox hunting.

I had people as my Sighted Guides, they were my eyes, guiding me. I even jumped over an old fence which was absolutely exhilarating. I still loved show jumping!

This got some really great media which helped us launch our ride from Brisbane to Sydney for RDA. I was also rewarded a lovely award by the Bythorn Hunt Club presented by Mr and Mrs Gallagher.

Things were really busy at this time. Organising and coordinating stuff, going over and over points for the ride, fundraisers in each town. None of this happens just because you're doing a ride. Lots of organising and coordinating on the home front is required. We were organising Woolshed Dances. We had wonderful fundraising evenings. We organised my friend Donna- Marie Killeen to speak and had a guest of honour, Mr Gordon Piper who was an actor in the well-known TV show at the time, A Country Practice. The venue was Vinegar Hill Woolshed. The place was packed to the rafters. We auctioned items, we had raffles going and we danced our little toes off. A great night was had by all.

As our fundraising rolled on; lamington drives and more raffle ticket sales, our major sponsors Ansett Pioneer and BP supplied our fuel.

Then it was time to organise our Sighted Guides. This was an easy one. Narelle Haywood was my Sighted Guide; she does the job ever so well. Then we had to organise trucks, truck drivers, support vehicle drivers, and the list goes on. The wonderful Ansett Pioneer carried our Team up and down the coast. We appreciate that so very much.

Just when things were nearly all organised, one thing stood out as not being quite right. My beautiful Guide Dog Donna had gone off her feed. I knew something was terribly wrong with her. Even though I sat with her each day and fed her out of my hand, she kept getting skinnier. Even if I offered her her favourite treats, she was still not eating. Something was drastically wrong; I could feel it in my heart.

I spoke with Guide Dogs NSW and they organised Donna to be picked up and taken down to Werribee. Why Werribee? That's where the wonderful veterinary clinic could find out what was wrong with Donna. As soon as they opened her up they knew straight away. Donna was riddled with cancer. They euthanised her on the spot.

I was absolutely shattered. I had lost my best friend, my eyes, my independence, my mobility. What was I going to do? How was I going to do this ride without my beautiful Donna by my side guiding me, looking after me? But the ride had to go on. There were so many people who had given up holidays and given their time to organise and attend fundraisers. So with a hole in my heart, we did the big trip up to Brisbane in preparation to start the ride. We stayed at the Moggill Riding For The Disabled.

The Moggill Riding For The Disabled is a wonderful complex. Our horses were trained each day. We'd ride out into the bush, getting them fit in preparation for our big trip from Brisbane to Sydney.

When we left Brisbane, I carried with me a letter from the Lord Mayor of Brisbane, Sallyanne Atkin to the Lord Mayor of Sydney. We were on our way.

The road was very busy as we rode to Southport. Many people were honking and pulling over to give us donations. We passed Sea World, Water World and Movie World. The excitement about turning up at Surfers Paradise Beach and swimming our horses was our days motivation. It was going to be so exciting because neither Narelle nor I had swum a horse on the beach before. Let alone swim our horses at Surfers Paradise.

We had the honour of being escorted into Southport by the Beenleigh Light Horse Brigade. Everything was going along really well until... one of the men's horses had a very big shy. That gentleman was in his 80's and he fell off! Oh my heavens, everybody and everything stopped. It was such a worrying time, but this spritely man sprang into action. One of the lads in his group said, "you're not getting back on Grandpa."

His reply – "just watch me. This is what we do. You fall off, you dust yourself off and you get back on. Someone find me a chair or something to get on," he requested. Then voila, he mounted up and we rode on.

We had many civic receptions on the road to the Gold Coast, and we visited lots of schools and parks where we spoke to various groups. It was really lovely, quite a spectacular day. I noticed a few threatening clouds out to the east, but I don't think they were going to worry us.

It was amazing! The swim on the beach at the Gold Coast was everything we expected. It wasn't just us that really enjoyed it. The horses loved it to.

Once I got over the whitewashes on the tops of the waves, in we went. We body surfed with the horses. It was a blast. All that could be heard was Nelly and I laughing non-stop! We came out of the water, took the saddles off and went in bareback. We took our boots off and had a really good swim. Heaps of media were there covering us swimming on the beach because it was such a rarity. It was so very, very cool.

Then we headed off to Murwillumbah where we were being hosted by the local Lions Club at the Showground. It was a good day for riding, and a great day for fundraising. At the function that evening I did what I normally did. We sold raffle tickets and I spoke about Riding For The Disabled Mudgee. Specifically all the wonderful things it does for our disabled community. There is nothing like having an animal in your life, whether it be a horse or a dog.

Most days I would do two or three presentations - talking about Riding For The Disabled and it's wonderful attributes. I got very proficient at public speaking. Come to think of it, I've never had any trouble speaking! The problem is stopping me.

Nelly was a wonderful Sighted Guide. Not only did she look after my beautiful horse and I, but she also described things of interest to me. At this time I only had a little bit of sight in my right eye. Nelly would direct me to the right place to see if I could get some visual picture of it. It was such picturesque country to be riding through. It was just beautiful.

Next we went through to Ballina, another lovely coastal town. More fundraising, more going through every pub in every town selling raffle tickets, getting donations. I think I've seen the inside of more pubs than most blokes would in a lifetime. On every ride we went to all the pubs. The locals were always so very generous with their donations and buying raffle tickets.

I am ever so grateful to the New South Wales Police. Every town we rode into we were escorted by a Police car with the lights flashing. Sometimes if it was a busy area, we had a Police car in front and behind. On many occasions we met up with the Police after our ride and they took us around fundraising. It was just amazing, how exceptionally kind and caring they all were and had the best interest of the ride at heart.

As the ride rolled on down the coast through lots of little hamlets and cities, we were always met by wonderful people. Generally, it was the Lions Club that hosted us for a barbecue or a dinner. Typically I'd speak, and we'd fundraise at each of the local pubs. This may sound monotonous, but it was such an amazing time.

During the ride it was bought to my attention that my six months had done its time with Riding For The Disabled Kellyville. I suspected I wouldn't have a job at the Kellyville RDA when I got back from the ride. Why? Because it was a government subsidised job because of my disability. So onwards and upwards. I didn't let it worry me that if I didn't get rehired at the RDA, that I'd definitely go back as a volunteer.

Down to Newcastle, again hosted by the Lions Club of Newcastle, I was speaking at the dinner meeting, fundraising, public speaking and doing the rounds at the local pubs to raise more money.

I'd never thought a ride could be spooky. But when we rode down the mountains through Weisman Ferry - it was really foggy, the air was damp and it sounded like there was something following us through the hills, something keeping pace with us. It was really off putting. I shared my thoughts with Nelly, she felt the same way. We were so happy and relieved to get down out of the mountains.

At Penrith we were met by the Mounted Police. They escorted us the 20 km into Luddenham Showground. We chatted with the Mounted Police as we rode and had a really pleasant morning. Soon after we arrived at the Luddenham Showground, more raffle tickets were sold then voila. The ride was over. It all happened that quickly.

At the Showground I was presented with a beautiful big bronze horse statute as thanks on behalf of Riding For The Disabled. It continues to sit proudly in my lounge room.

COURAGE

By Bob Cooper, 1991

The rains have come at last,
And in the west the anxious dreams have come to fruit,
As has Sue-Ellen's quest.

And by some lonely road, a hoof mark fades away,
For courage is forgotten swiftly in this age and day.

The mulga trees tipped silver grey, stand mute upon the plain,
The cautious black faced wallabies peer through
the saving rain.

And all along the way she rode, life beats its endless pace,
But there's both joy and sadness on Sue-Ellen's
suntanned face.

The joy is for the fact, that in those people that can't cope,
She stirs a light of gratitude, of reverence and hope.

The sadness is for times now gone that may not come again,
For times are ever changing, in her life, and on the plain.

The generous contributions by the folks along the road,
Who took the task to heart and helped to
share Sue-Ellen's load.

But as she says her sad farewell, to this ride that's now gone,
Her heart is on the battle that she'll always carry on.

*

INDEPENDENCE

"There is always hope. Never give up.
Never stop believing."
Sue-Ellen Lovett

Hectic & Eccles

Eccles & I

Independence, no independence, Guide Dog, white cane!

Relying on people truly isn't a choice. I needed some training to help me gain independence. I had spent six months at Gillies Plains in South Australia, at the Blind School to learn Living Skills, to cope with being blind. During this time, I had white cane training. I must say, I struggled with using the white cane. It felt really foreign, alien like. Plus it does something I especially don't like... it draws attention to me. The white cane really didn't make me feel enabled.

But there was a method to this madness. I had to do the white cane training before I was allowed to train with a Guide Dog. This excited me immensely. A beautiful Guide Dog could be my eyes. This was going to open the doors that open the world to me. So look out, here I come! I can't wait to start training with my new Guide Dog.

Then it all happened!

It was about 9am on a Monday morning in 1981 when a lovely gentleman called Ray Joyce who worked for Guide Dogs Victoria turned up at our place in Werribee with my new eyes! A beautiful German Shepherd Guide Dog called Donna.

This was quite a special dog for me to be working with as Guide Dogs normally use Labradors, but they were trialling the German Shepherd as they are used heavily in Europe, and they thought they would see how it went in Australia. The fact that I had trained sheep dogs and horses was the reason they allowed me to work with this beautiful dog.

Under Ray's guidance we spent the first week getting to know each other. The first few days were really spent bonding I suppose. We didn't do much work with a harness or anything like that. Come day four, we did a little bit of work with a harness up to the little shop a block away and back. It was so cool. I could walk with this beautiful dog and I didn't have to hold onto someone's arm! She guided me up to the shop, we got some milk and I said "home Donna," and she walked me home. You have no idea how liberating and amazing it was.

Then that weekend Donna went back to Guide Dogs with Ray. I was devastated. But she did return on Monday and we did more of the same. Up to the corner shop and back, lots of commands; left, right, straight to the curb Donna and she would stop and I would give her the command to cross the road. Ray would correct me if I made a mistake, but it was pretty awesome.

This beautiful dog and I were bonding really well, so when it came to the end of week two, Ray allowed me to keep Donna at home. Well, was I excited!

Oh my! I had homework! Ray wanted me to teach Donna something before he returned. What the hell am I going to teach a Guide Dog? So, we played ball and I told her to pick the ball out from amongst the whole heap of wine glasses. And then the pièce de résistance. I taught her to play dead. Very proud of this! It didn't take long though mind you. Clever dog.

When Ray arrived Monday morning to start training he asked "what did you manage to teach Donna?" I said we played lots of ball games and so forth, did lots of sitting and staying, but I didn't go anywhere with her in the harness. Then I told Ray about how I taught Donna to play dead. Well holy cow he was not impressed. "She's not a trick dog," he said. My response was, "you told me to teach her something, I had no idea what to teach her." But it was a command, I said bang and she played dead. I thought it was pretty cool and I thought we were both very clever.

Come week three we were walking confidently up to the Werribee shops. We taught Donna all my usual routes, like going to the bank, hairdresser, not so much the shopping centre, but key points that I would visit on a normal weekly basis which worked wonderfully. Then we did some train travel, and this was quite liberating. But I felt quite uncomfortable on the train and actually quite vulnerable.

Then the start of Week Four was a little bit of a shake-up. We were going out training on the Monday morning and Ray mentioned do you know anybody who drives a yellow car. I said no, definitely not. He said well that car was there last week and it ended up being at a lot of places where we went and Ray thought they were stalking us. This was very, very, scary! So he rang the Police and the Police addressed the situation and the yellow car disappeared. Phew! That really put the wind up me. When you can't see, you are really so vulnerable. But the lovely thing about Donna being a German Shepherd was that people were wary, which I felt really happy about.

Things progressed from there. We flew to Sydney and caught the bus back to Mudgee from Werribee. It was so cool. Yes, Donna went on the plane and bus with me. I had my wings, and I could go and do whatever I wanted. I was independent.

To celebrate my new independence, I did something extra special with Fred, my white cane. I buried it! Yes, I dug a hole and buried it in the garden at home in Werribee. I had my independence with Donna; I had no need of Fred anymore. Plus, I really didn't like using the white cane.

On one of my trips home to Mudgee, Dad picked me up from Dubbo and we drove home quite late at night. I'd been planning on doing a fundraiser for Guide Dogs and wanted my Dad to be involved. It was how to spring it on my Dad. I will talk more about these long-distance fundraising rides later. Right now I need to share with you how it played out.

I was just sitting chatting with Donna in the lounge room, Dad was reading the local paper. I said, "I'd like to ride a horse from Mudgee to Melbourne to raise money for Guide Dogs." I may have Mumbled it the first few times I said it because I knew what my Dad's response would be. He ignored me so I said, "Dad! You're not listening."

"Well, speak slowly and clearly" he replied.

So, I blurted out "I would like to ride a horse from Mudgee to Melbourne with a Sighted Guide, to raise money for Guide Dogs. To say thank you for my independence and mobility."

No prizes for guessing what my Dad said. A flat out "NO!"

"You can't even ride around the lucerne paddock without tripping over a bale! So how do you think you are going to ride a horse from Mudgee to Melbourne?"

I interrupted my Dad and said, "Well my idea is to get your Lions Club involved to organise fundraising events each night in the different towns we pass through.

"No, just a flat no. This is not going to happen." He was adamant.

I knew what I had to do to get a yes. I tailored my reply

accordingly and said, "okay, I'll go to Rotary and ask if they'll support the ride from Mudgee to Melbourne."

Well did that change my Dad's mind! The next night the Lions Club President came and had tea with us, and the rest is history.

So, in 1984 with the help of the Mudgee Lions Club, my Dad driving my horse truck and my wonderful friend Helen Parks as my Sighted Guide, we headed off to Melbourne to raise money for Guide Dogs.

Oh, for those of you who were worried about where Donna was, she came with us of course. She was in the air-conditioned car while we rode the miles during the day using six Australian Stockhorses. They were amazing.

The ride was 1200 kilometres and took 36 days. We raised $36,000 which meant six lovely new Guide Dogs could be trained for six visually impaired and blind people. Donna was a hit everywhere we went. She worked so well in every and any situation.

Then in early 1985 Donna lost her appetite and stopped eating her food. Even though I'd sit and feed her little bits of meat out of my hand, things weren't good. So we took her to the Werribee Veterinary Clinic and they x-rayed her. We weren't ready for what they found. Cancer! They tried to operate, but the cancer was too big. They euthanised Donna on the operating table. I was devastated. I wasn't just losing my best mate; I was losing my independence. I can't describe in words the hurt. But the old saying, "life goes on" is relevant here, and it did.

Enter stage left a little creamy bitch called Tara. For this lovely dog I went to the Guide Dogs Centre in Victoria for a month of training. It was eye-opening! I was bored to snores, but it was a great learning experience.

It was very hard for Tara, and to this day I feel guilty as I needed my mobility and independence, but I didn't want Tara. I so badly wanted Donna back, my beautiful German Shepherd. But that wasn't possible, so I had to knuckle down and do my best with Tara. She was super easy to work with, no fuss at all.

We did lots of cool things like dog psychology while we were at the Guide Dog Training Centre, and lots of obedience work. It was much more intense than the first time I'd trained with Donna. I think this is why I'm so adamant about how Guide Dogs, especially mine, are treated. I don't allow people to talk to my Guide Dogs, or pat them. Such actions can distract them, and I may get hurt or killed because my dog is being distracted. I get that most often, the person doing the ignorant or naïve distracting has no idea of the possible consequences of their actions. And guess what? I don't care! It's my safety and my Guide Dogs safety that are my concern. I think this makes me a good handler.

Tara and I did quite a few wonderful things together. She was such a nice quiet achiever who just got on with life. The average working life of a Guide Dog is six to seven years. I had Tara as my Guide for eleven years, as I didn't want to go back and re-train with another dog at the Guide Dogs Centre in Melbourne.

When it came to retiring Tara, I had intended to give her to a retirement village or something like that. She would have fitted in beautifully in such a place, but by that stage she had become a little incontinent. So instead, I gave her back to Guide Dogs to find a home for her. It was so cool when many, many years later, on one of my fundraising rides, Tara and I crossed paths again!

It was lovely to have the opportunity to apologise to Tara for not being as loving as I should have been. I had been obsessed with the loss of my beautiful Donna. Grief is just such a hard thing. Everyone copes with it differently. It was lovely to catch up with her. She was tone deaf and I think she was suffering from dementia, but she was a very healthy elderly lady. Thank you Tara for the joy you brought to my life.

Then I met my new Guide Dog, the magnificent Eccles. Wow what a spectacular dog. Whenever the harness was on, he transformed into my Suit and Tie guy. He never goofed off. He was always the absolute professional. We travelled the world together! We went to the World Equestrian Games in Denmark, Paralympic Games in Atlanta and in Sydney and travelled to New

Zealand numerous times. Let the journey begin with this beautiful animal.

When Eccles entered my life, I was training quite hard for the Sydney Paralympic Games. So, I was backward and forward to Melbourne training once a month and down to Sydney for training. It was relentless, and this beautiful dog did not miss a beat.

We travelled all over Australia doing public speaking engagements. It was just so enjoyable travelling around with my best mate. He was so confident through the airports and getting on the plane. He would curl up at my feet and not move until we were ready to disembark. Such a great travelling companion, especially when we went shopping! He never said "no! Don't put that on Visa."

I was always, always so proud to be out with my wonderful Eccles.

Everyone who met him loved him. But if someone tried to pat him while he was working, he would duck his head or turn away so they couldn't touch him. He knew the rules. Everyone else didn't understand, and everyone loves to break rules like: let's pat the Guide Dog, let's see if we can distract the Guide Dog. But Eccles was on the job, he didn't worry about anybody else, he was just focused on looking after me.

So, the trips continued down to Melbourne training with Mary Longdon. We were continually back and forth from Mudgee, Melbourne and Sydney. Then bring into the mix when I was appointed to the Paralympic Games Board by The Honourable Michael Knight. Every month we had Board meetings, sometimes every two weeks. So, we were down to Sydney to Board meetings which was really just so very cool. As you can imagine I'm pretty shy, it takes me awhile to get comfortable. But by the second Board meeting I had found my voice and I was amongst friends with a mutual interest to host the best Paralympic Games the world has ever seen. I have no doubt in my mind we did exactly that. We hosted the best Paralympics ever.

During some of the presentations in the boardroom, there

would be some moaning and groaning! It came from under the table. The monotone voice delivering important information was boring apparently and Eccles had no problem voicing his opinion.

With each Board meeting it became more and more apparent that there was a major shortfall in the budget for the Paralympics. How are we going to meet the budget? How are we going to host the best Paralympic games the world has ever seen with that amount of money? The only way I knew to make a difference was to offer to do another long-distance ride. This time Melbourne to Sydney to raise money for the Sydney Paralympic Games being held in 2000, PLUS - to raise public awareness. The meetings and chatter about making such a ride into a reality started in 1997.

The ride was discussed at length. Unlike the other rides I'd organised the wonderful thing about this one was that it wouldn't be organised and coordinated by me. It would be organised and coordinated by the rather sizeable Public Relations Department of the Paralympics Organisation. This made it bigger than Ben Hur! Sometimes it all became quite overwhelming: the personalities involved, the knocking of heads, people not understanding how simple it could be, and people making it all too complex.

The Head of the PR Department was a lovely lady called Mary. We got on really well. There was also a wonderful guy who came on the ride with us, Steve, and a lovely young lass. They spent the whole ride with us. They went ahead and made sure everything was organised: our accommodation, the press, the public speaking venues etc. Most days I gave three to four presentations about our ride and the upcoming Sydney Paralympics. I would always mention it was going to be the best Paralympics the world has ever seen. That message plus rallying everybody to come and take ownership for Australia running the best Paralympic Games EVER, was on my lips each day for weeks!

So, now it's time to start the ride! Mudgee to Melbourne here we come. We headed off from Mudgee. As per usual, the horses had been in work building their fitness for about four to six weeks prior to the ride starting. The wonderful Mr Richardson and his amazing friends in the Australian Sock Horse Society came to the party with magnificent Australian Stockhorses for me to ride. I am so grateful for this gentleman being in my life. He has been a Godsend, a mentor and such an amazing gentleman with such a big heart.

So, we leave Mudgee with all the horses who are as fit as fiddles. As well as my beautiful little mare Mudgee. We head for Melbourne. We take two days to travel down to the Mounted Police Headquarters in Melbourne. Our horses are stabled here for the next five days while we do public relations and get everything organised for heading out on the road.

How amazing is Winnebago! This incredible company sponsored our ride. They gave us an amazing Winnebago to live in for the five weeks on the ride. It was so cool. They took the double bed out and put in three bunks either side down the back of the Winnebago. Voila, now all our team is accommodated in the Winnie! It was comfy, it was fun. My bed was over the driver's seat.

The Winnie had a spacious living area, solar panels and a generator for power, a great kitchen for cooking and was just so comfortable. The fact that everybody could live together was even better.

On this ride Eccles and I did, no exaggeration, hundreds of interviews in hundreds of different places to hundreds of different people! From school children to the local Lions Club, to speaking to the Politicians in Canberra at the National Library. It was a pretty amazing ride, and by my side all the time was the wonderful Eccles.

Each day we spent anything from five to thirteen hours in the saddle. Nothing much changes on the rides over these long distances. Except for the beautiful people and the fundraising options and being given donations that can be auctioned off. It's the same thing every day. Except just different beautiful people.

When we got to Kyabram we were met by the local Mayor. He took us for a tour of the area. It's a really huge dairy area, it was excellent. This was especially interesting for me as I'd worked at a dairy in Mudgee for many years growing up. The layout of that dairy was what they call a Herringbone Dairy. I worked for two people, Reg McAdam and Warwick Haymes. They were both into different areas of Dairy cows. Warwick had Friesian Cows, and Reg had beautiful Jersey cows.

At Warwick's I think we milked seven or eight hundred cows. At the place we toured in Kyabram they milked a couple of thousand head of cows, each day, twice a day! To do this volume they used a machine call a Rotolactor. The cows walk onto a big circle platform which rotates around. It is all automated and computerised. Each cows ear tag is read when they enter the Rotolactor, which not only allocates to that cow the right amount of feed but it also records how much milk that cow produced. It was one hell of an organisation. Just amazing. All our team loved it.

A secret though! While that was all very amazing, there was something at that dairy I was itching to go see. The poddy calves! So, Eccles and I toddle on down with the owner to meet the poddy calves. Oh my God they were gorgeous! And they all were coming up looking at Eccles' nose. Not so good for Guide Dogs protocol, but it was very cute. Then something unexpected happened. The owner said to me, "Would you like one?" Well obviously, I said, "yes please." So now on the ride we had six horses, a Guide Dog and... one poddy calf! It was so cool. Each morning Eccles carried the poddy calf's milk out to it. I'd fed it, then Eccles would carry the empty bottle back. I could hear him licking the left-over milk from around the teat as he caried it. Very sneaky, very funny.

Everything was going swimmingly and then my Dad turns up for his stint on the ride. "What the bloody hell is the calf doing on the ride!" Oopsy! Dad wasn't impressed. But he soon settled in to helping look after our cute little poddy calf.

It was rather funny when we got to the Inglis stables in Sydney. The guy at the Inglis stable said six stables and we said plus one please. He said, "but you've only got six horses." My reply, "yes, six horses plus a poddy calf." I think it is possibly the first and only poddy calf that's been at the Inglis stables.

Eccles was such a star. When we finished the ride Eccles, Mudgee and I went up in the lift in the Sydney Town Hall. Eccles guided Mudgee and I out onto the Sydney Town Hall balcony for the Civic Reception with the then Mayor Frank Sartor. We were presented with a big bunch of flowers which Mudgee quickly proceeded to try and eat.

Animals never cease to amaze me. That evening we were invited by Frank Sartor to a special fundraising dinner, 460 seated guests in the magnificent Sydney Town Hall. We took Mudgee back that night to Sydney Town Hall, up in the lift, through the bowels of Sydney Town Hall into the auditorium. Eccles led Mudgee and I down the red carpet passed all the seated guests. Richo held Mudgee for me while Eccles took me up onto the stage. I spoke and had a presentation with Frank Sartor and The Honourable Michael Knight. At the conclusion Eccles guided me back to my beautiful Mudgee, then out of the auditorium.

Eccles was my companion, all the time leading me into the arena to do competitions. On a flight to Sydney, on a flight to Denmark, on a flight to New Zealand. It was always Eccles and I. He was the most awesome Guide Dog you could ever have. He was always so confident and reliable.

Eccles and I were often in the car with our coach and friend Judy Cubitt. We might have been travelling to ride a horse, look at a horse or have a lesson on a horse. Jude became very attached to Eccles and Eccles loved Judy. After the Sydney Paralympic Games Judy was diagnosed with Parkinson's Disease. It was at this time that Eccles was looking to retire. So, I gave Eccles to Judy. He loved living with Judy. All the things he couldn't do as a Guide Dog he could do with Judy. He was spoilt rotten.

Judy's Parkinson's progressed quite quickly. She only had Eccles for a few short years before she needed to go into a retirement village. Eccles went to live with the magnificent equestrian - Carolyn Lieutenant. There he lived out the rest of his life with Carolyn and her beautiful dog Georgie. My mate passed away when he was fourteen. He had a wonderful life and was always loved. Thank you so much Judy and Caroline for enriching his life and loving him. Mind you he was pretty hard not to love.

Hello Jag! After Eccles retired, I started working with a beautiful dog called Jag. I changed his name when I first got him, his was yucky and not at all nice enough for a lovely handsome chocolate Labrador. Jag and I bonded very quickly, and he was a great work dog. Instead of the typical four weeks initial training together, Jag and I knocked it over in in two weeks. He was such a clever dog.

Jag and I spent most of our time doing trips to Dubbo or the odd trip to Sydney and public speaking engagements. When Jag retired, he went to live with a lovely family, Anna and Howard. He lived out his days as one very happy dog.

Then enter Prada, another lovely chocolate Labrador which I trained in less than two weeks. Again, an exceptional Guide Dog. I used Prada in town in Dubbo, travelling to Sydney, a little bit the same as life with Jag. Plus we did lots of dressage competitions, where he would lead me into the arena or around the venue.

I suspect for you in the grand scheme of things, this all sounds like lots of small chores. But no, not to me. To have your independence and mobility and be able to do ALL these things by yourself is AWESOME! Independence and mobility is the biggest thing having a Guide Dog has bought to my life. If I wanted to get on a plane and fly to Sydney or get on a plane and fly to Queensland to do a speaking engagement, I could do it by myself, with my best mate. We should never take this thing called INDEPENDENCE lightly. It's massive.

Prada retired at Christmas time and is with a friend in Mudgee where he is still living happily. He is a very cool, very clever dog. Another dog with a big personality.

After Prada, Matt and I went down to Sydney and trialled a couple of other Guide Dogs. None of which were suitable. Then a few weeks later Guide Dogs rang me about a lovely little black bitch called Amani. Oh wow what a classy little girl with a great work ethic. She was a bit of a sniffer. Oh how she loved sniffing, a lot! But still a wonderful work tool.

Something I was noticing that was happening with the last two Guide Dogs I'd had was that I was losing my confidence with them! I would rather go into town with somebody as a Sighted Guide than use the Guide Dog. So, my Guide Dogs started to get used less and less. Amani probably felt that more than any of the other Guide Dogs. Confidence is such a huge thing. Especially when it starts the downward slide. Being totally blind was getting really scary, and town was a very busy place.

So, I made the decision early in 2019 to retire Amani. At that time the NDIS had entered my life and had given me the ability to employ someone to help me and be my Sighted Guide.

I must say, my journey with Guide Dogs has been a pretty amazing thirty-eight years. I am so very grateful for what they brought to my life. I am also now very grateful to the NDIS for what they have brought to my life. It is the most amazing independence I have never known.

Now, to get around the farm, much to my horror, I use a white cane! This is so I don't run into things, and also, we have lots of not so lovely brown snakes! You'd hear my cane, I put a bell on it so it jingles. Hopefully that noise or the tapping of it is enough of a deterrent to keep any snakes away. I also have my beautiful horse Johno, who we have trained to be like a Guide Dog. I give him commands, like to do my Guide Dog, and he takes me where I've asked him to. To the tack shed, to the dressage arena, "Johno Mounting Block".

Animals bring so much joy and love to our lives. For me the extra lovely thing is... I haven't lost my confidence with my beautiful horses. Thank God.

*

QUESTIONS MOST PEOPLE AREN'T GAME TO ASK! PT4

"Life is a choice."
Sue-Ellen Lovett

DO YOU GET SCARED?

Oh my heavens yes!

There's quite a lot of things that frighten me. Snakes in the garden is a biggie. I've had numerous encounters with snakes. I've been struck by three brown snakes over the past 20 years of living here on the Macquarie River.

But I don't think anything compares to the fear you have when you get lost in your own bedroom! It's a horrible feeling, gut wrenching panic, until you have some sort of sensibility come into your head and you think logically and work out where you are. Although I've probably running into the glory box in the meantime or hit the door with my head, it's just such a horrible feeling there's nothing I can do to fix that one. My sense of orientation is really crappy so when I stand up I have no idea which way I'm facing.

I used to have a great sense of direction.

How do you deal with losing your confidence?

Oh my heavens this question cuts close to the heart.

I suppose my confidence has come and gone, especially as I was losing my sight. It did a lot of more coming and going from the fear factor of not fulfilling a dream or being able to do what you would like to do. Then the itty-bitty shitty committee thoughts would get in my head and undermine my confidence even more. I'm not sure when that started appearing, but it's been around for a while. My way of coping with this is just keep moving forward, maybe a little sideways, but always one step at a time forward, small steps so I am not over faced.

My unceremonious buster off Johno which broke my knee would probably be the biggest clincher as far as losing my confidence has been. It's been a hard track back, especially with Johno being ill, but that's in the story for you to discover.

Confidence is just so brittle, it's definitely two steps forward, one step back. It is critical to keep positive, have a good mindset and make your goals attainable. Oh my heavens this is such a biggie. I share more on this in the story.

How do you know what shirt you are putting on?

This is a biggie for going out, but I'm sure if you asked any of my friends most of my shirts are all the same. My work shirts live in a cupboard, and it really doesn't matter what comes out of that cupboard on a work day. But if I'm going out there is an app on my phone that will tell me the colour of the shirt I'm putting on.

I'm quite conservative. I like what I like and especially colour wise and who would've thought that would've minded to a Blind Chick what colour she was wearing. But there are certain colours

Do you wear make up?

Holy cow! No that would be too scary, I would look like Bobo The Clown. The closest I get to wearing make-up is probably some Sorbolene face cream. I tried using mascara but kept poking myself in the eye. Imagine me trying to put eyeshadow on! Lordy be, I'd look like a rainbow.

Any embarrassing moments with your Guide Dog?

This one is embarrassing only to me.

I was going shopping with my wonderful mother-in-law Lee. We pulled up in the car park, I got out with my beautiful Guide Dog Eccles, put the harness on him, did the clip up, gave him a pat under the chin and said "Walk On." But Eccles didn't move. It was like, what the hell is wrong?

In that time Lee had come around the car and could see what was happening and she couldn't contain herself she was giggling and laughing that much. I couldn't work out what the hell was wrong, why my Guide Dog wouldn't move. Well in shopping centres they have steel rails that coral the shopping trolleys, I had attached Eccles with his harness around one of these rails, hence he couldn't move. I was so embarrassed, but it was oh so funny. I only ever did that once.

ANY OTHER SPECIAL EMBARRASSING MOMENTS YOU CAN THINK OFF?

Oh yes there are many of them but one that is very fresh to my mind happened only recently.

My beautiful friends Jacqueline and Tash sent me a gorgeous gift box of things. An amazing surprise. I was on the phone to them while I opened all these wonderful gifts, there was at least 15 things wrapped in bubble wrap inside the box. It was quite a cool experience and loads of fun. I had to open everything and smell it; it was tactile for me as well. As you could imagine I love things that smell beautiful.

So, I get to this bottle, a little squirt bottle with a round lid on it, and they say open it. I smelt it and I had a wow moment, "oh that's not ….. " and at that moment Jacqueline said put your finger in it, so I did. But I didn't wait for the rest of what she said, "put your finger in it and feel it". Oops, I'd already wet the tip of my finger, put it in the jar and then put my finger in my mouth. Well gee wiz, didn't I get a surprise. It was definitely not something you put in your mouth, yuck! Okay, I need to wait for instructions.

DO YOU GO TO THE MOVIES?

Before Covid we used to go to the movies quite a lot. Matthew loves the movies, but I don't get as much out of it. But Matthew is awesome at describing to me what is happening. When we were at the movies watching Chocolate Matthew was describing what was going on and the people in front turned around and in no uncertain terms told Matthew to shut up, if he wanted to talk to go outside. While we probably haven't been to a movie in a good three years, anytime we do we always try now to sit well away from other people so Matthew can tell me what's happening.

Why do you always sign off on your Facebook posts with 'Loads of love and hugs'?

Oh wow that's an easy one.

Because I don't think there is enough love and hugging in this world. There are so many people out there that are lonely, and they need to know that someone cares and that someone can send them love. Love is such a beautiful kind thing and it's cheap and easy to give. You can send it in a note, you can send it on Facebook, you can tell someone you love them.

Try it, it makes you feel good.

*

DRESSAGE

"Always do your best – you don't need to be perfect."
Sue-Ellen Lovett

Hectic & I at
Sydney Royal Show

Desi, Terry Snow & Team of
Living Markers at Willinga
Park - Dressage by the Sea

Eccles, Hectic & I

What is dressage? I've never heard of it...

A few months after the Ride to Save Life to raise funds to put in three helipads, complete with fuel dumps and lights, at the Mudgee, Rylstone and Gulgong hospitals I received a letter from Mrs Pearl Bachelor. She mentioned a competition coming up that she thought I would be interested in. It was in an equine discipline called dressage, which I had never heard of. She sent a couple of pieces of paper with letters on it, lots of rectangular arenas with letters and directions of what you would do at each marker.

Well WOW! That seemed blinking confusing.

So, I did a bit of research into this dressage stuff. Apparently, it was ridden in an arena - a rectangle shape space, typically grass or sand, that was 20 meters by 60 meters, with letters of the alphabet at various spots around the outside. The rider's job was to get their horse to accurately do various movements inside that arena space, like trot from K to M, or canter a 20m circle at B. It could be free walking, trotting, cantering, half passing, halting, backing or canter pirouetting!

WOW! I never knew walking was free. But I was keen to try and sort this stuff out!

I organised how this arena was supposed to be set up, and I began practising in the... lounge room! Don't laugh, I didn't have anything I could ride my horse in at all that even resembled a dressage arena, all I had was Dads lucerne paddock. So off around the lounge room I'd go, doing my best free walk, trot, and canter.

So, I practiced walking and trotting, I learnt what a leg yield was, then there was this thing called a shoulder-in, so I learnt what that was too. I worked all this stuff out. Then one day Mudgee Dressage Group was hosting the State Championship Event and Mrs Bachelor had suggested I contact a lady called Judy Cubitt. I invited Judi out for afternoon tea so she could tell me more about dressage, and how, or even if, I was doing the movements correctly.

Well Judy thought my gorgeous stallion Hectic moved quite nicely. My walk, trot and canter were fine but... some of the other movements required quite a bit of tweaking, especially the walk pirouette. I did a handy turn on the forehand, but that was not what was required. It was a turn on the haunches that was required. So, with Judy's help, we mastered doing that fancy turn.

Judy wasn't one to mince words, "Why are you doing this? And what's the go with your eyes?" Ha ha, lucky I'm not delicate. So, I explained to her my condition - Retinitis Pigmentosa, how it affected my vision, and the prognosis was that at some stage in the not-too-distant future I'd be totally blind. So, I was in a burning hurry to learn as much as I could about this dressage gig.

A pretty cool friendship started straight away and with Judy's help and after a couple months, we headed down to the Australian Riding For The Disabled Dressage Championships at Hawkesbury.

Gee whiz! I had never met any dressage riders before. They make the horses look ever so pretty! White saddle cloths, white boots, everything pristine and beautiful. Dad and I had our horse truck parked under a shed with the lovely Lesley-Ann Taylor from South Australia. Lesley was very kind to my Dad and I, plus she gave me lots of hints and help. Apart from Judy, she was my only friend when I first started doing dressage. I will never forget her kindness.

Well, what an interesting event. All these people training and plaiting their ponies. Hectic had no mane. Not because he'd rubbed it out... I had cut it off! I always hog my horse's mane because I prefer no mane. All my horses have spectacular necks, from being well trained.

We got through the first couple of competitions. Seeing as all this country kid has ever done was chase cattle, I thought we did okay! I think we got a second or third, then came the freestyle to music. Holy hell, no idea how we put it together. Our music was The Man

From Snowy River. When we got to the arena, we were told that instead of the arena being 60 by 20 meters, it was 20 by 40 meters for this test! The music did not fit the smaller arena. Holy cow! What do we do?

I remember Mrs Bachelor saying to me, if you need a hand get in contact with Judy Cubitt, so I did. Well Judy saved the day! She re-cut my music, and we were set! We did our first freestyle to music, which I must say I enjoyed immensely. I love riding to music. It is the icing on the cake. In fact, I don't think it needs icing, but it's pretty cool in any case.

Okay keeping in mind that it was at the end of 1994 that I rode my very first dressage test, Hectic and I had never seen an arena before competing in one at the Championships at Hawkesbury. Imagine my surprise when Mrs Bachelor suggested a much bigger event than Hawkesbury. She convinced me to try to qualify for the Paralympic Games in Atlanta in 1996. Holy cow! The Olympics had never been on my radar! I had never ever thought of representing

Australia in a discipline that I hardly knew anything about.

What are you getting yourself into girl?

And there have never been such true words thought in my head, ever. What have you got yourself into? Training camps every few months, lots more competitions. I had only ever competed able bodied. I had my beautiful stallion Yarrahapinni Hectic who was very, very clever. And under the watchful eye and coaching of Judy Cubitt we improved immensely. We went up through the grades quite quickly and in no time at all we are riding at FEI level, which is International Level Prix St-George and Inter One. It was a cool journey, and I loved the training. However, I had a little problem with all the costs involved. But I was convinced that if there is a will, there is a way.

Dad took me back down to Hawkesbury for the following years Australian Dressage Championships. Sadly the Riding For The Disabled Dressage Championships were being held at the same time. Once again under the guidance of Judy Cubitt we were much more prepared and ready to compete.

Unbeknownst to me Judy had organised a really big surprise for me that night!

My wonderful horse Hectic and I were going to do a display during the Grand Prix Dressage Tests in front of all the able-bodied riders. Judy had also organised eight people from Riding For The Disabled to stand at the markers, which was a great idea. They each wore long white coats which made me riding to the markers easier to see. (At this time, I had only 2% sight in my right eye. I would scan for the markers, looking for the white coats.)

Oh, my heavens! I could only just hear the music over the generators with the big bright lights. But my stallion Hectic was a true showman and he mentioned to me - just sit there and I'll look after the rest. It was a blast! I loved every minute of it, and that exhilaration and that feeling of absolute ecstasy happens every time I do a freestyle. It is amazing! We did our freestyle to the cheers and coos and whistles of the people watching. It was a blast! Thank you so much Judy Cubitt, for bringing so much joy and happiness to my life.

A few weeks after a competition at Riding For The Disabled and selection for Atlanta, I was put on one of the high-performance squads which was very exciting. This also meant going to Melbourne for training camps every few weeks, which was a huge learning opportunity for me.

Our coach for the Paralympics was a very English lady called Mary Longdon who was quite analytical and straight down the line. An amazing coach.

During this time Judy also introduced me to an amazing lady called Carolyn Lieutenant who was Australia's leading dressage rider at the time. Caroline was also an amazing judge. She was the full package, judge, rider, and coach. What she didn't know about dressage, nobody knew. But Caroline was hard line. You listened, and you learnt. I was privileged to have lessons with Caroline learning so much and she also allowed me to ride some of her own beautiful horses namely Temuchin and Champ.

Unbeknownst to me, Caroline was petrified about teaching me! Judy told her: "give her a hard time, you are not teaching a disabled rider, you are teaching an accomplished rider that needs to learn more about dressage." And this is exactly what Caroline did. The journey was amazing!

One of the amazing things that Caroline introduced into my life when I was riding Temuchin was two wonderful movements called Piaffe and Passage – of which Temuchin was a particular master. Caroline taught me to Piaffe and Passage on Temuchin. What a blast! I think I was floating on cloud nine for at least a week and a half after those rides. I could continuously feel these movements happening underneath me. It was magnificent! I had never felt anything like it in my life!

The energy, the connection, the incredible power of a partnership with another animal all the while no amount of force is being used, yet this magnificent animal responds to my aids and does even more snazzy dance moves with such grace than I could have ever imagined. This horse-human connection I felt with Temuchin, it touched me to my core. I was forever changed.

Caroline was also good enough to allow me to use her

beautiful Temuchin to film a documentary for A Current Affair. It was wonderful! With Caroline's guidance and Judy there backing everything up, and on the back of this beautiful horse, we moved around like a we were dancing. How lucky could a girl be? This journey was mind blowing! Everyday learning something new. I was so privileged and honoured to be coached by Caroline and to have the privilege of riding her horses as well, so very, very fortunate.

In 1995 there was another selection round for the Australian Team going to Atlanta down at Werribee in Victoria. I took my wonderful Hectic with me. Ro, the wife of the gentleman who bred my wonderful Hectic and my Dad also accompanied us. Ro was also good enough to lend me her beautiful horse Astral who was just such a gentleman, like Hectic - a true star.

Two horses doubled my chances of qualifying for the Team, plus riding someone else's horse demonstrated my ability to perform on horses other than my own.

By this time my Dad and I had built a dressage arena in the front paddock, so now I had somewhere to practice. I practiced daily on Hectic and Astral. I practised our movements, our timing, our freestyle, and then came the day for us to be heading south. We loaded the two horses on the truck, Dad drove, and my Guide Dog observed out the window all the way to Werribee.

Well, it was a blast! I was so excited to be there! The Asian Pacific Games were being held in Werribee at that time. There were horses everywhere. It was an eye-opener for this country kid.

Ok, we were riding for international selection now! I must tell you, I thought this was important and a great honour, but I didn't realise how much was riding on it, on behalf of other people.

The next morning Ro and I went to get Hectic ready and warmed up for our lesson with Mary before competing. But something was wrong. Hectic wasn't right. Someone had drugged my horse! Hectic couldn't walk in a straight line. It was as if he had had two bottles of champagne and had started on the third. I was devastated! I didn't know what to do.

Mary was absolutely livid with the situation, she yelled at me and said, "You will ride him, you will make a point, you will ride him!" So I did, and I competed. Some of the time we were on top of the logs outlining the arena and some of the time were actually in the arena. I was devastated. My Dad was in tears, Ro was horrified. How could this happen?

At the same time as our qualifying event was being held at Werribee in Victoria, so to was the Asia Pacific Game.

So, after I had finished competing with Hectic, Ro and I went and saw the Asia Pacific Games vets. If I knew then what I know now this wouldn't have happened. But I asked them to come and take blood samples. Yes, they took blood samples, but they kept them both. I should've kept one of the blood samples. You can guess what happened - somehow the blood that we had taken from Hectic went missing, hence we couldn't prove anything!

My Dad wanted to pack up and go home then and there. He was disgusted, devastated, and so upset for all the hard work we'd put in. After that incident Ro and a fellow competitor's husband, Rex Skinner, slept outside our horse stables for the rest of the competition. We weren't taking any more risks.

There was one very big highlight for me though. I'd been given the honour of riding Ro's lovely horse Astral. So Astral and I did what we'd practised at home. We did all the movements expected of us plus two-time changes and three-time changes. Ro had been struggling with the changes with Astral, so in our freestyle I deliberately added higher degree of difficulty movements. We did six two-time changes and six three-time changes. Ro was ecstatic and so proud of her beautiful Astral, but she had a major question for me. How was I able to complete the changes on Astral? I had trained him at home.

Even with someone trying to make things more difficult by drugging my horse, we still made it onto the shortlist for Atlanta. I was so proud to get even this close to representing Australia. I never dreamt that this country kid would achieve this!

In February 1996 it was apparent that the relationship I had at that time with John was over. I asked him to leave my home. This was a liberating time. It was time for me to grow and become independent and focus on representing Australia.

Also, it was a really special time as my sister Lizzie moved in with me to spend time together and support me leading into Atlanta. My God what an amazing girl! Full of life! Full of vigour! I loved having Lizzie around so much. When we were growing up we were never that close. I was always jealous and insecure. Lizzie was born when I was nearly five, I didn't take her arrival very well. I felt as if I didn't count, but I knew deep down I did. I allowed these silly insecurities to blow my mind and prevent me having a lovely relationship with my sister growing up.

Back to the road to Atlanta!

After making the shortlist our intense training continued. Every fortnight Judy Cubitt would come and give me lessons. If I wasn't having lessons with Judy, I was down in Melbourne training at Mary's on one of her horses. Getting confident at riding other horses was especially important as an Equestrian Paralympian because you don't get to take your own horse. The host country provides the horses and the horse you get to compete on is chosen at random, it's drawn out of a hat.

Also, while all this training was going on Lizzie, and I were hunting for second hand furniture. When John left, so did lots of the furniture. I had a three-bedroom cottage to furnish! We bought old lounges and covered them. We bought an old bed which Mum helped us cover the bed head and make it look really flash by putting buttons on it and pulling them back through, making it look as if it was quilted. It was a very, very cool time in my little cottage. Have I mentioned yet that I love craft?

Things were motoring along nicely with redecorating the house. Peter, my wonderful little brother, built me a four-poster bed out of Oregon and I dressed it with lace. Mum made me some beautiful curtains and a magnificent bedspread. Keep in mind that this amazing lady is totally blind! Mum is so very talented. And before you know it, the cottage was old worldly, and it suited me perfectly.

Then there was some mind-blowing news! Very exciting news my wonderful coach Judy had been invited to be a Judge at the Atlanta Paralympic Games, which meant she could no longer coach me.

Carolyn Lieutenant picked up a lot of the slack, as did a lovely international rider called Glenn Fryer. Both helped me a lot with lessons. Glenn would come to Mudgee for our lessons. I was also travelling every few months down to Melbourne to have lessons with Mary Longdon. Things were progressing well. Albeit many were worried about my sanity given my marriage had just fallen apart. But I had my horses, I was okay. We were on track to Atlanta.

Do you need a break??
Time to grab cuppa??
If so, see you back here ready for the rest of this journey to Atlanta!

During this time, I went to Kew in Melbourne, to the Victorian Guide Dogs training venue, to train with a new Guide Dog. His name was Eccles. Golden ears with freckles on them Eccles was always so professional. He was never a stubbies and singlet dog. He was my Suit and Tie guy. He was an absolutely amazing Guide Dog, he never let me down. My independence soured under his guidance.

What a dude! And oh, so very, very clever.

Eccles and I graduated from the training school in only three weeks. Typically, you train together for a month, but we knocked their socks off. We bonded quickly and worked together perfectly. We were the A-Team. I loved him. He was just so clever; it was as if he could read my mind.

So, Eccles and I were off on a massive journey. We were off to America! We were representing our beautiful country at the Atlanta Paralympic Games. Bring it on! How exciting. WOW!

What a journey.

While Mary and I were travelling to the airport after one of our training gigs, we stopped to visit one of Mary's long-time friends. They had quite a few dogs, so we thought it best to leave Eccles in the car while we were in visiting. Well guess what! We forgot Mary had a big packet of unshelled peanuts in the car. When we got back in the car there was not even one shelled peanut left! Someone had eaten them all. Every single one, even the husks! Oh, my heavens! I was about to get on a plane to fly back to Sydney, then to Mudgee. What was going to happen? Oops! There was lots of farting and people looking and pointing and giggling. I could hear tummy rumbling. I thought "Oh my heavens Eccles, keep it together! This is not going to be good Public Relations for Guide Dogs if you poo in the plane!"

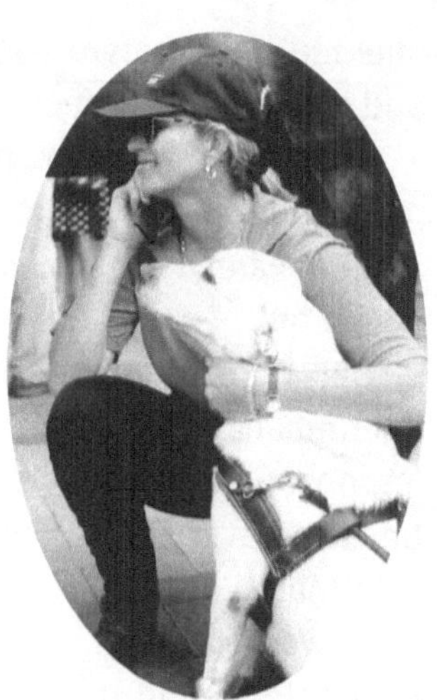

Poor Eccles, he had a tummy ache for a little while. Soon enough everything passed and got back to normal. But after that we were much more vigilant about not leaving Eccles untied in a vehicle.

Well things were hotting up! We were heading down to Mary's to train on a monthly basis. I became such a frequent flyer you would have thought I would grow feathers and wings. The learning experience was massive. Mary and I used to have a lovely time together. Often clashing though! Yes, two passionate women meant that sometimes we disagreed, but she was generally right.

The cost was starting to build up though. How was this going to be sustainable or achievable? $1,000 a month! I just couldn't see this being achievable. I needed to find a way to make this happen.

The New South Wales Academy Of Sport granted me a scholarship for $1,000, which was a great help. The Mudgee Dressage Group held a fundraiser which raised $5,000 for me.

Hazleton Airlines sponsored my trips from Mudgee to Sydney, which was a huge saving. A scholarship for $1,000 from the Australian Disability Sports Council was also a great help. Thanks to everyone it was all now achievable.

Early May at the Intercontinental Hotel in Sydney the Australian Paralympic Committee held the launch of the uniform to be worn in Atlanta. After this Press Release there was going to be the announcement of the Australian Team members to represent Australia in Atlanta. Tensions were high! Nobody knew! There hadn't been any notification beforehand giving you pre-notice of whether you had or had not been selected. We would all find out together on that day. I don't mind admitting, it was a killer! The waiting was so hard... and then I heard it! My name was announced - Sue-Ellen Lovett in the Australian Equestrian Team!

WOW! Man, oh man! I was so excited! We are off to Atlanta! We are going to represent Australia!

Mum and Dad took me down to a motel the night before we flew out. We went to a lovely restaurant for dinner. We didn't stay out late as it was going to be an early start. Also, we couldn't give Eccles a lot of food nor a lot of water as the flight was going to be a long one, 17 hours. We toileted him a couple of times before we went to Kingsford Smith Airport for our flight. Mary Longdon was accompanying me, which was excellent. There were lots of tears. Tears of joy. Tears of anticipation. There are tears now. Just thinking about it brings back so many overwhelming feelings. Wow what a privilege. I'm going to be representing Australia!

Eccles was an awesome traveller. He did not disgrace himself in the 17 hours we were on the plane. But the stewards are wonderful! They asked us if we would like to take the stairs off the plane down onto the tarmac to see he would like to relieve himself. So we took Eccles down off the plane and walked him to a shady spot on the tarmac. He looked up at us in such disbelief. He wanted a garden, after 17 hours he was still happy to wait. So we were taken in, we went through customs and found Eccles a garden. We were also accompanied by two security guards.

They picked up what Eccles left behind just to check we weren't carrying any contraband. I thought that was hilarious! We flew from LAX through to Atlanta from Atlanta we then went down to Jackson County where we were hosted by an amazing family called the Johnstons. Some of the crew stayed with Shirley Ruth who supplied the horses for us to practice on.

The hospitality was monumental! Every night we dined out. We did speaking engagements, we visited hospitals. It was just more than I could ever have dreamt of. And we met some of the most beautiful people.

One of my highlights was meeting a young patient who was bed ridden. Hanging around his room were the most beautiful oil painting. They were so impressive. Especially to me as they were tactile! I could feel the beautiful spruce trees he had painted and the silky water deer. I bought a painting as I have never ever been able to appreciate art until this beautiful man's art entered my lie. He is so very gifted.

It was getting closer to the time that we would be going into the Paralympic Village in Atlanta. A lot of it was being pulled down as we moved in because the Olympics had only finished two weeks before hand. We had one day to settle into the village and then the next day we went down to the venue where the equestrian events were being held to meet our prospective horses. Keep in mind our horses were drawn out of a hat.

My roomie on this trip was Mandy. She was a wonderful girl who had thalidomide as a child. Mandy was a laugh and a great person to be sharing a room with. We had many a fun hour spent together and then there was another beautiful person, Sue Hayden. She used to read me stories which was lovely. Just such a great team of girls and then there was Margaret. She had MS. Margaret and I were competing against each other. I just had the best time. So, bring on the horses!

We had all put a lot of work into training for the Paralympics. We had trained by riding different horses of different levels and different heights and sizes. This had been a critical part of our preparation so we'd be ready for whatever horse we might draw in Atlanta. It was just a little disappointing and yes, a good craftsman should never blame the tools, but they got nice quiet little horses, for the nice quiet little disabled people! That's how it felt. The organisers had no idea of the standard of riders they were dealing with. The European riders and the English riders were amazing, and our Team members were no slouches, but we had to work with what we drew out of the hat.

The first two horses I drew out of the hat were not suitable at all. They were a bit forward and they didn't listen very well. When you are visually impaired it is easier to be asking a horse to move on than to try and pull it up. So, by this time I'd ridden for two and a bit days and now I only had one and a half days left till I'd be riding for our country. In the warm-up test the day before the competition, a little chestnut horse who had been worked too hard by another country and tied up, became available. So that was it. That horse was the one I had to ride. She was a little bit hot for me and a little bit naughty, but she was who I drew.

We all had a good laugh about the blind rider's arena! It had a big fence around it. Well gee-whiz! But I must admit, I was glad when I rode in there for my warm-up test, because as I was coming across the diagonal the little chestnut mare bucked and bucked and bucked! I rode for eight seconds! But... I didn't get a score for my eight seconds, and I didn't get a very good score for my dressage either. It was an appalling test if the truth be known and not something I was proud of.

Overall, I think I ended up midfield over the two competitions. I wasn't terribly impressed. But it was on the world stage, and you can only deal with what you were given.

The opening and closing ceremonies of the Paralympic Games were amazing. I was one of the flagbearers for the closing ceremony which was extra special because Atlanta handed the Paralympic Flag to us, as Australia was the next country to host the Paralympic Games in 2000. That was a very proud moment, and I got to meet the wonderful Honourable Michael Knight, Minister for the Olympics and President of the Sydney Organising Committee for the Olympic Games, who was a lovely gentleman.

Wow what a journey! Then it was time to pack up and head for home. What a welcome home - Lizzie had put things everywhere welcoming me home. It was amazing. I was a little burnt out, over faced and disappointed because we all tried so very, very, hard. It was very disappointing with the horses we were given, but these things only make you stronger. I couldn't wait to get back on my beautiful Mudgee and just go for a ride down the road, quietly in my own head and in my own time.

Well three weeks down the road the phone rings and I come in and I get a message on my answering machine – "Good morning Sue-Ellen, this is Shirley from the Honourable Michael Knights office, Michael would like to speak to you. I'll try you again later." I thought one of my mates must be playing a practical joke on me, so I deleted the message.

The next day I got in a little earlier, about 10ish, so when the phone rang this time, I answered it. "Good morning Sue-Ellen, it's Shirley from Michael Knight's office. Michael would like to speak to you if possible." I said, "oh sure, who is pulling my leg?" I was about to hang up, thinking someone was playing a practical joke, until she said, "Sue Ellen I'm about to put Michael Knight through." So, I stayed on the line!

Well guess what? It was Michael Knight and wow, what did he want with me?

Well, it became very apparent very quickly what Michael wanted. He wanted to appoint me to the Board of the Sydney Paralympic Games. Holy cow! I'm just a country kid. I have no experience on a Board! Michael thought differently. He said, "you have lots of experience with your public speaking and your fundraising, and we would be proud to have you on our Board." Of course, I said yes! And so began the start of a new journey.

Wow! This country kid is on a Board for the Sydney Paralympic Games!

*

Never Say Never

Cascador, Guide
Dog Prada & I

"Never say that you can't do something,
or that something seems impossible,

or that something can't be done, no matter how
discouraging or harrowing it may be.

Human beings are limited only by what we allow
ourselves to be limited by: our own minds.

We are each the masters of our own reality,
when we become self-aware to this:

absolutely anything in the world is possible."

By Mike Norton

*

Vision is Much More Than Seeing

"If there isn't a light at the end of the tunnel,
bloody go down and light it yourself!"
Sue-Ellen Lovett

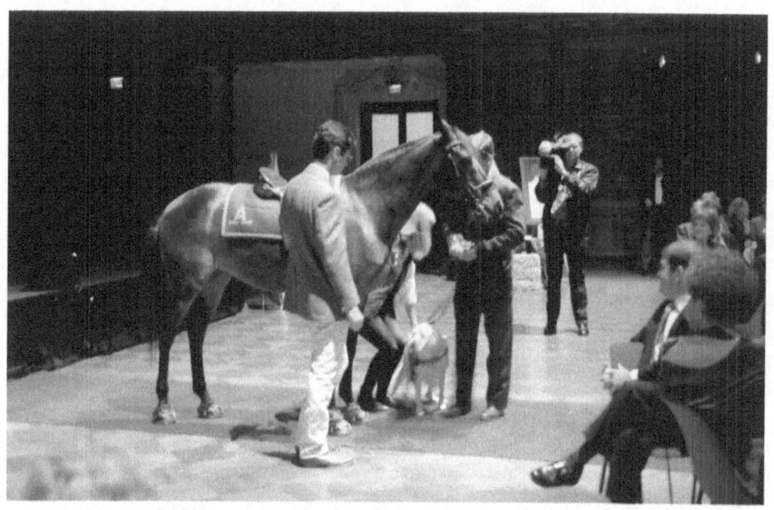

Town Hall Finale - Mudgee, Eccles & I, with sighted Guides Bruce
Richardson and Robbie Aitkin

As a child growing up my Mum and Dad spent quite a bit of time travelling, mainly down to Sydney. Naturopath appointment, herbalist appointment, anybody with a cure. My Dad and Mum were desperate to save my mother's sight. She had a hereditary disease called Retinitis Pigmentosa that was sending her blind.

Desperation gripped them both as they travelled the country looking for answers, help or a cure.

They went to a Genealogist, to track the disease. They couldn't track it any further back than my Mum. In her family her brothers and sisters don't have it, neither did her parents. It remains a mystery how then it was possible for my Mum to end up with this hideous hereditary disease, that slowly takes your sight away, leaving you in darkness.

All these things I found out as time has gone on. It was never discussed in the family, that Mum was losing her sight, going blind. Mum drove for many years and I can remember many a time us driving home, me in the back of the car. One occasion in particular was when I was lying on the back seat of the old Holden. We were driving down the hill to Kaludabah, our family home. All of a sudden there was feathers everywhere. It was like someone had busted a pillow. I said, "Mummy! Mummy! I can see feathers everywhere! Everywhere there are feathers!" Mum told me to go back to sleep. Apparently, she had hit an emu. The silly creature was playing chicken with her. Well, he lost out big time!

Dad went to work on the farm each day and Mum went to work in town. Dad drove us kids and Mum to the bus stop and she started catching the bus into work. At the time I didn't know why this big change happened. What I learnt years later was that because Mum was losing her sight, she also lost her driving license. This clipped her wings somewhat. But the old saying goes, "if there's a will, there's a way." She worked for many, many years with nobody knowing she was slowly going blind.

Then one day my parents were called into infant school. I was six years old, in first class. The Principal wanted to talk to Mum and Dad about me. When they arrived, the Principal didn't mince words. She said, "Mr and Mrs Lovett, we think your daughter has an intellectual disability."

Mum and Dad said "I don't think so. Like what?" But with further looking into the issue, it was discovered that the kid couldn't see, that was the problem. As a wee child I used to run into table legs all the time, which was put down to me being a clumsy child. The reality was not only did I have the same disease as Mum, I also had extreme short sightedness.

You see, at home I spent all my time on the horse. Guess what? My horse had two beautiful brown eyes and it didn't run into things. So guess who was safe on their horse? Safer than being on her own two feet. Hence, I have spent my life chasing that elusive dream of independence and having wind beneath my wings, riding my beautiful horse. But as time went on, my sight deteriorated.

I used to go out mustering with the station hands. My beautiful horse Silver and I never went through gates ... we jumped everything. We were as one. As my eyes deteriorated things got harder for me to navigate on the ground, but easier to be safe on the horse.

Eventually came the day when I was 12 years old, I went to an Ophthalmologists in Sydney. That Doctor diagnosed me with having Mum's disease, Retinitis Pigmentosa. I was born with it.

Officially, at school I wasn't the best or the smartest student. But I got by. But I excelled when with my horse. As soon as I got home, off I'd go on the horse, up the hills to our private sanctuary - the bush. The beautiful animals and the fairies at the bottom of the garden, and the magic of freedom.

When I was about 19, I went to a Macquarie Street specialist in Sydney. This Doctor did a thorough examination of my eyes. His words to me were, "Go out and live your life to the fullest. Experience and do everything you want to do, because you are going to go totally blind." This was a little bit of a shock to the system. Like holy cow! I wasn't ready for it! That day we travelled home from Sydney, the next morning a whole heap of friends and I got on our horses. One of my friends had their guitar with them as we all rode our horses up to the tallest hill in the area. We sat on the top of that hill while my wonderful friend played his guitar. He played lots of beautiful Cat Stevens songs. It was such a memorable moment, celebrating life and enjoying a sunrise together.

So life goes on! Everyone has their cross to bare. It is just a matter of how you carry it.

Mine is going blind. It is not going to stop me from having the most amazing life that I can have. I may have inherited this disease from my mother, but it's not the only thing I inherited. I inherited three other traits from my parents: stubbornness, bloody mindedness and determination. Three wonderful things to inherit, plus the ability to dream big and to make dreams come true.

When I was a child, I believed that there were fairies at the bottom of the garden. I still believe that miracles can happen, and that I can achieve anything I set my mind to. These beliefs have stood me in good stead.

From the outset I was determined that mere blindness wasn't going to stop me from doing the thing I love most in the world, riding horses. Not just riding them, but I love jumping with them. My beautiful horse Silver and I used to do six bar jumping. We jumped a height of 5'8". She was 14, I was 16.

After our jumping phase I did lots of showing and so forth. I even had a go at camp drafting. I had a wonderful stallion, Hectic, that I showed, plus he stood at stud. As my eyes got really bad and I went totally blind, I discovered the wonderful discipline of dressage. For this I am eternally grateful. Dressage has been just such a wonderful place for me to keep riding. It allows me to be independent ... and knock people socks off!

As a Blind Chick and her beautiful horse dance into the main dressage arena, it doesn't get much better than that.

*

WHO IS SUE-ELLEN LOVETT?

*"If you expect what you want to land
in your lap, think again."*
Sue-Ellen Lovett

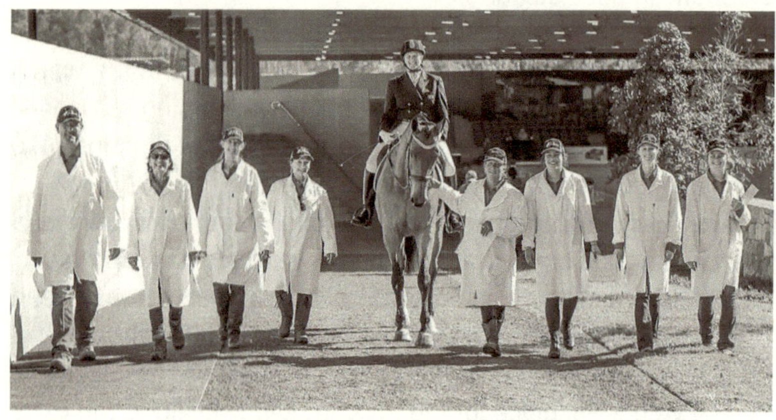

Living Markers Team, Desi & I, at Willinga Park
From left to right: Matt, Donna, Prue, Jacq,
myself & Desi, Nel, Lily, Denae & Sarah

This is a lovely article that I thought was worth sharing with you.
Regional Lifestyle Magazine - Spring 2019

By the time Sue-Ellen Lovett and Desiderata enter the indoor arena at the Sydney International Equestrian Centre the stands are full of spectators. The thud of each footfall of the rounded warmblood gelding can be heard padding rhythmically in the sand as the crowd falls into a hushed silence. They have all come to see the blind lady ride dressage.

"Whatever you want to do with your life, get out and do it now, because you're not going to be able to later on."

These were the words of an ophthalmologist Sue-Ellen saw when she was 19. At 12 years old she learned that she had inherited Retinitis Pigmentosa from her mother, more commonly known as Tunnel Vision. The specialist gave her a full prognosis which confirmed the worst. She should expect to lose her vision completely and all the abilities that usually go with it, he said. He was not to know of the exceptional strength, determination and talent of the woman sitting in his inner Sydney clinic that day.

Sue-Ellen went on to have a stellar equestrian career spanning decades and one that withstood the progression into total blindness. Four consecutive years qualifying at FEI level, the highest possible dressage level, to compete against able bodied riders at international competitions. Two consecutive Paralympic Games in Atlanta and Sydney. A team bronze medal at the World Dressage Championships in Denmark in 1999 - she was ranked fourth in the world in Para-Equestrian dressage at the time. Five times national Riding for Disabled Australia Grade 4 Dressage Champion. Sue-Ellen is currently ranked in the top ten percent of dressage riders in the country.

"I won't let other people decide what I can and can't do," she explains. "It's not a reason to stop living, it's not a reason to stop having a go and my parents taught me that from the beginning. It is probably more of a reason to do what you want and do what you love. I'd love people to see my ability, not my disability."

Sue-Ellen has just come in from the stables on a lucerne and wheat farm west of Dubbo. The property is run by her husband, Matthew, and owned by his parents, but for many years it has also served as Sue-Ellen's training ground. She uses her cane and her horse to move independently around the farm and today her black Labrador Guide Dog, Armani, is lying in the shade on the lawn. Sue-Ellen tries to limit her use of Armani on the farm during the warmer months when the risk of a snake bite is high. Snakes are a dangerous part of life for any Australian, but especially when you can't see. Sue-Ellen has been struck by Brown Snakes several times on her boots.

Over the years her Guide Dogs have afforded her a degree of independence and mobility that would not otherwise be possible, but Sue-Ellen admits she is still more comfortable on a horse than on her own two feet. She was drawn to them from the beginning, as the early stages of her visual impairement resulted in what appeared to be 'clumsiness' as a child.

"Horses gave me the freedom and independence to do everything because they're not going to run into anything," Sue-Ellen remembers. "I was very much a typical country kid and really all I wanted to do was be at home with Dad riding my horse. And every time shearing came around I had the worst tummy ache in the world and by the time the school bus was gone I was better."

Her horses lead her up to the tack shed where she expertly lays her hands on the riding gear by feel and from memory. Her home and her stables are kept neat and orderly for this reason. It is then onto the arena where she uses the morning sun to orientate herself and begin training. She sets up the exercises and the patterns, Desiderata takes care of the corners. Sue-Ellen has educated six horses to FEI dressage level, and it is clear her blindness affords her a unique connection with these animals. It seems that her reliance on instinct, feel and other senses, actually makes for clearer communication with a horse. Even that perhaps, on some level, the horse senses her reliance on him and the symbiotic nature of their relationship. "The training is a real buzz," she says. "I would like to think my horse and I can relate on a different level."

Sue-Ellen has adapted to each of the challenges that have come with degenerative eyesight over the years. What started out as vision that resembled looking down the barrel of a pen has incrementally progressed to total blindness. At each stage of the disease Sue-Ellen has refused to accept limitations. Upon losing the ability to detect contrasts she enlisted a team of Living Markers to hold large LED lights at various points around the arena during competitions. She has since lost the ability to detect light and now rides to sound or through counting strides. "At home I usually don't know where I am in the arena," she says. "After I lost contrast it was devastating, and I stopped riding but we just knew we had to find a way."

Once Sue-Ellen successfully made the transition to Living Markers she returned to the professional dressage circuit in full force. She is currently preparing for her first Grand Prix in April next year. "It's just a matter of working out ways to do things," she explains. "When I'm competing at international competitions riding to sound it can be absolutely mind-blowing for the crowds, the stands fill up. I'm just so fortunate, there are often tears when I ride, and it's not because I'm sad it's these tears of joy that I have no control over. It absolutely rocks my boat, I'm so passionate about it."

Growing up on a 21,000 acre farm outside of Mudgee afforded Sue-Ellen her 'can do', no-nonsense approach to challenges. It was an idyllic childhood as a farm kid riding and exploring the green rolling hills on the banks of the Cudgegong River. Her deep attachment to horses began as a baby. "I was riding from before I can remember, before I could even sit up," she says. "My Dad used to sit me up on a little orange cushion on the front of the horse and take me out mustering. When I got big enough and if he had a beast that didn't want to stay in the mob he'd sit me on a post with my little orange cushion and off he'd fly, bring the beast back in and then pick me up off the post. I've been so fortunate, all the way through I've lived my dream."

Sue-Ellen's competitive horse riding began with Pony Club and she soon became a fearless show jumper. "My horse and I would jump everything in sight," she recalls. "I never opened gates I jumped them, I set up a cross country course and would go around it bareback, no bridle. I've always been as one with my horses. People say you only get one good horse - that's rubbish, my life has been full of amazing horses." She dabbled in many disciplines, including camp drafting, but eventually settled on dressage and quickly transitioned to a professional career.

She also began long distance riding to fundraise for causes close to her heart. Her rides now total over 16,000 kilometers and have raised more than $3.1 million. With a Sighted Guide to assist her, Sue-Ellen has been seen riding 'Mudgee', her little brown stock horse, across large swathes of the Australian landscape. Such was her connection to the mare that at the conclusion of one long distance ride, Mudgee rode in a lift inside Sydney Town Hall and walked the red carpet alongside Sue-Ellen to make an entrance to a dinner with 460 seated guests. "That little horse did not miss a beat," she says. "She was pretty special."

Her most recent 'Ride Against Cancer' was coordinated in memory of her late father, John Lovett, who passed away from cancer eight years ago. "It just ate him alive," she said. "A horrific death, really cruel and very sad." All her previous rides had been completed alongside her father, so it was her first solo ride and also the first ride to be completed since she was declared totally blind.

With the help of a support crew and two Sighted Guides Sue-Ellen rode 800 kilometers across the Central Western NSW outback. She raised over $70 000 for the new Western Cancer Centre in Dubbo. "It was just so wonderful, because Dad's Lions Club, the Mudgee Lions Club, coordinated the ride," she says. "My husband Matt helps out a lot and he supplies all the lucerne for the training of the horses and for the rides. I've got amazing friends that helped - organising all the water, feed and packing. It's about making a difference and that's been part of my family all the way through, my parents have always been very community minded."

Sue-Ellen and her team also managed to train six ex-racehorses to use on the ride and successfully rehomed them along the way to raise awareness for the Racing NSW Rehoming Program. "Nothing happens in my life without a team," she says. "The rides wouldn't happen, the competitions wouldn't happen. I'm just so very grateful that people give up their time to make these dreams come true."

Aside from her horse riding, Sue-Ellen has also made extensive contributions through leadership positions, representation and community engagement. She has held positions such as Board Member of the Sydney Paralympic Organising Committee, appointed in 1997 by the Honorable Michael Knight. She has also been recognized by the Australian Government and Her Majesty the Queen for her efforts. Sue-Ellen continues to draw strength from a tight network of family and friends to maintain her busy schedule and career. "Sometimes it can be really difficult and frustrating not being able to see, and also lonely," she says. "But I'm very fortunate with the people around me."

*

Questions most people aren't game to ask! Pt5

"I love my rose-coloured glasses."
Sue-Ellen Lovett

So, you believe in Fairies and Magic!

Every day there is magic happening around you if you just take time to look at it and observe it. Being loved is magic, being in love is magic. The bond and working with a horse is magic, the birds in the garden is magic. My life is so full of magic fairy dust and fairies. I'm so grateful, so happy. They all bring joy and laughter and put a smile on your face.

Do you use your white cane anywhere other than on the farm?

That is a definite no.

For personal reasons my Mum uses a white cane, she is also totally blind. But because I have had a Guide Dog for so many years, I feel more comfortable going shopping with my Guide Dog or doing a speaking engagement with my Guide Dog. I feel quite self-conscious with the cane but that's my problem, no one else's. It is a great mobility aid and right now as I dictate these answers onto my iPhone, I am using my white cane to walk to the gate. But I don't use it in public. It's my hang up.

ANY EMBARRASSING MOMENTS
WITH YOUR WHITE CANE?

That's a big yes.

Before you get a Guide Dog you have to have white cane training. This is so you have another sort of mobility as well as the Guide Dog.

I have had many, many embarrassing instances with my white cane. One was when I did my white cane training in Adelaide. You had to catch a bus into Rundle Mall, the main centre of Adelaide. I'd learnt a special route to take so when I came up to the traffic lights and I ran my cane forward and upward. Ooops, I'd run it up a lady's leg! She wasn't impressed. I was most embarrassed. So, the white can in public with me can be scary stuff.

WHAT ARE YOUR THOUGHTS ON
DOING THINGS PERFECTLY?

Personally, I don't like perfection.

While I endeavour to do my very best with everything I do, I don't like that word 'Perfection'. Why? Because I don't think there is any such thing. Just do your very best and you know what, that's enough. You're enough.

DO YOU HELP MATTHEW ON THE FARM?

Not nearly as much as I used to.

It is quite a thrill when he trusts me to drive the tractor and Matthew is on another tractor behind me. We hook up by our phones and he gives me directions where to go with the tractor telling me to go left or right. He's always telling me to go faster but I'm not comfortable doing that. I just poke along probably at walking speed but it's still a thrill. The Blind Chick driving a tractor, whoohoo bring it on!

IS IT HARD WHEN PEOPLE SAY
"NO IT'S OKAY I'LL DO IT?"

Oh wow this is one of the hardest things for me to do, just sit and do nothing.

I like to participate. Okay I'm slower than usual, but I do my best. It's lovely to be part of something that's happening with a team of people, even if it's just a little thing like when the truck is being packed to go away for a competition, I'm wiping the saddles down and cleaning the bridles. Give me a job. I love to be part of the team.

DO YOU EVER FEEL USELESS?

Oh absolutely!

It's not hard to make someone with a disability feel useless. I spend a lot of time trying to make people see my ability not my disability, but there is quite a lot I can't do. But that's my life and that's how it is, I just get on with it and do the best I can. Hopefully by doing so people can see I can be useful.

DO YOU GARDEN?

Oh I love my garden.

I spent quite a bit of time in the garden in spring. However, in summer I generally don't go near the garden unless I have someone with me. We live on a river and we have lots of brown snakes. I've encountered quite a few since Matthew and I have been married these last 22 years. But yes, I love my garden. I used to have a ripper of a veggie garden. I'm thinking about putting another one in so I'll see if I can get someone who likes veggie gardening to join me, we can do it as a team.

*

DARE TO DREAM

"To dream of success is to set a goal
of where you want to be.
To wake up, take action, and achieve
it is what true success is all about."
Idowu Koyenikan

So, dare to dream!
Let's make those dreams come true.

*

HOW DREAM COME TRUE

"There is no 'I' in Team.
Teams are what make my dreams come true."
Sue-Ellen Lovett

This is a biggie, a GRAB A CUPPA moment.

Do I enjoy competition? Absolutely. I love showing off my beautiful horse and our ability not our disability.

Is it a challenge? Absolutely.
Do I get nervous? Absolutely.

But let's start at the beginning

Training at home by myself can often be fraught with a few potholes. As in, I'm not doing a movement at the exact position, and as you know dressage is a very precise discipline. If the test says to do an eight metre circle at B, then that circle is meant to be eight metres and start exactly at B. As you know there are no straight lines in a circle, so that means there are many things to consider when riding a test.

I try and make it easier for myself when I train at home. I work a lot when I have the opportunity to have eyes on the ground or a coach counting strides between the movements. This helps a lot, especially if you have a horse with lovely rhythm and regularity and they don't get tense.

As soon as a horse shows tension, their rhythm and the regularity change. So it is really important if you can keep your horse calm and keep that rhythm and regularity, which makes counting so much easier.

My biggest Nemesis would have to be the centreline! When I walk with no horse under me, I list to the left. So when I ride a horse, I also list to the left and the right, because I have absolutely no idea what is straight. This is where having the amazing Living Markers come in.

So when I have the opportunity to have a coach and someone who can call the letter C, we do lots of work on setting up the centreline and counting strides, but mainly we focus on trying to get me to ride straight. This is quite the challenge when you are totally blind.

I never ride the full test at home. I ride bits and pieces. Why? So the horse doesn't ever get to know the test and anticipate what's to come next on competition day. There is nothing ore embarrassing than a horse knowing more than you do, ha ha.

For me to learn a dressage test is really quite difficult. I have to rote learn it first. I do this by listening to it on my iPhone. I always learn the trot section first, I go over it and over it in my head. I draw the pattern on my leg with my finger, as I ride the pattern in my head. Then I learn the walk, which is quite easy. It's generally a diagonal and maybe a couple of walk pirouettes and then into the canter. Then I learn the canter section. All of this learning and mental rehearsal is done at home in the lounge room, in the comfort of the lounge chair. But I have to admit, it takes ages for me to remember a test. I'm definitely not the sharpest knife in the draw.

I absolutely love, love, love the training part of dressage, the teaching the horse new movements. I find this so gratifying. Always my training approach is... it's 'One Step At A Time' and 'Ask Don't Tell'. I always invite the horse, I don't tell them. Training this way gives me tingles up my spine. I just so love training these magnificent animals.

So now we know the test and have been practising it in the dressage arena at home. But there's a chink in my training. I NEVER EVER get to ride a full test prior to a competition! Why? Because there are never a spare eight people to act as Living Markers at home to practise with. This is somewhat of a challenge, but this is how it is and what I do in preparation to ride the best dressage test I can.

I start packing the horse float probably two weeks before we need to leave. I don't cope with rush, and I don't cope with pressure or stress. So it's important for me to do things as I think of them and be prepared.

Leaving things to the last minute just does not rock my boat, in fact it makes me feel quite ill inside. I do not cope with the pressure and the stress of now, now, now. I like to take my time and to be organised. The added advantage of taking time to plan, pack and be organised is that the whole lead up to the competition or event is more enjoyable.

So we know our dressage test, we have been practising, the horse float is packed – we are ready to go!

But before all this can happen you need to have a driver! So I put out my feelers to organise a driver and possibly a few extra helpers to come along with me. I am so grateful to the NDIS who helps me pay the driver and an assistant to help look after me. I am so very grateful. It is really amazing the independence the NDIS has given me.

Having the ability to be able to pay people to help you, makes the world of difference. I don't have to go cap in hand to everybody asking for assistance anymore, I did it that way for years. I am so grateful to the beautiful people who helped me for so many years with a glad heart.

So we head off to the competition. It could be to Brisbane, Sydney, or just to a local competition in Dubbo. Regardless of where it is nothing much changes in my preparation other than the distance we travel to get there.

All the same, things need to happen once we get there. One of the wonderful girls who helps me will go out and find eight Living Markers to stand at the letters in the arena. Without these Living Markers I cannot do a dressage test. The importance of these amazing people is massive, they allow me to fulfil my dream of riding a dressage test.

Once the eight people have been gathered, they are all allocated a letter in the dressage arena. Each get a copy of the dressage test with their letter coloured in in pink highlighter, so they know when to call their letter.

My Competition Coordinator goes through the dressage test with each of the Living Markers, over and over again until they have it down pat and they get used to calling the letter out loud, loud enough for me to hear it. Imagine you are one of my Living Markers and you'd been given the Letter B. You'd stand at B and call out your letter over and over again, B, B, B in time with each stride of my horse. This gives me the direction of where I need to ride to. Yes, being a Living Marker is a massive responsibility and they all do such a wonderful job.

Now you understand why, without the Living Markers I can't ride a dressage test.

Then it's a matter of getting me organised and saddling up my horse. I like to tack up myself, but one of my friends always does a gear check to make sure I have everything on properly and not back to front or upside down, which often happens!

My horse is led to the mounting block, I mount, then my coach takes me out into the warm-up area. Are there nerves at this stage? Yes, but just a few. What's interesting is at this stage the things I worry are things like: do we have enough Living Markers or will I be at the dressage arena on time? Yet all of these things I really have no control over! I need to get better at just letting my wonderful friends do the job they do, to coordinate and organise. I know I have no reason to worry about such things because - I've never been late to a dressage test!

Counting down the time, it's nearly time to walk to the arena. I might do one last trot, an extension and maybe throw in a couple of flying changes in the canter, and we're ready to go.

My wonderful coach takes me to the dressage arena. We walk right around the arena and as we go past each of the Living Markers my coach lets me know who's there and I thank them very much. I cannot emphasise how grateful I am to these amazing people, they totally rock.

When we get to the judge's car we stop and say hello, then continue around to the letter A.

My coach centres me in the entrance where I wait for the car horn to blow to let me know the dressage test has started. For the tests I ride, most of the entrances are at a canter, so I go from a halt straight into a canter. As soon as that horn blows my wonderful Living Marker at C starts calling the letter C every stride. Up the centreline I count about 14 strides and then the person at B starts calling X. As soon as they start calling X, X, X, I can tell by how close their voice is that I'm getting close to where I need to halt and salute the judge. I have probably between five and six strides to go, so I canter for three more strides, and then half halt, half halt and halt. I put the reins into my left hand and salute the judge with my right hand.

At this stage I have a big sigh, I take a deep breath in and breathe. We are in the arena, and it feel so good, in fact its magical. Then for the rest of the test my wonderful Living Markers call me around the arena. Because of the amazing Living Markers, I have the ability to ride an extremely accurate test.

But this is only the start of what I have to juggle in my brain! I have so many things to think of; the rhythm and the regularity of my horse stride, keeping a lovely soft consistent contact through the reins and keeping my right hand quiet. (My right hand is also my Nemesis). I focus on not asking my horse for more than I would ask at home, Ask Don't Tell.

Counting the strides as I ride helps me orientate, as does listening to the letters being called. Breathe, remember the test, remember the movement, how many strides are there in that half pass, oh that's right twelve, go straight... There are so many things to think about. For me the biggest one is... remembering to breathe!

There is one thing I always do when I ride a test that I never have to work hard to remember. It comes naturally. What is that you ask? The smile on my face does not move. For me riding a test is pure magic, it's living the dream. The test seems to take no time at all, I ride from Living Marker to Living Marker smiling and listening to the lovely letters being called. Oh my Lord how very grateful and blessed I am to be doing this. I'm living my dream.

We are going across the diagonal, we're doing two times changes, we do another diagonal, then three times changes. As I hear the Living Markers calling the letters this is a real comfort to me. I know where I am, I know what I'm doing, I know I am accurate.

In no time at all the canter work is finished and we are heading back down the centreline to finish. I can hear the letter C being called; I count my strides; I listen to the Living Marker at B to start calling the letter X. There is its, again half halt, half halt and hold then salute. We are finished! I have tears running down my face, these tears are not of sadness, they are tears of elation and gratitude. I am so grateful. I have just done another dressage test! This totally rocked. This is what dreams are made off. For me though, my dreams don't come true without the help from beautiful friends and a team of Living Markers.

Often, I'm not the only one crying! I think everybody feels the elation and how very special it is for the Blind Chick to ride a dressage test. The magic between the horse and the rider, that communication, the love, is real.

After we come out of the dressage test, we generally all sit round and have some champagne. As you do! This sharing some bubbles has become a bit of a ritual.

There is always one of my crew who want to go get my dressage test and read me the judge's comments. I don't mean to be rude or disrespectful, but I really don't care what the judge says! I just experienced a magical moment of riding a dressage test and all that matters to me is that I am happy with what my beautiful horse and I have just achieved.

Probably the hardest thing about all of this getting ready for a dressage competition is the what if's and that itty-bitty shitty committee that can be in your head a few days before a comp. I do get a little anxious before we go in the arena, like I've said before, I worry about things that are out of my control. So it really is a waste of time me worrying about them!

At a competition we are surrounded by the most positive, beautiful people. People who have given up their time to make my dream come true. None of this can happen without the Living Markers. Nothing happens in my life without a team and people believing in my dream and helping making it happen.

Never think things are impossible! If there's a will, there really is a way to make it happen. If you want it badly enough, you can make it happen.

I haven't competed in over two years. Am I looking forward to competing again? Yes. Is there any anxiety or anxiousness about competing again? Absolutely there is. I wouldn't be human if there wasn't. But I look forward to the challenge and Lola and I doing our first dressage test together. That will be so special. I know Lola will do me proud. She is just the most spectacular horse, and we have a lovely bond. I can't wait for the day Lola and I do our first dressage test.

A very special thank you to all of the people over the years who have been my Living Markers. I am so very grateful to you all for enabling me t compete because you're there. You helped make my dreams come true. I thank you from the bottom of my heart and I send you all massive hugs and love.

*

SYDNEY 2000 PARALYMPIC GAMES – WHAT A YEAR!

"Most people wing it, start flying."
Sue-Ellen Lovett

Rock of Gibraltar, Eccles & I

Matt & I on our Wedding

Well, what a lead up, and what an amazing amount of work.

After the 1996 Atlanta Paralympics, there was another amazing competition. It was going to the World Championships in 1999 in Denmark. Oh my lord, that was a blast! It was wonderful and my Guide Dog Eccles took me with the Team. Great time, lovely people, and lovely horses.

Winning a Bronze in Denmark with the Australian Team and being ranked individually 4th in the World helped me qualified for

Sydney 2000. Keep in mind that all the horses for the competition were drawn out off a hat. They were not horses we had trained with prior to the competition.

This was addictive! I was loving the dressage. The horses we used at the Sydney Paralympic games were provided for us, the horse we rode was drawn out of a hat. This meant you couldn't take your own horse.

So, under the watchful eye of my super coach Judy Cubitt, I had to prepare to ride a horse I had no experience on. How did we do that preparation? We did miles of travelling to different locations to practise riding different horses, so I could develop the skill to ride whatever horse I'd be allocated at the Game, hopefully!

What a treat riding so many generous people's experienced dressage horses. I felt very privileged to ride both of Carolyn Lieutenant's school masters, Temuchin and Champ. I had many, many lessons on both of these beautiful horses leading into the Sydney Games. Paul Biancardi in Terry Hills also were very generous. I would go down for weeks at a time and stay with the family and ride their dressage and eventing horses. I am so very grateful for the time and effort the Biancardi family put into me qualifying for Sydney, so grateful.

I was also honoured to be given Ro Barton's beautiful horse Astral to train on. Astral was an advanced dressage horse so he gave me lots of wonderful things to practice. I was fortunate to be competing my lovely stallion Yarrahappini Hectic at the time. He'd been bred by Mike and Ro Barton at Wellington and was quite a star in my life. I trained him up to Grand Prix but we only ever competed Small Tour Pre-St George and Intro One.

At the time of preparing to compete in Sydney I was still a member of the Board of the Sydney Paralympics. It quickly became very apparent that there was a shortfall in the budget. So, I put together a proposal and presented it to the Board to rectify this. My idea was to do two or three long distance rides to raise public awareness and money for the Paralympic games. I'm not sure what they initially thought of the proposal, but we ended up doing two rides. The first one in 1997, the second in 1998.

Perhaps suggesting these two rides wasn't my brightest idea, as I was also training to qualify for the World Equestrian Games (1999) in Denmark, and for the Sydney 2000 Paralympic Games.

But ... the shortfall in the budget for the Paralympic games was massive. Unlike the Olympics, which was totally underwritten, so we needed to do something.

But... I had another goal in doing the rides, one that was equally as important as helping fix the budget shortfall. I believed we needed to make the Paralympic Games the PEOPLE'S GAMES! We needed to give the people ownership. We needed to make the public aware of how amazing the Paralympic Games are and thus pack the stands while the Paralympians competed.

Steve Cumberland + Dad

So it began, our first of the long-distance rides - from Melbourne to Sydney. This was 30 odd days in the saddle plus on most days I would do 2-3 presentations at various locations: schools, Lions

Clubs etc. Wherever I could do public speaking, I would invite the public to the Paralympics. Paralleling the ride, I was doing TV appearances and radio interviews as well. And in between all of this, we were on the horses 3-4 hours a day. It was massive!

In the back of my mind, I was thinking; 'oh my heavens, I hope I'm not letting the Paralympic Equestrian Team down by not training my dressage, because this long-distance ride was a big, big commitment.' The horses had to be in work six weeks before the ride, building their fitness. But thankfully it all worked out in the end. I had my bum in the seat of the saddle every day, sometimes two different horses a day on the ride. This riding different horses was the experience I needed. That's how I reconciled doing the ride.

We had mini training camps at Jill Rickard's property at Kurrajong Park in North Richmond, Sydney. It was lovely, Jill had the ideal situation. She had multiple bedrooms, a nice kitchen and bathroom on the ground floor of her home, where all us girls stayed, and of an evening we would go upstairs and dine with her, Pat, Jill and Carolyn.

We were so very fortunate to have Jill as our Coach leading into the World Equestrian Games in Denmark and Carolyn Lieutenant was the Assistant Coach.

So, every camp at Jill's we would get a loan of peoples' horses that were at various stages of their education. Plus, we got to train on Jill's beautiful horse Peaches And Cream, a lovely little Palomino. Jill competed at the World Equestrian Games on another horse that I remember riding and absolutely loved to death. A beautiful grey horse called Liebling.

Jill and Carolyn also organised a German Coach to come out and do some training with us. He was really quite good. I did find it a little disturbing though when he was giving us a lesson in English, but he'd be discussing us with his German friend in German! I found it most disconcerting. But that didn't take away from the fact that he was a very good coach.

At the training camps at Jill's, the girls and I had the most wonderful time. There was a lovely rapport between all the riders, and if I remember rightly, some cheeky bugger, no idea who it was, but I think she might have had a Guide Dog, sewed up some of the Assistant Coaches clothes and short sheeted her bed. Now I must tell you, Carolyn Lieutenant is not someone who you would joke around with by such antics as short sheeting her bed or sewing up the arm holes of her nightie. But I did, and I still giggle about it to this day.

Well how funny! About six months after that training camp, I received a phone call, it was Carolyn. It was so cool to hear from her. She had just tried to put her brunch coat on and hadn't realised I'd sewn up the arm holes on that as well. Ooops! But I think it made her smile. It sure as hell made me smile.

Always, never far from my side, was the wonderful Judy Cubitt. Judy was there with me for every lesson at Jill's place. Jude was the queen of organisation. She looked out for all the girls and made sure everything ran smoothly. She went to the airport, picked up and dropped off people. She was the lady that made it all run so smoothly.

It's amazing when I think about it, all of this has come about because of me doing a ride in 1984 and meeting two people at the Riding For The Disabled people at Wagga Wagga, Willie Singleton and Maureen Turner. The difference that this amazing organisation has made to my life over the years is incredible. I would not have attended World Equestrian Game in Denmark or the Atlanta and Sydney Paralympics if I had not been involved with the Riding for the Disabled earlier on.

So the camps continued, as did practising riding different horses. To further support our preparation for Sydney Jude organised in early 1998, or late 1997, for us to ride some of the horses at the Orana Equestrian Club in Dubbo. This Judy organised through a lovely lady called Lee Manny. So off we all went to Dubbo where we were hosted by John and Lee at their beautiful property between Dubbo and Narromine. Their son Matthew was there, he was sort of a nice guy, helping get our luggage out of the car. While he didn't have a lot to say, he was really quite shy, he was a nice, nice guy.

So, the next day we went into the Dubbo Showground where quite a few of the local Dubbo ladies brought their beautiful dressage horses in for me to ride. I had a lovely time riding all these amazing horses. One horse was owned by Peter Green, a mare. A seriously striking looking white warmblood cross called Valkyrie. Not only was she gorgeous to look at she was beautiful to ride and so very, very clever.

A lovely lady called Sharon Kirby was there, I also got to ride her horse and the beauty owned by Jan Cookson. Jenny Beechey had a magnificent horse who was educated to Grand Prix. The list went on. It was just such an amazing time, meeting people and honing my skills to be a better dressage rider. Always under the watchful eye and coaching of Judy Cubitt.

After we'd been in Dubbo for three days, it was time for Jude and I to head off. Before we left though I invited Lee and family to the Paralympic Ball I was hosting in Mudgee, in about a months' time. I also asked Matthew if he would like to come. He was quite noncommittal and thought he might prefer to sit at home and watch the Rugby Test match. No worries.

The Sydney Paralympic Board Committee meetings were every two weeks, so I got lots of air time flying from Mudgee to Sydney. It was fun, I got to know quite a lot of lovely pilots. Guess who said yes to being my partner at the Ball? Yes, a wonderful Hazleton Airlines Pilot. But the night before the ball I got a phone call; "sorry Sue, I've been sent to Wagga Wagga, so I won't be able to come to the Paralympic Ball."

No matter. I got seated up on the main table with the Honourable Michael Knight and his beautiful wife Ann, and the list goes on. It was a really wonderful night.

The incredible James Blundell was our MC for the night. Not only did a local poet narrate the famous poem "In the Droving Day's" by Henry Lawson, but my little mare Mudgee was used as an actor. It was a hit and the scene was amazing. We had bales of hay and stockyards set up in the auditorium at the Country Comfort resort.

But the real mine blowing part of the evening was about to happen.

The lights were dimmed, the smoke machine started, and I entered the auditorium on my stallion Hectic in the total darkness and mist, except for a spotlight shining just on us. Judy was in my ear giving me directions every stride: What to ride, where to ride - half pass, left two strides. flying change, half pass right two strides, flying change, canter pirouette, trot.

We had such a small area to do a pretty magnificent display in. It was... oh my, it was awesome! Hectic was just a star. When we finished my Guide Dog Eccles came running up to us and we walked together to the edge near the auditorium. My beautiful stallion bows and my Guide Dog Eccles lead Hecco and I out of the auditorium.

Everyone went crazy! It was amazing! Then we had all the children from Saint Matthews School entering into the auditorium to one of the Paralympic songs and chanting "Aussie! Aussie! Aussie! Oi! Oi! Oi!" It was such an amazing night.

It was a pretty cool night on so many levels. After all the formalities had finished, I went around with Eccles guiding me and found Judy, Lee, and family. While talking to Judy and Lee I just happened to enquire of Lee if Matthew had come to the ball. She said yes, he's at the end of the table. So I gave Eccles to Judy and went and found Matthew. I asked him to dance. Wow, we danced all night! It was just perfect. We had so much in common. He a farm boy, me a farm girl, and we enjoyed each other's company immensely. We sat and talked for hours after the ball and then Matt came and visited me.

So, time marched on. More rides, more training camps, more Board meetings. It was full on! We ended up doing a ride from Melbourne to Sydney raising $1.1 million for the Sydney Paralympic Games, and the public awareness was massive. We had such a great following! Then two years later I did another ride, Brisbane to Sydney, which wasn't quite as successful as the first one because we had the Paralympic PR machine behind us doing that ride, which was quite mind blowing, but it still raised much needed funds so was pretty cool as well. Then in 1999 we headed off to Denmark to the World Equestrian Games.

Life was hectic. Amongst all of this, I was full time doing public speaking gigs and doing TV and radio interviews as much as I could. I was the Paralympian face in front of the public. I kept inviting the public to the Paralympics. We wanted to host the best Paralympic Games the world has ever seen. Come along, it is going to be amazing!

Then suddenly, the Paralympics is nearly here! While we were moving into the village the security was very high. There were sniffer dogs when you walked in to make sure no one was carrying anything metal or illegal. It was full on.

We settled into the village, then we went out to Horsley Park where the equestrian event was to be held. Oh my Lord, what an amazing venue! All the girls got to try their horse that was drawn out of a hat. Some people drew amazingly well-educated horses, others not so well educated. It was so generous of the Australian Equestrian Community to loan beautiful horses to the Paralympic Games. We are so very grateful because without this generosity the Paralympic Games Equestrian would not have happened.

The first two horses I tried were not suitable for me. They were a little bit too forward. When you can't see that isn't a good thing. I'm better with something you need to ask to go, rather than having to pull it back. So that was Day One. Day Two came along and a lovely horse called Rock Of Gibraltar became available, so I took the ride on Rocky, an Australian Thoroughbred. He was amazing! Beautiful temperament, very handsome, and owned by a beautiful couple Ray and Merl Speakman from up the coast. He was a star, an absolute gentleman.

Rocky and I got on like a house on fire. He was just wonderful. At 21 years young he had a little bit of arthritis which was worrying him considerably. I could feel it in his gait. His paces were a little bit irregular which the judges would have noticed. So, each day I was at the vets trying to get something to help Rocky cope with his arthritis. But we couldn't quite nail it. There was always just that little bit of an irregularity there. And those amazing eyes of the International Judges picked it up. But we got some very cool placings. We got a fourth and fifth which I was very pleased with.

It was also pretty cool because being on the Board of the Sydney Paralympic Games I also had passes to go up into the VIP area. To be able to get away and sit and have a coffee was really lovely.

The Sydney Paralympic Games was everything that the Board wanted it to be. It was the best Paralympics the world has ever seen. All the athletes still speak of the Sydney Paralympic Games with fondness and excitement.

While we were competing and so forth, I missed out on a few of the lovely events that the Board members had been invited to, but I was there as a competitor. I was there representing Australia. And you know what? It doesn't get any better than that. Representing your country totally rocks!

It was also a pretty big year for Matthew and I as we got... married! Plus, we built a house on Matt's family property which is between Dubbo and Narromine. Such an exciting year! It was massive. In fact, our wedding was covered by the New Idea magazine, they were the official photographers and did a lovely story. It was like a bit of a fairy tale.

Belinda Ingram, Bradley, me, Matthew, Sarah Haywood, Anthony Manny

*

WHEN I HAVE FELT MOST ALONE –
YET I WASN'T!

"This too shall pass."
Sue-Ellen Lovett

Sarah (niece) & I

Sometimes over the last 30 maybe 40 years with going blind I have felt very alone, and I've not known where to turn. Up until 15 years ago I always had somewhere to turn. I could ring my Dad. I could talk to my Dad. Dad my hero, my confidant, my everything.

I think the hardest thing about going blind is you think you're the only one living through a hard time and it's crap, but it's dark, it's difficult and it's scary and who wants to be with a blind person? It's like, what's my worth? Why am I here? This is just shit.

With the process of going blind you go through the five stages of grieving.

I used to laugh with one of the guys from Guide Dogs who would ring me often. He was a wonderful gentleman called Ben Schwartz. He rang regularly and we'd talk about how I was feeling. It was when I was going through a pretty dark time... please excuse the pun! Then Ben would ask me how I was feeling. Dah! I spent a lot of time in the angry stage and the resentful stage and the pissed off stage!

Ben would quietly ask me "have you asked someone for some help, do you need someone to talk to?" I didn't think I had anyone to talk to other than my Dad. But Ben was a wonderful sounding board as well as an amazing friend. I found out during our conversations that he also had Retinitis Pigmentosa and was going blind!! Yet, he was so strong and stoic for me. I will be eternally grateful to that wonderful man who made such a difference and always took the piss out of me and made me smile. I apologise for the language, but that's how it was.

For example, one of his favourite things when he knew I was mentally in a dark place was to say something like "oh my heavens, the amazing Sue-Ellen Lovett needs help." Then he'd laugh. Then we'd both laugh. Then we'd discuss the situation. But most of the time Ben listened without judgement.

The thing that helped me the most, was having someone listen, REALLY listen. He didn't interject while I talked it out, he sort of let me work out why I was so dark and struggling within myself, by letting me talk it out while he listened.

So needless to say, the darkness hasn't got any better, but my coping mechanism has. Except for when we buried my Dad on 16 April 2010. That was the day he died. That was the day my dreams took a dive. I had talked to my Dad about everything. We had plotted and planned all my rides together. Dad was beside me on most of my rides or if not, he was on part of them. He had never said that I couldn't do anything because I couldn't see. He was always there to support and enable me. If I fell and scraped my knee, he was there to listen to me.

Dad never mollycoddled any of us kids. Lizzie and I both have the same disease as Mum, the Retinitis Pigmentosa. Pete didn't get away unscathed. While he doesn't have Retinitis Pigmentosa at 14 he had a brick wall fall on him which crushed both his legs. He lost his left leg from gangrene as a consequence.

My little brother is up there with Dad as one of my heroes. Most people have movie stars or singers as their heroes, but not me. Mine are my Dad, my little brother and the amazing George Richardson. George also believed in me, he helped make my dreams come true.

I speak of George in other parts of my book, but Mr Richo had the most amazing influence on my life. I rang him about doing the long distance rides. He was always there to help organise the horse truck, run me to Scone for meetings with the Stockhorse Society, and take me to look at a horse truck that's being built for us. The generosity of this amazing and beautiful man knows no bounds. He also supplied horses for my long distance rides. Keeping in mind that I did 10 long-distance rides, that all except the last ride had Australian Stockhorses supplied by George. He used to breed these magnificent horses at his Eurella Stud in the Capertee Valley, three hours west of Sydney. This Stud is still in the family, Managed by his son Bruce. Bruce also accompanied me on one of my rides. It was the Melbourne to Sydney 1,200km one to raise money for the Sydney 2000 Paralympics.

Over the years I think people's kindness has been the thing that has had the most impact on my life. The beautiful Linda Lord from Poseidon Equine coming to my aid to help Johno at such a critical time as he, we, struggled with his neurological degenerative disease, called Equine Shivers. This wonderful lady contacted me with the sole reason of making a difference and helping Johno.

Our struggle got brought to the attention of the amazing Linda because a gorgeous lady from way back in my past called Jean Finley contacted Linda. Interestingly we'd used one of Jean's horses in my long-distance ride from Cairns to the Gold Coast. It was a beautiful little Australian Stockhorse mare called Masala. Jean had been following Johno's and my journey on Facebook. When I shared a post about Johno's diagnosis of Equine Shivers, Jean contacted Linda and told her of our plight. At the time Johno was getting colic every 10 to 14 days. Our situation was like living a nightmare. It was quite unmanageable.

These amazing, beautiful people that come into your life fleetingly, maybe for a month, a year, 10 years or even just an hour, they make such a difference.

One of these beautiful people is called Rosemary Barton. Ro was more than a Guardian Angel for me for a long time. It was when I was qualifying for Atlanta and Ro lent me her magnificent Australian Stockhorse gelding Astral. He had been schooled up to medium level. He helped me qualify for the Sydney 2000 Paralympic Games. Ro even put her life on hold to travel down to Melbourne with Dad and I and support me during that quite stressful selection process to make the Sydney Team.

It is incredible, an absolute level of kindness and trust with someone, when they give you their pride and joy. That's how I feel about Ro sharing her beautiful Astral with me. As you know, Paralympic Equestrian riders draw the names of the horses they compete on out of a hat. So I needed to learn, then practise the skills of being prepared for whatever horse I might draw. Astral was critical for me to learn those skills and to have me qualify for Team Sydney.

As if helping make sure I qualified for the Paralympic Team wasn't enough, the wonderful Ro then helped me with my wedding dress and preparations for the actual wedding day. Keeping in mind Mum is totally blind, so that sort of thing wasn't possible for her to do. Ro took me to dress fittings and helped me plan things, right down to what decorations should go on each table at the reception.

Oh my heavens. I am so grateful to so many beautiful people. My worry is I'm not going to be able to tell you about all of them.

I am so grateful to the amazing people who have come and gone in my life, people who touched my heart and made a difference and helped make me the person I am today.

Another amazing man that came into my life was Paul Biancardi. I was introduced to Paul and his family through my awesome coach Judy Cubitt. Paul offered me the use of three of his dressage horses to train on, in preparation for making the Sydney Team. Judy and I would travel to Paul's property at Terrey Hills, on Sydney's northern beaches. There I'd train under Judy's expert guidance on his beautiful school masters. Paul and his lovely wife looked after me for weeks on end.

One extra special memory is doing a riding demonstration on Hectic, and a speaking gig for the company Paul was the Head of, at his home. Oh my heavens, such amazing memories. It was hilarious because after my presentation had finished, I'd dismounted from Hectic, and Matthew brought my Guide Dog over to me. That should have been simple enough. But no! Everyone watching thought Matthew was a blind person.

More recently a wonderful friend of mine Kathy Williams was visiting, and she happened to mention a lovely gentleman called Terry Snow. Next thing Kathy sent Terry a message about her blind friend who was wanting to get her horse trained to Grand Prix level, but who didn't have the funds to do so.

Then, out of the blue, I received a call from the amazing Terry Snow. Why was Terry calling me? He was offering to sponsor my training! As you can imagine when I go to a competition I have not just the eight Living Markers, I have quite an entourage. So the costs of fuel, accommodation and lessons, all add up. Terry was incredibly generous. His sponsorship paid not just for my lessons, but for the accommodation and other things as well. Whenever we'd go to his magnificent Willinga Park to train, we stayed in his family's glorious beach house at Bawley Point.

Talk about an amazing man with an amazing vision. He told me he expected a few people might question his choice of sponsoring a Blind Chick. But he said he didn't care. He wanted to help me achieve my dream of riding at Grand Prix Level. And he did!

I did my first Grand Prix test at Willinga Park in February 2019. That was the most amazing accomplishment I have ever had. While I had trained many horses to Grand Prix level, I had never ridden at that level. THANK YOU, THANK YOU Terry for making my dreams come true and believing in me. You, your beautiful wife Jeanette and your family treated me with such kindness. I am so very grateful.

There is something in my life that you may consider very repetitious. Yes, it is repetitious, but it's important to me. What is it? I spend a lot of time saying 'thank you' and being grateful. This is because I can't make my dreams come true on my own. I can't ride, train, do a long distance fundraising ride or a speaking gig, on my own. It is always a Team of people that help make these things happen. They show their commitment to me through their empathy and understanding. They encourage me to keep moving forward, one step at a time.

If I was hit by a bus today, I would have no complaints about what I've accomplished with my life, or the direction it has taken me. I've often been asked if I was given the option to draw the cards again would I do the same things? Probably yes, but maybe with a few little tweaks. My blindness has shaped the person I am today. I'm happy in my skin.

I think as humans we are very lucky. We have people coming and going in our lives all the time. While some may stay for a long time, others move on. I believe people come into our life for a reason, and it's generally when we need them the most that they appear. They may step in and make a difference, then be on their way again. This to me is how I think life works. Why the timing of it always seems so perfect, I have no idea.

This brings me to another beautiful person in my life, someone who has been in my life on and off for at least 20 years. Her name is Jacqueline Thompson. We typically speak to each other on a daily basis. It's amazing, she often says exactly what I'm thinking. After those occasions of being so mentally in tune, connected somehow, she often says "we are so on the same page." Jacqueline's ability to take my babbling out a whole heap of words and then turn those words into something extraordinary is exceptional.

She knows that I don't feel comfortable telling people about my achievements. Yet she can craft the most engaging combination of words in such a way even I want to meet this Sue-Ellen Lovett chick! She doesn't just make me sound amazing; she makes me feel amazing.

There is so much love and so much support between us. We worked together on Johno's last book, titled Walk in My Shoes. It was so cool, such fun. Jacqueline was our eyes. We work so well together. She believes in me. I believe in her. It's not just her professionalism that drives her attention to detail. I feel it, it's her protectiveness of me that fuels her preparedness to go above and beyond to ensure that every line of text in my books are as good as they can be, and that those words reflect who I am.

She's been incredibly vigilant at ensuring she never edited any content without, as she calls it, my permission. To that end she has become a master at fixing the weird words or the gobbledygook that happen in my phone's process of converting my dictation into text. But, oh my Lord! Sometimes that text Jacqueline has to make sense of is just plain rude, seriously strange or absolutely hilarious – for all the wrong reasons!

Friendship is one of those things you can't make happen. It is one of those magical things that just happens. Some people have friends that'll be with them for life. I'm sure Jacqueline and I have been friends in another life. We're on the same page so often and we love the same kinds of adventures. Jacqueline has been very instrumental in not just helping me pull this book together, she has helped me confront things that I probably would have left as they were, in the shadows, in denial. Too painful to deal with.

I had been struggling to write a particular chapter. Really struggling. Isn't it amazing when someone hurts you and even years later you still struggle to understand it all, let alone put it on paper. But gently, gently, lending me her strength, Jacqueline reminded me to take lots of deep breaths and she kept nudging me at the right moments to keep telling my story. She kept listening. My beautiful friend helped me write that tough chapter. Listening to it on playback I have to admit I am very proud of how the pain and trauma that had been there for sooo many years, has now translated into something so positive.

So beautiful Jacqueline, thank you for bringing so much love, joy, and magic to my life, for making me smile, making me laugh and making me cry. The tears are generally tears of joy for the beauty you bring to my life. I will be eternally grateful for your friendship. Thank you, my lovely friend.

Last but not least, my amazing husband Matthew. You have been there through some of the toughest of times of my life. You have never molly coddled me or over protected me. You are always there with tough love when I need it. You give me that veritable kick in the butt that I need at the time, to brush myself off and get going again.

Thank you for believing in me and knowing how important horses are in my life. Your investment in the beautiful Johno, a horse, a mate, that we only had for two years and two days, that we both loved. Johno touched our hearts, that time was such an amazing journey together.

Now we have gorgeous Lola in our life. I shall never be able to thank you enough Matt, for believing, for trusting, and for helping make my dreams come true.

Now I can't go without mentioning our contraceptive... cat! Beautiful Thunder Paws is so named because he curls up between Matthew and I at the night. Never the twain shall meet! Hee hee. We can both cuddle

Thunder Paws, that's how he thinks it should be. He was found in the shed quite unwell years ago. Now he is the love of our life, our fur child. He makes us smile and laugh on a daily basis.

It's the little things that count, the love, the kindness, a smile. Okay I can't see your smile, but I believe a smile makes a difference to people, and it costs you nothing. So, when you get a chance, send someone your love, your kindness, give them a smile. This behaviour makes the world go round and makes everybody happy.

*

LIFE!

These aren't my words, but they are wonderful words of wisdom.

Please take time to read and digest them.

SOMETIMES LIFE SUCKS

Horses break, you fall off, poles come down, events get cancelled, and sometimes it just never stops raining.

There are days you want to scream, cry, shout, hide or just disappear, but people will always come along and cut you down with four little words … "it could be worse."

And all of sudden you feel guilty for letting something "so trivial" affect you, when there are people going through so much more.

So, you shut the feelings down, you push it away and refuse to let it surface because you don't feel you deserve to be disappointed, or upset, or angry, or frustrated.

But as time passes that feeling is still there, it's just silently chipping away at you inside with nowhere to go.
The more you ignore it, the worse it feels.

Those feelings of frustration, anger, disappointment, heartbreak … they need to be felt. You can only move on when you are ready to, and if you're still holding onto all those feelings, that will never happen.

One person's worst day might be another person's best.
Putting out someone else's light won't make
yours shine any brighter.

Be kind, always. People are fighting battles
you know nothing about.

Anon

*

QUESTIONS MOST PEOPLE AREN'T GAME TO ASK! PT65

"Listen to your dreams not your fears."
Sue-Ellen Lovett

IF YOU WERE SIGHTED, DO YOU THINK YOU WOULD HAVE MADE THE OLYMPIC DRESSAGE TEAM?

Oh, that one is an easy one. Absolutely not. Definitely not.
I'm not in that league and it never has been a burn. I was so grateful to be given the opportunity of going to the Paralympics Games and World Championships, that rocked. But I don't think I would've been a good enough rider to be an Olympian.

WHY LONG-DISTANCE RIDES ON HORSES?

Mainly because it's something I can do with confidence. Okay I need a Sighted Guide and we need truck drivers and PR people, but I can ride a horse. To be able to ride a horse and raise money at the same time - bring it on! I just love doing that.

ARE YOU DEAF TOO?

People don't necessarily ask this, but they do assume that people who are blind are also deaf. A lot of these people begin to speak slowly and louder than usual. Please shed this assumption if this is you, and speak to the person who is blind as you would with anyone else.

I can't imagine your life

People who say this type of thing typically see my life as being really hard and challenging. Yes it is both of those at times but it's also full of love, joy and the most amazing adventures. Being blind is no excuse for not living. I just get on with it like everyone else. Life is for living.

You Are Inspiring

Thank you, but all I'm doing is living my life.

I'm so sorry for you

Why? I have an amazingly full and happy life. What's to be sorry for?

Don't ignore me

Often if I'm with someone, they're guiding me, people don't speak to me, they speak to my guide as if I'm not even there. If you see a person who is blind with someone, please speak to them as well. They can answer for themself.

*

BETRAYAL, TRUST AND VULNERABILITY

*"In a mirror you can see what is on the outside,
but all the important things happen from the inside."*
Sue-Ellen Lovett

I think one of the hardest things about being blind is trust. Trusting people, plus how vulnerable you are because you are so very reliant on people's honesty.

I am so very grateful I have some of the most wonderful friends, they've always looked out for me. Not that they needed to! It's just what they did, because that's what friends do.

I never ever thought I was vulnerable, or that any of my friends would be dishonest or take advantage of me. Well, I was in for a very, very stiff learning curve. It hurts to this day that someone I trusted and did right by, didn't do the right thing by me. They even turned the tables on me, making me look like the bad person!

Matthew always says to me that I look at life through rose coloured glasses. I agree. I like to think the best of people and not have a cynical thought. I like to think and feel that I am surrounded by goodness, not dishonesty and manipulation. How this next story pans out is probably a lot of my own fault. Possibly being too trusting. Plus, not being open and upfront with my husband.

I wanted to buy a new saddle and I knew what Matt would say. It would be a flat out no! So, I thought if I got a loan through the saddlery, I would be home and hosed. I could pay it off over a couple of years, Matthew would be none the wiser, I would have my new saddle and it would all be hunky-dory. Well hunky-dory went very pear-shaped.

So, I went and purchased the saddle. I didn't give them my address, I give them the address of another person, my friend. That friend was with me when I bought the saddle. The first payment had to be made at the Post office, which I was not able to do, so my friend offered to drop the payment in. I was grateful for their offer and as they'd need my credit card to do that I didn't worry. I didn't need it, I'd only needed it for the original purchase at the saddlery. All I needed to do was pay it off over two and a half years.

Two years slipped around quickly. While at that friend's house helping her pack, her husband gave me my mail, the loan statements, that got delivered to their house. I slipped it in my jacket pocket. That friend drove me home. Before she left, I put my jacket on the back of a chair and went to the bathroom. On my return we said our good-byes and she left.

I went to get the statement from my pocket to ask someone to check it, but the envelopes were gone! I thought that was peculiar. Yes, alarm bells should have gone off then and there. But they didn't. Again, me being trusting and thinking the best of people, which is a good thing. But sometimes it's a bit dumb.

So, another month or two goes past and my friend's husband drops another statement in the mail up to me, I thank him very much. That afternoon, a lady that had her horse on agistment in my mother-in-law's stables next door came out to check her horse. I asked her to please check my most recent statement. I just said "it was for $5,000 and everything should be paid up for the saddle. The account should be all squared away."

Well, I was not prepared for what was to come next. My friend opened the statement, and she was looking at it for a while. Nothing being said. I asked "it's all okay, isn't it? It's totally paid out, I owe nothing." She said "Sue-Ellen, this account is maxed out for $5,000!"

Holy cow! I nearly died. I didn't know what to do. I had done this with Matthew not knowing. I have been a fool! A total fool! Absolutely not knowing what to do, I felt sick. Okay $5,000 for some people is not a lot of money, but for me on a blind pension where you live on the smell of an oily rag, $5,000 is a huge amount of money.

How the hell was I going to pay this back?

I slept on the problem that night. I was gutted. I was busted. The only thing I could do is ring the person concerned. Well, the explanation was interesting - "Oh I have a card exactly the same, I must've been using your card." Now excuse me, but how does that happen when her pin number would be different to my pin number? And she knew my pin, as I'd given it to her to make that first payment.

I explained to her that I had spoken with the Police. To this day, I still have the paperwork in my draw which details of the withdrawals from my account from places I hadn't been to at that time, like: Canberra, Sydney and Mudgee. I live in Dubbo! I was gutted. I thought she was a good friend. Any case, within five days the money was back in my account. Thank heavens!

I did tell my husband Matthew what had happened, but it took me about a year to pluck up the courage to admit to him what a fool I'd been for doing what I did and apologising for not letting him know in the first place.

But what a cruel lesson. I am in a very vulnerable situation. Anybody who is blind is dependent on other people's honesty to do the right thing. I still trust people. I still give friends my pin number because I can't use the handy teller machines without their help. I just hope I never run into another person that would think of embezzling money from me. I try to always do the right thing. If anyone does anything for me, I pay the costs involved like the petrol, accommodation, meals .... I spend most of my time relying on people. I often feel like a burden. I am so very grateful for all the wonderful friends I have now, and those I've had over the years.

I thought this story was worth sharing because, I would still like to be friends with this person. I have forgiven them. I won't forget, but I've forgiven her. But she keeps me well away, at arm's-length. I'm not quite sure why. Perhaps its guilt.

*

THE DAY FROM HELL

"Don't talk about it – do something."
Sue-Ellen Lovett

Cascador, Guide Dog Prada & I | ©Noni McCarthy

My good friend Jackie Cantrall and I had been planning a trip down to Camden to look at a prospective new horse for me. A lovely big grey warmblood called Cascador.

My mother-in-law Lee watched the video the owner provided of him doing a dressage test. She said he had a little tension, but that it was still quite a respectable test. Jackie said he looked really lovely.

So Jackie and I left Dubbo really early one Thursday morning and travelled the six hours to meet Cascador. We weren't going to visit him until late afternoon, so we thought we'd pop into a local pub for lunch.

This is where our day started to go pear shaped!

Jackie and I walked into the pub and went to the restaurant area inside. After Jackie read me the menu and we decided what we'd like, we put our order in. Then we were asked to leave the restaurant area: "Please sit outside." I was appalled. I was upset. We did not leave the restaurant area. Jackie and I took a seat in the restaurant, ate our meal, then left, albeit still shocked from this experience. The day was not going to improve.

We went out to a lovely family property and rode Cascador. He was what a bit doughy, lazy, and not that responsive. But I thought, 'well that's the sort of horse I need... We'll come back tomorrow and ride him again.'

So, Jackie and I went looking around Camden for a possible motel. On our way out of town Jackie spotted one, so we pulled in to enquire about vacancies. Jacqui said the people in the office watched us get out of the car and put the harness on Prada. When we walked in and booked a room the lady was very, very pleasant. Until she informed us that "you are very welcome to stay, but the dog must sleep outside." Oh my heavens! It's getting better by the minute! We explained to the lady that it is illegal to refuse entry to a Guide Dog. It is illegal to refuse entry to a Guide Dog anywhere; except a quarantine area, eg: a zoo. Her demand was out and out discrimination.

I had a card, supplied by Guide Dogs Australia, which I gave to the lady to read. It states the rules and regulations around Guide Dogs. She read it, but it made no difference. She said, "the dog is to sleep outside." Well, I'm sorry 'the dog' did not sleep outside. We bought Prada into our Motel room, put him on his mat, gave him some water and dinner and he didn't move all night. Guide Dogs are trained to be very clean, unobtrusive and to do a job - which is to guide and look after me.

Jackie and I went and laid on our respective beds discussing the days repercussions. The experience with the horse was okay. The experience of being refused entry because of my Guide Dog at two places was not. I was very upset and not sure what to do about this. But I said to Jackie, "what do you feel like for dinner?" She said, "let's see if there's some Thai." So we found a nice Thai restaurant and thought we'd slip down there about six thirty for dinner.

After we drove to the restaurant, Prada guided me inside where the waitress escorted us to our table. As Jackie was reading me the menu the waitress returned, but not to ask us for our order. Instead, she said "the owner would like you to leave please." I replied, "I beg your pardon?" She continued, "the owner would like you to leave please. You cannot come into the restaurant with a dog." We started explaining how you cannot refuse a Guide Dog entrance to a restaurant. By this stage, I was in tears. My beautiful friend Jackie took over my battle of trying to explain to the waitress that what she was requesting was illegal. The owner refused to come out and talk to us, so Jackie and I just sat there.

I was determined not to leave the restaurant. This day had been a shocker. Three times I was asked to leave the premises because of my Guide Dog. It was horrible! It was not acceptable! I was still in tears, but I said to Jackie, "we are not leaving!" Eventually they did serve us. We ate, paid, and then left the restaurant.

Back to the motel Prada came inside with us, where he got on his mat and went to sleep. I was still devastated. There are no words to describe this day from hell. "What am I going to do?" I thought to myself. "This is not good enough! If this happened to a young person with a Guide Dog, it could be enough to destroy their confidence in using their Guide Dog!"

So, the next day I made two phone calls. I rang Guide Dogs Australia and put in a formal complaint, plus I rang Human Rights And Equal Opportunities and put in motion a complaint that they would handle for me. The formal complaint against the motel, restaurant, and pub.

Guide Dogs Australia were wonderful. They liaised with Human Rights And Equal Opportunities. I didn't want a payout. I didn't want anything other than an apology and that they do a public awareness campaign with Guide Dogs Australia in their town, Camden.

After a few weeks I received a really lovely letter from the owner of the pub. They apologised and let me know they were attending the public awareness session run by Guide Dogs Australia in Camden. I also received an apology from the motel.

Daily for about a week the Human Rights And Equal Opportunities personnel liaised with the owner of the Thai restaurant. He continued to refuse to even admit that he had asked me to leave the restaurant! After the seventh letter from his solicitor, which again was not an apology, the lovely girl from Human Rights And Equal Opportunities rang me and explained that the owner of the Thai restaurant was frightened that I was going to sue him. I asked her to please explain to the gentleman that "If I do not get an apology, I will indeed sue him."

The next day I received a lovely letter by email from the gentleman at the Thai restaurant. He was very apologetic, he admitted that he did not understand about Guide Dogs and that he was going to attend the public awareness session.

I asked the lady from Human Rights And Equal Opportunities to please contact the three lovely people who took the time to say sorry and admit they were at fault. They all attended the public awareness session run by Guide Dogs Australia in Camden. It was terrific.

The next day we visited with Cascador, and I had my second ride. He was not quite as doughy as he was the first ride, but he was certainly a horse you had to ask to go. Well, this is another story altogether. I did end up buying Cascador, but he ended up being quite the monster, quite dangerous. It was frightening. I was at a competition the week after I had bought him and many of my friends said, "Oh no Sue-Ellen! He will not suit you."

I was devastated. What a trip.

*

ONE DAY AT A TIME

Remember those choices we talk about.
Keep making good choices.

"Although time seems to fly, it never travels
faster than one day at a time.
Each day is a new opportunity to live your life to the fullest.
In each waking day, you will find scores of blessings
and opportunities for positive change.
Do not let your TODAY be stolen by the
unchangeable past or the indefinite future!
Today is a new day!"

By Steve Maraboli

Remember to be kind, drop somebody a message, let somebody know you love them and care about them, and don't forget to spread the smiles. We want to create a pandemic of smiles. So, keep smiling.

*

DESIDERATA – 2017

"Reach for the stars and land in the clouds."
Sue-Ellen Lovett

Desi, Guide Dog Armani & I | ©Kathy Hyde (Dubbo)

I had admired this lovely horse from afar for many a year. He was a Warmblood Arab Cross, ridden by a lovely lady down in Albury called Debbie.

Low and behold, I heard he had been sitting in the paddock for a couple of years and had been doing nothing. So, I approached his lovely owner Sandy Croghan and asked if she would be willing to sell him. She said yes, but if I would like I could trial him first.

When Desi arrived home, he was extremely fat, think love handles! He was six axe handles wide and seriously thick through the neck. Poor big guy - he could not bend at all! So, my first priority was ... Desi on a diet! Secondly ... he had some soundness issues.

We started simply by me taking him out to the dressage arena and just hand walking him for about 30-40 minutes each day. This was getting very tiring (for me). So, one day I got the mounting block and voila, on I got and off we went walking around the arena. Naughty me, a nice quiet walk with a halter on but no bridle, no saddle, no helmet! I trusted him and savoured the Desi and I special time together, building our bond. Ooops, someone saw us! I got caught. Matthew came out and man oh man did I get ripped into, mainly because I didn't have a helmet on. The fact that I was riding a horse with no bridle and saddle was another issue altogether.

But I did point out to Matt that Desi was so fat he couldn't run out of sight on a dark night, even if he wanted to. He was incredibly fat and incredibly unfit. Just walking around the arena was a major effort for him.

After about three weeks I decided I needed to get the vet to come and do a vet check. The results weren't good. In short, my vet said "definitely not, he has issues in his front feet, he is unsound, probably manageable but not fixable."

Have you heard or seen things on a horse called Hibernomas? They're nasty festering sore like things and Desi didn't just have one, he had a few of these horrible benign tumours. One had eaten half of his penis away, one on his near side hock, and another inside his mouth. Ugly, nasty, horrible things, but I got those cleared up quickly. My vet Don wasn't keen for me to buy him, he said "Desi is high maintenance, and you will not be able to see when things break out on him. I would suggest you didn't buy him."

Then I had another vet come out, Brad, who did x-rays on his front hooves. His words exactly were, "No Sue, this is not going to work."

So, I rang my wonderful Farrier Christian Munge who went in and had a look at Desi's x-rays. I said to Christian, "if you say we can manage this situation and get him sound and out of pain, I will buy him." Christian's reply was, "yes, we can do this."

So, I bought Desi.

Under Christian's expert shoeing, Desi slowly became sound. He spent four months with what they call Rocker Shoes on. These are shoes that have been bent in a slight curve at the front of the shoe which elevates the front of the shoe off the ground which helps improve the sole growth and improves the passage of blood through the hoof, which aids the overall hoof health. This was exactly what Desi needed. Plus, he was shod every four weeks, instead of the typical six, to maintain his hoof growth and the correct angle of his pedal bone. Everything needed to be looked after so very carefully. Christian was definitely the man for the job.

Desi went from strength to strength. When I bought him, he was a dressage horse at Elementary level, with a few extra tricks. But that's what they were ... tricks! Those movements weren't established, and they weren't correct. So we needed to find a good trainer.

I had been speaking to a young lass that I used to teach many years ago called Sam Hyde. Sam had been bringing a lovely young coach up from Yass, down near Canberra, to have lessons with. Her name... Jana Poppe. I asked Sam if we could organise for me to have lessons and if Jana would be able to come out and give me a hand. This was the start of a wonderful journey between Jana and I.

Nothing happened quickly with Desi. You would teach him something today and tomorrow he would tell you he had never heard of it in his life! So you'd start again. Little things like the shoulder-in took him nearly two years to get right. Just asking for the angle and keeping it and keeping the rhythm and regularity.

But Jana never gave up. Taking us slowly, we progressed through the ranks and were up doing Small Tour which are Prix St-George and Inter One Dressage Tests. But it was such a slow journey! Desi's constant reply to my inviting him to do something we'd trained on before was always, "but I have no idea what you're talking about!" Then we would have a discussion, sometimes an argument. Then Desi would respond, "oh that's right, I remember now." And off we'd go again. Jana's patience and consistency made it all come together for us.

Apart from being a great coach and a great mate, Jana also helped problem solve when it got to the stage that I couldn't see the big LED lights anymore. The LEDs had been critical in giving me direction in the Dressage arena. But I could no longer see them! Jana figured out a way to keep me in the dressage arena, competing. We tried having a musical instrument be the sound at the arena letters that I rode to, but that didn't work. Then we tried something that did work... people with voices standing at the arena letters.

I remember one day in particular, we'd just come home from a competition where yes Desi competed, but not with me riding him. A friend rode him because there was no way I could navigate an arena now that I had lost all my sight. I was at the sink making dinner and I was... sobbing. Matthew walked in and he saw me crying. He asked, "what are you blubbering about?" My reply, "I should be riding and competing Desi. I don't know how to cope with not being a rider."

Matthew's exact words for me were, "stop blubbering and find a way."

So, we did! We positioned eight 'Living Markers' around the arena where each of the arena letters are. The Living Markers would call their letter and I rode to them, to their letter. WOW, WOW, WOW, I could ride a dressage test once again. It absolutely rocked. To this day this is still how I ride a dressage test, with my beautiful Living Markers.

Let me bring to life what riding with Living Markers while being blind is like. Just take a movement, for instance pirouettes on the centre line. Let me share with you what happens. As you ride past K, you start counting seven strides until you get to A.

On the eighth stride you are part way through a turn down the centreline. Then you ride six strides, then you do a half halt and a half halt and go into your canter pirouette to the left. Counting eight strides of your canter pirouette, you then go straight for six strides, and do a flying change. Six strides and then another two half halts and a canter pirouette to the right, counting your eight strides in your canter pirouette. Cantering forward and all the time the Living Marker standing at C is calling C - C - C - C continuously. They do this continuously, so I know where I am in the arena. As I travel towards K, the calling begins K - K - K - K to give me direction. The Living Markers are calling their letter non-stop while I am in the arena.

As well as listening I have to count strides, so I know where movements start and finish in the arena. All this noise is critical for me to pay attention to, I don't want to get lost or accidentally ride over the edge of the arena into someone's lap! This is how I navigate; I've still got to concentrate on being a rider - riding my horse and not looking like a sack of potatoes while I do that. Talk about brain overload!

Thanks to my wonderful sponsorship with the amazing Terry Snow, I was going down to Willinga Park and having lessons with Brett Parbery. That was very beneficial, to be training with one of our leading riders in Australia. What a wonderful opportunity.

Terry and I had set a goal for ourselves. I was going to get to ride Grand Prix! So, I needed another coach, as well as still having lessons with Jana. A good mate and wonderful lady in Orange, Cathie Drury-Klein, had ridden at Grand Prix level, started training us. Desi and I were struggling with our one-time changes in the canter, especially our timing and accuracy. Cathie is what I would call an analytical coach. She broke everything down to steps and timing, we improved out of sight.

In no time at all Cathie had me practicing Grand Prix movements, plus we were starting to crack those elusive one-time changes. Each time we visited Cathie and husband Trevor for our two-day sessions, we improved so much, and our accuracy was getting better.

In the five years I had Desi, he came such a long way, and we had such a lot of fun. Plus, we had a lot of followers! Everybody loved Desi. We were called Team Desiderate and were sponsored by Willinga Park and The Snow Foundation, all of which was made possible by the amazing Snow family.

I think this is worth a mention. When we finished our daily training, we'd go back to our beautiful big stable at Willinga Park and unsaddle. Then Desi would guide me to the wash bay so I could wash him off, scrape him off, and then he'd guide me back to his stable. What a clever lad. The trip to the wash bay was one of many destinations Desi was taught to do. Another was him guiding me from the paddock to the tack shed. This was especially important, as I didn't have any assistance. I was riding by myself. So every day it was up to Desi and I to get to the arena safely by ourselves, ride, get back to the tack shed, bath him and put him away. So, it became... Desi and the Blind Chick.

But don't think he was Mr Perfect for a Blind Chick, because he wasn't. Sometimes he was a bit sneaky. He would go visit other ponies around the stable. But I was aware of what he was up to because I count my strides. I knew how many strides before he had to turn. He only tried taking me on a joy ride once.

Desi, Gladys Berejiklian, NSW Premier & I, at Willinga Park

One of my magical moments with Desi was when Karen was cleaning out Desi's stable and I was walking Desi around the round yard, just for some exercise. I asked Karen for a leg up, keeping in mind he just had a halter on, I thought we'd just walk around the round yard. Well, we went from walking, to trotting, cantering, one-times changes, two- time changes, the odd canter pirouette thrown in and back to a walk, a little bit of passage and piaffe. All in just a halter and bareback. Such an amazing horse, so much trust.

Oopsy! I got caught by Bret Parbery riding without a helmet.

I think the highlight of Desiderata's career was riding a demonstration at a CDI, an international competition, at Willinga Park. We were the lunchtime entertainment. The extra challenge with this amazing ride was I only got to ride the full Grand Prix test the night before! Yes, as bizarre as that seems, I'd never ridden the whole test before. Why not? Because at home I don't have a spare eight friends to be the Living Markers.

So, on the Friday night before the big day, at about 6 o'clock a whole heap of mates, Roger Fitzharding, Dena Gracie, Geoffrey Spears, Janelle Waters, Trevor Klein, Jacqueline Benn, Mark Dowling and Matthew all got in their living marker positions. Desi and I started riding the test but man oh man I was tense! I was overriding and stressed to the max. It was horrible.

The next day our eight Living Markers, all with their white coats on, were ready for us to ride our first ever Grand Prix test. No pressure!

I think we were a bit of a crowd pleaser, the Blind Chick, and her beautiful horse Desiderata. It was such a blast. I rode the test. I don't think you would mark me very well as a competition test, but we did all the movements, and my Living Markers were amazing. I am so very grateful to the guys and girls who gave me their time. And to the amazing Snow Family from the bottom of my heart I am so very grateful - thank you for making this amazing dream come true for a Blind Chick. It sure was special.

The next day we left Willinga Park and dropped Desi off to Nina Boyd in Canberra to start the next chapter of his life. It was time for me to get a new dance partner to train through to Grand Prix. Desi was to be sold. He was down there for two months and didn't sell, so he went to Queensland and is living with a lovely lady up there. He still belongs to me but I'm so happy he is loved and being looked after so well.

*

THE CHALLENGE RIDE
AGAINST CANCER – 2018

"Life is full of challenges."
Sue-Ellen Lovett

Jana Poppe, Me
& Jo O'Brien

Crew names in chalk on
the Gulgong Pub wall

Vashka, Me
& Amani

We started and finished this 800 km ride in Dubbo. The route was Dubbo, Geurie, Wellington, Goolma, Mudgee, Gulgong, Dunedoo, Coolah, Binnaway, Mendooran, Gilgandra, Collie, Warren, Trangie, Narromine then a photo finish at the Dubbo Racecourse.

I think 'The Challenge' suited this ride right down to the ground. It was fraught with loads of challenges right from the get-go.

It was an 800km ride through Central Western New South Wales. 15 days in the saddle visiting 15 towns. We raised just over $80,000.

The idea of doing this ride was hatched when friends Jac, Janelle and I were watching videos of one of my other rides, one of them suggested "Why don't you do another ride?" Obviously, Matthew wasn't in ear shot when they said that!

This ride became our 10th long distance fund raiser! It may be the last ride I do.

For me by far this was the hardest ride so far. Why? Because it was the first ride done without my Dad by my side, or a phone call away.

Firstly, we had to decide where we'd ride from and to. The why we'd ride and raise money I already knew. Money was needed for the Oncology Unit at the Dubbo Base Hospital; they were desperate for funds to fit out their new Wellness Centre.

Next, we had to decide what horses we were going to use. I did speak at length with the Australian Stockhorse Society and then my friend Janine rang me with an absolutely awesome idea – "Why don't you contact the people from the thoroughbred rehoming program about using ex-racehorses?"

So, I contacted them and had a chat. They were very keen but had no concept of what was required doing a long-distance ride of 800 km with horses that weren't fit.

At that stage Scott Brodie was Thoroughbred Rehabilitation Manager for Racing NSW, which meant he was running the Racing NSW Rehoming Program for ex-racehorses, and doing a wonderful job. Arrangements were made for us to go and meet the six horses they'd selected for us. This meant travelling down to the lovely property called Bandanor, owned by Racing NSW in Capertee, which is in Central West NSW.

We'd been told the horses we were to look at were 'in work'. However wonderful Scott had no idea how fit long-distance ride horses need to be. He thought the horses would walk the 800 km. No! We trot and canter, horses must be fit. So, my wonderful friend Jackie Cantrall and I went down to Capertee, basing ourselves out of the Capertee pub.

We had the best time at the Capertee pub; amazing meals and quite hilarious navigating going upstairs with my Guide Dog, the corridors were quite narrow. We had an awesome time there and during the day we trained the six horses they gave us.

Thank heavens Jackie is a very confident and competent rider because some of the horses were too playful for me. I don't cope well on horses I don't know. So Jackie and I would change mounts and finish off doing the miles to build up their fitness. We started very slowly, introducing the horses to 10 km sometimes 12 km a day, just building up the distance slowly and getting to know them.

Of the six horses the next priority was to decide which two were the safest, least spooky, best temperament ones best suited to … me! So it was that the two beautiful horses that had been breed at the Godolphin Stud and had had successful racing careers that I chose as mine, were Vashka and Spilsbury.

Vashka was so handsome he was the pinup boy for the Racing NSW Rehoming Program.

It was very generous of Racing NSW to donate five of these horses to us, so we could sell them on the road while doing the miles. It was wonderful, all the horses went to great homes. The only one that was never for sale was the pinup boy, Vashka.

Once Jackie and I had done a few miles on each of the horses, which took us only about a week, each of our wonderful support team took a horse home to train it from there. Jana Poppe, one of my coaches, took a very handsome young gelding home to train in Orange. A couple of the other girls on the ride, Jac Benn and Janelle Waters, took Lilith and Aussie, both very nice types and handy horses to have around. Jo O'Brien took Go Dragon, a beautiful big strong horse that could go all day. He had such a beautiful temperament.

We all had the horses in work for about a month. I had Spilsbury and Vashka, working them at least five days a week. If I didn't have someone to ride with me I lunged them. They had to have the miles under their belt to get fit, 800 km isn't a walk in the park.

The ride was coordinated by my Dads old Lions Club, Mudgee Lions Club. Les and Lee Liesfield, Lion's Club Members, were on the ride with us the whole time. They also helped map the roads and worked out the best routes for us to take. On all our rides we tried to stay off the main roads and only go on dirt roads. Planning this and making it happen is a big job.

The Lions Club also organised the evening functions where we did lots of fundraising plus talks at schools. All the events were good fun.

My wonderful friend Janine Turner also helped a lot with navigating and deciding on what local roads to use. Janine and friend Tony had a very good knowledge of the local roads which was invaluable.

We had a massive Cocktail Party fundraiser before we left Dubbo at the Castlereagh Hotel. This was hosted by the beautiful and so very generous Mandy and Nelson Kelly who own the pub. Oh my heavens what a night! It was amazing. We raised around $20,000 before we'd even left Dubbo!

On the evening of the auction Janet Wattes and Gabrielle Arnold took charge and organised the raffle. My beautiful niece Sarah Forgioni helped with the auction. It was such a cool night. People were so generous.

The Guest Speaker for the event was Dr Florian Honeyball, Head of the Oncology Unit at Dubbo Base Hospital. His talk was so riveting and inspiring it helped motivate people to give generously in the auction.

How did we get items to auction? Easy! Two of my wonderful friends Lyn and Bridget took me around to different businesses in town gathering auction and raffle items. We had a hoot doing this. They are such awesome girls and great company. I am so grateful for their friendship and all their help.

The preparation and fitness training of the horses was wonderful. All the horses handled the 800km amazingly well. They adapted brilliantly when you think they are racehorses and not used to long distance rides.

We left Dubbo from the Bunnings car park. The wonderful Dugald Saunders, our local member and a great friend, came to see us off.

I was on tender hooks the morning we were due to start the ride because the lass who was doing our escorting and publicity had gone AWOL! She arrived about an hour and a half late, which put us behind time. The horses were all very anxious from just standing around. As were some of the people!

We were very grateful to have a wonderful Vet riding with us that first week. Dr Andrew Clark, plus his beautiful wife Nicole, daughter Jade and son Lachie all came along. They were all such great support. Jade was in charge for the first week, along with my beautiful niece Sarah, organising and coordinating the feeding of the horse's morning and night. This is quite a big job.

Our first day was Dubbo to Geurie. Holy cow it was fraught with interesting challenges! There's that word again. Firstly, we had to work out how to get over the Mitchell Highway safely. There was a great big culvert which is like a big ditch. None of the horses were keen to go over the culvert. Thank heavens for Andrew and Jana and their wonderful horse skills.

We also got bogged! Who'd have thought you could get bogged in a drought, but we did. And again, Andrew Clark saved the day. Not only is he an amazing vet, but he's a master at getting vehicles out of bogged situations.

Each night on the ride there were barbecues hosted by either the Lions Club or a local service group. A great time was had by all.

We had some amazing weather, beautiful weather some of the days. On other days oh my heavens, it felt think we were in the middle of a cyclone! Trees were being thrown around, limbs were broken off, it was quite frightening. The worst of the weather was when we were riding from Gulgong to Dunedoo. My wonderful Sighted Guide Jo O'Brien was stuck with me, literally, I was not leaving her side. As we rode, I kept my leg as close to hers as I could, so I could feel confident. It was truly a frightening ride, but the Australian thoroughbreds were so good under terrible and extreme weather conditions. They were such good horses.

We had the pleasure of catching up with Mr Jim Bowman, Hugh Bowman's Dad on the way into Dunedoo. Hugh grew up in Dunedoo and rode the legendary mare Winx to an unprecedented 33 consecutive victories. Jim also joined us and helped with the

Dunedoo fundraiser. Hugh donated an amazing photograph of Winks crossing the finish line with him riding her to yet another win. Hugh and Wink's trainer Chris Waller had both autographed it. His generosity was so greatly appreciated.

The beautiful Kerry O'Leary organised this amazing Dunedoo evening function. She also spoke about the Oncology Unit which was so interesting.

Keep in mind this ride was done in a time of drought. The hospitality and the generosity of the country people was amazing, totally amazing.

We swapped over crew members at Binnaway. Oh my heavens! What a town, what an amazing heart this beautiful town has. In all of my previous nine long-distance rides I don't think we have raised so much money in one evening. What a function, what beautiful country people, what incredible generosity. And oh my sore feet! I danced the night away. I love dancing and happily danced with anybody that would dance with me. I had so much energy to burn. We raised over $20,000 in that one night! I'm still totally blown away by the generosity of this beautiful town.

At Binnaway we lost our amazing truck driver and her truck. The beautiful Lyn Jarvis not only drove our spare horses, she also washed down the horses after we'd ridden. What a beautiful lady. She had her lovely kelpie with her on the ride who was a bit of a star.

It is amazing the beautiful people that come out of the woodwork to help you for a good cause. I'm so grateful to Lyn for not just offering her truck but for driving it and supporting the ride.

It was at this changeover of teams that my wonderful friends Jenelle Waters and Jacqueline Benn joined us. Jenelle bought her horse truck, which we used for the rest of the ride. Driving the truck was my mate Steve Cumberland. Steve is definitely a gluten for punishment. He has done nine of our ten rides. He is either by my side as a Sighted Guide or driving the horse truck or support vehicle. I am so grateful for his friendship over all the years. You don't get mates like him every day.

We were momentarily short a Sighted Guide for the second week, until the wonderful Jo O'Brien organised for Carina, a lovely young girl from Canada, to ride with us. Oh my heavens! She was quite a horse woman, very capable. We had a lovely time.

The second week of the ride absolutely flew by. Being surrounded by people I work with all the time, and my best friends, was totally awesome. My wonderful mate Jackie Cantrall joined us riding into Coonamble. You may remember it was Jackie who helped me train the horses for that week down at Capertee. It was lovely to have her along for the day. Jackie works at Taronga Zoo here in Dubbo and while not able to get a lot of time off, it was great to have her part of the ride.

When we got to Warren oh my heavens what a reunion. My wonderful friend Narelle Hayward lives in Warren, she had done three of the rides with me. We got to catch up with Narelle and her beautiful daughter Sarah. It was Sarah who was Flower Girl at our wedding. It was such a cool night.

Jo O'Brien had a lot to do with organising an amazing function at Warren. It had great entertainment, amazing food and a super-duper auction.

When we were riding into Narromine the Honorary Mark Coulton, Federal Member for Parkes, was going to come and ride with us but we weren't able to coordinate getting Mark in the saddle. He and his family gave a wonderful donation to the ride which was so appreciated.

Our last day was from Narromine to Dubbo. Apparently, this was a very pretty ride, riding alongside lots of healthy crops.

These horses were absolute super stars. They did their job really well. Not surprisingly we had no problem selling the five Racing NSW had donated to us. I am still in touch with two of these beautiful horses: Jenelle and Jac still own Aussie and the beautiful chestnut mare Lilith is owned by a lovely friend of ours Abby Stubbs. Abby does show jumping with the bold little mare, they do really well together.

Vashka went back to racing New South Wales and Spilsbury was sold to a lovely show home.

It has been really rather lovely, people from Godolphin have stayed in contact with me since the end of the ride. They wanted to find out where the horses went. I was impressed with how diligent they are in looking after their horses after the horses have finished racing.

I was also impressed with the Godolphin generosity. We so appreciate that they gave a ticket for two people to their official box on race day in Sydney for the Melbourne Cup. That was so very generous. They also donated many other items that we were able to auction or give away.

We finished the ride at Dubbo racecourse. It was a very quick finish. We drew a raffle, enjoyed a couple of glasses of champagne and it was all over! Time for everyone to head home.

A massive thank you to the team that participated in this Ride Against Cancer for the Western Cancer Council Foundation. We raised a whopping $80,000. This money will help fund critical cancer research. Wouldn't it be wonderful if because of the money we raised, that a cure for a type of cancer was found!

Although this ride was fraught with challenges, I remain so very grateful to the people that took time out to make it happen.

*** * ***

Before I sign off on this chapter, I think it's important to mention what happened to me after the ride, because of what happened during the ride. It could happen to anyone. It's not that it's all about me or unique to me. This could have happened to you.

I think it's important to share what can happen after you work so hard towards something. When that something finishes you spend a lot of time reflecting on it. Reflecting on what worked, what didn't, where things went wrong, what you could've done better, what you should've done better.

This is painful for me to share. It still upsets me. You'll soon know why.

I am so very grateful to my lovely friend Jac Benn who listened to me for many days, me sobbing, crying, and trying to talk through what had happened to me. And how what happened had made me feel.

I don't think I have ever had a blacker time in my life.

The thought of suicide crossed my mind. Yes, that's something big to admit. This was the first time in my life when emotionally I could not see a light at the end of the tunnel. I didn't know if I had the energy or the will to re-light it myself.

This ride was not one of the best rides I'd ever done. Although we met the ride objectives of raising critical money for the Western Cancer Council Foundation, that money going to assist in setting up a Cancer Research Unit in the Oncology Unit of the Dubbo Base Hospital, I was left in a serious black hole.

If the only paragraphs that you read in my book are these ones about what helped me get out of that darkness, that'll make me very happy. One day you could do for someone what my friend Jac did for me.

As I talked, cried, and sobbed - it was what Jac didn't say that I found the most helpful.

I had no idea how to get rid of the overwhelming, suffocating darkness that followed that ride. When the darkness started to clear I realised something quite magical. My beautiful friend hadn't stopped me from talking or crying, she'd simply encouraged me to let it out, talk it out. She'd simply listened while I cried and talked. I'd felt violated, betrayed, undermined. I felt totally discombobulated. I wasn't myself. My world had tilted off its axis.

Never underestimate the importance of how you treat people, and how people treat you. I think respect is a massive thing. As is being honest and being kind. Massive.

I have taken many things away from this ride. One of which is probably never to do another long-distance ride. I'm sure I will find a way to keep helping people because that is why I am here on earth. To help others and to make a positive difference wherever I can.

THANK YOU

By Bob Cooper

The weary ride is over, but the battle rages on,

For cancer still holds all the cards,
when the money raised is gone.

But the generous nature of some folk,
will help to ease the pain,

For they gave their hard-earned dollars,
from the steep hills to the plain.

And the ride itself is arduous, for the bush is rarely tame,

There were personal conflicts out there,
let's say human passions blamed.

But the task at hand was so worthwhile,
that good reason came out best,

And those that joined the party knuckled down to face the test.

The wiry ponies faced the miles, as only horses can,

They were toughened by hard tucker,
and the driving force of man.

And Sue-Ellen set a cracking pace,
for she had the guts to cope,

Knowing full well that the hand of time,
lays a heavy hand of hope.

So from town to town the eroding miles,
filled the coffers of the quest,

Ever closer came the target that this blind girl had to best.

There were saddening sights as she made
her way across this dusty land.

For every town held its own grim tale,
of cancers searching hand.

A small child lost in the mulga scrub,
to a parent wracked with pain,

A girl of three with cancerous eyes, that will never see again.

A money box from a mother's hand,
from a child lost days before,

An anguished husband's generous cheque,
and a wife hell see no more.

A crippled woman walks across to
the campfires wandering light,

And gives part of her pension, so what did she eat that night?

There is so much more than this pen could write,
to the kindness received,

But it would not do them justice,
it must be seen to be believed.

So to every town and person, Lions Club, farrier, and vet,

Who gave unselfishly their aid, rest assured we won't forget.

For the dark side will grow brighter
through your generous bequest,

And Sue-Ellen and her helpers,
thank the good folk of the west.

*

CH
castlereagh hotel
LIONS INTERNATIONAL
THE CHALLENGE 2018 Ride Against Cancer
THE CASTLEREAGH HOTEL PRESENTS ...
Cocktail Party
SATURDAY, 22ND SEPTEMBER 2018
6.30 PM
Canapés and free drink on arrival
GUEST SPEAKERS
DR FLORIAN HONEYBALL
SUE-ELLEN LOVETT
Sue-Ellen Lovett is a Blind Paralympian and cancer survivor.
Riding approximately 800km throughout Central West NSW to
raise money to fight this dreaded disease.
ALL PROCEEDS GOING TO THE
DUBBO INTEGRATED WELLNESS CENTRE
FEATURING
ENTERTAINMENT BY ISAAC COMPTON
MONSTER AUCTION • SILENT AUCTION
THE CHALLENGE MERCHANDISE FOR SALE
TICKETS $70.00
PURCHASE AT
WWW.123TIX.COM.AU/EVENTS/1835
123 TIX

JOHNO

"Is what you're doing what makes
you smile, makes you happy?
If not, change it."
Sue-Ellen Lovett

©2CPhotography

Today he did everything! Wow what a spectacular morning. Two days in a row. No horrific westerly wind with dust clouds where you can hardly see.

Just walking out onto the veranda and I hear Karen pull up. I give her a shout and ask her if she would mind going and moving the sprinkler and I will go catch Johno. So, the white cane and I head off down to Johno's yard when Karen yells out, "he's in the breezeway eating." So now I know where he is, I don't have to stand and listen to find him.

I make my way down the lawn towards Johno's yard using my white cane in front of me for guidance. Also, its handy to hunt away brown snakes. As we live next to a river, we have quite a few brown snakes, so if I make as much noise as possible, hopefully I scare them away!

I make my way through Johno's gate down towards his stable where I can hear him quietly eating. I walk down and give him a good morning cuddle, put the halter up over his nose and do it up at the side. I step back so I'm positioned at his shoulder and put my right hand on his neck, about halfway along his neck, and say "walk on Johno, to the tack shed." Johno then guides me out his paddock gate into the house yard and up to the tack shed. Here he stands, not being tied up, he is ground tied, just being a responsible young man standing where he has been put.

Teaching Johno how to be ground tied, and not wander off, was all part of him learning a series of disciplines which as humans we'd put under the heading of manners.

This is a special day for us. Why? Because it is the first day of me going and catching Johno by myself! Generally, Karen is there keeping a watchful eye on us both. Not today. After giving Johno a brush and some fly spray, which I apply firstly to a brush then brush it on him, on go his brush boots, saddle cloth and saddle. Even when I girth him up, he does not move a single hair. He stands patiently.

I step quickly into the tack shed with Johno standing outside. I put my top boots on, helmet on and tuck my gloves in my pocket. I pick the bridle up, take his fly veil off, undo his halter and let it drop to the ground. I put the bridle on his head, do up the throat latch, the drop noseband and flash strap and we're ready to go.

By this time Karen was back from moving the sprinkler, I said, "okay we're ready to go." She said, "okey-dokey." So, I put the rein in my left hand, my right hand went on Johno's neck and after some little clicking noises Johno guided me out to the dressage arena. Johno walks us out through the pine trees, does a slight left, then a slight right and we go straight for about one hundred meters. Then I feel the road under my feet, it's seven strides and we've crossed the road. We kept going straight, then up a bank, turned left and Johno walked me along the outside of the round yard. We stopped when we got halfway around the round yard, time to check his girth and do it up a little more.

Then I got a bit of a surprise. I asked Karen a question, "would you like to take him now and put him on the mounting block?" She replied, "no, no. You do it." So, I went back and took my position at Johno's shoulder, holding the rein about 12 inches from the bit I put my other hand on his neck, gave him a little click, click and said, "mounting block Johno, to the mounting block." He guided us to the mounting block and stood. This was only the second time he'd done this by himself. Karen had been training him to go to the mounting block with a clicker, it has worked a treat. We only had to get him to take one step back to be perfect. What a clever boy Johno.

I then quietly get up onto the mounting block, put my left foot in the stirrup and mount. Johno stands quietly and then I take a little contact with his reins and invite his head around for his nose to touch my left foot. Then I invite his head around for his nose to touch my right foot. We do these exercises for a few minutes then walk on into the dressage arena. Such a good lad.

Once in the dressage arena I'm very reliant on the sun for my orientation. While the sun is shining on my left shoulder, I know I'm on the right rein, all is good. When I get onto the short side, the sun's warmth is on my back.

Karen set a timer and we do five minutes each side adding up to 20 minutes at the walk. Then we do some trot and canter work. In the walk we address getting Johno supple, doing some lateral work, leg and shoulder yields and just keeping his body lovely and supple. Then we quietly go into the trot, oh my heavens this horse has a trot to die for! It's like floating on air.

Johno is such a willing and beautiful horse to ride. He is any young ladies dream horse. Obliging and kind, he just wants to please. We do some lateral work in the trot, then I ask him to go into the canter. We do some canter work then a couple of half passes to the left and to the right. They feel super amazing.

That is my favourite word for this horse, he never ceases to amaze me. Then we do some half passes to the left, getting even better, bigger strides. Oh, what a feeling!

Then we start doing quite a bit of transition work, trot to canter and canter to walk. I get him a little bit more on my seat rather than my hands. I have pretty lazy core muscles. I should be at the gym doing workouts, but I don't. Johno and I will sort it out. But core muscles are so important, to be using core and not hands is so important. I must improve my core muscles, so I'm not putting weight on Johno's mouth. He has such a beautiful and very responsive mouth.

You may ask, how do we know when to turn? Well, I leave that up to Johno, he's the one with the eyes. He has been well orientated around the arena in the walk, we do well and can do a competition corner in the walk, and in the trot every now and again. I think we do a good corner, but again, I'm never quite sure where corners are!

But as soon as I have my Living Markers' eyes helping me, I can count strides and know exactly where I am in the arena. That will come very soon, but I need to get a little more confident with what Johno and I are doing until I asked for other people's help. Canter is going extremely well, lovely big, bold, upbeat canter.

So, we get to the end of our riding time and do a 5-8 minute warm down, at the walk. Then I pull up on the northern end of the arena, give him a big pat and say to him, "mounting block Johno, mounting block." He then walks to the gate at the arena, goes out and lines up with the mounting block without me touching his reins and guess what, he lines us up perfectly.

We didn't need to go back or forward even one step. I then dismounted, let his girth out a little while Karen undid his noseband and flash strap so he could have a carrot as his reward. What a clever boy! He did it all.

All that was left to do was for him to guide me back to the tack shed.

Karen walked with us to the tack shed where I give him a well-earned bath, sprayed him with fly spray, put his rug and fly veil on then walked with him back to his paddock for a lovely big well-earned biscuit of lucerne hay.

This was our second day of Johno acting as my guide horse. I am totally reliant on Johno from the time I reach him in the paddock, to the time he returns there after his training and wash. What an amazingly clever horse. I do believe he enjoys every moment of our training. He is always so happy. Ditto, the smile never moves off my face. I am so very blessed to have such a gorgeous animal in my life.

'Johno and the Blind Chick', a perfect example of how dreams do come true.

After our ride Karen asked what I was thinking about while I was riding? I said that was an easy question. I was thinking how very, very, lucky I am to have such a beautiful horse in my life, and to be living my dream.

*

QUESTIONS MOST PEOPLE AREN'T GAME TO ASK! PT7

"The bravest thing you can do is ask for help."
Sue-Ellen Lovett

ANY EMBARRASSING MOMENTS SADDLING YOUR HORSE?

Oh my heavens yes!

I've put boots on upside down, saddle cloths around the wrong way, the saddle on in the wrong position, you name it, I've done it.

One of the best ones happened recently. I'd brought Lola up to the tack shed, saddled her up and I was about to put the bridle on. I was so proud of how well I'd taught Lola to ground tie, so I thought!

Obviously, I hadn't taught her to that well because when I turned around, she was supposed to still be only about six or eight inches away from me but oops, there was no horse! She'd gone.

So here was me walking through the garden listening and following her footsteps. I was panicking because I don't have a yard to tie Lola up in and our house yard just goes out onto the cropping paddocks or straight out onto the highway.

As I walked across the garden all I could think of was me face planting into a tree and Lola getting out on the highway. Then I heard my beautiful mother-in-law's voice asking which way did Lolo go? I pointed in the direction where I could hear her hoofbeats and Lee followed her across the garden. My heart, oh my heart, I thought I was going to have a heart attack I was so scared. Thankfully Lee caught Lola, who'd stopped to munch on some grass, and I took her back to the tack shed. Hence no more ground tying, okay.

ANY SPECIAL MOMENTS IN YOUR LIFE OTHER THAN REPRESENTING AUSTRALIA?

You'll notice all the special things in my life all have horses in them.

I think the long-distance horse ride we did from Cairns to the Gold Coast to raise money for Riding For The Disabled in 1988, 2,400 kms and 54 days in the saddle was extra special. We'd swim the horses on the beaches we rode to at the end of that day's ride. We had the most amazing time.

We finished the ride at the Gold Coast on the beach at Surfers Paradise. How many people get to swim on the beach at Surfers Paradise? It was beautiful and amazing, and Narelle my Sighted Guide and I had the best time.

We even had a poem written for this ride by the amazing Maureen Turner.

RIDE FOR MOBILITY

It's a different world from our world,
The world Sue-Ellen Lovett sees.

It's a world of lilting birdsong,
And the smell of flowers and trees.

It's a world of being helped along
By folk just being kind,
Of going where her Guide Dog leads,
You see, Sue-Ellen's blind.

And yet our Sue-Ellen has answered
A call to see if she can
ride from Cairns to Brisbane,
A Ride For Mobility.

She is helping the Mudgee RDA
To keep its coffers full,
And all she asks from us at home
Is to get behind and pull.

We know that money's short these days,
And rather hard to find.
But not as tough as facing life
Handicapped or blind.

So if you can spare ten dollars,
Or five, or even one,
The riders at our Mudgee RDA
Will continue having fun.

by Maureen Turner

WHY DID YOU GO TO A BLIND SCHOOL?

I went down to Adelaide to the blind school for a couple of reasons. The first one was for the Independence. Learning to be independent while living at the school was really cool. I did some wonderful woodwork and got to learn how to use a white cane so I could then take my next step forward, getting a Guide Dog.

I also met an amazing man who was the then Head of the Blind School. I wish I could remember his name because he inspired me to have a voice. I have tried to be like him and have a voice for the blind, the disabled, and the elderly. I want to be a voice for people who are afraid and scared.

DO YOU KNOW WHAT COLOUR YOUR HAIR IS?

Good question.

Kimmy, my hairdresser, has been doing my hair for years, she knows what I like. She always says I look as hot as mustard, so who can argue with that! I'm happy to go with what Kimmy does, it always seems to get nice comments. At the moment I'm trying to grow it out, but oh my heavens, it's driving me crazy.

DO YOU MIND NICKNAMES?

No not at all.

From when I first started doing my long-distance rides in 1984, I've always been known as the Blind Chick, and it sort of stuck. I have no problem with it. I have a friend from Canberra who calls me Blindie, my husband sometimes calls me Blinky, but it's all in fun and love. No harm is meant and I'm okay with it.

ARE YOU LOOKING FORWARD TO HAVING A NEW GUIDE DOG?

Absobloodylootly!

It will be so nice being able to go down and feed Lola and not get zapped by the electric fence. It will be so lovely with my Guide Dog guiding Lola and I out to the dressage arena and back, and not getting lost in the garden. Being able to walk to the front gate at the end of our driveway, which is a kilometre down and a kilometr back, just because we can, will be wonderful.

I look forward to all of these beautiful things. I'm not sure what Thunder Paws is going to think of the new Guide Dog but I'm sure he will adjust.

Just to put you in the loop Thunder Paws is our fur baby, a beautiful champagne coloured long-haired cat, the other love of our life.

*

BRING BACK THE KID

"Never stop being curious.
Let the child within you SHINE."
Sue-Ellen Lovett

For those moments when you don't have a horse

Why?

Growing up I think I took a lot for granted.

I never questioned why I had this amazing connection with horses.

Why they would follow me?

Why they wanted to be with me?

Why I could sit for hours in the paddock surrounded by horses and be at peace.

I never questioned why it was so easy to train a horse, or ride bareback with no bridle or saddle.

Why was it so easy?

Why did I feel so at peace, so as one?

Why I could go and muster a wild stallion and his 50 or 60 mares, and put them in the yards, draft him off into a pen, put him in a race and sit under him while I dressed his leg wound? Yet he had never been touched by man! He had never been touched by anyone. But he trusted me, he let me put a halter on him and heaven knows why, he just stood in the race letting me sit under him and dress his leg.

When my father came home and saw us, thank heavens he kept driving passed us. He had seen where I was sitting and while furious at my actions, he knew not to interrupt. If he did, his intervention could have caused me to get injured. It would certainly have interrupted the magic and trust between the stallion and I. This time with the stallion was such an amazing experience for me. It was all about trust, love, intent and being present.

As a kid all those things came naturally. I was always present when I was with my horse, they were my one and only, my love, my focus. We were invincible together. I would get on my horse at daybreak and not be home until the sun set. I can remember many a time galloping home on Silver, no saddle, maybe a halter, wind in my hair, shirt flapping on my sides. We were as one. I was at peace. We were soaring. It was magical.

Where have those days gone?

Okay, things started to change. We went to Pony Club and started telling horses what to do, we had different expectations. Our approach of "Ask, don't Tell", we Asked the horses what to do which means working together, rather than Told them, went out the window. Then you get a little bit older and start having lessons. The expectations go up again, more demand, more telling, less asking, more force.

Where has the "Ask don't Tell" gone?

Where is the pleasure?

Where has the fun gone all of a sudden?

It's all become hard work and it is all get it now, now, now, more, more, more!

These changes have probably gone on for a very large part of my life. Until probably the last eight years I just did what everybody else did, I conformed. As time went on I still loved my horse, I was still enjoying my horse. But then everything started to change. My methodology of how I worked with horses changed. The relationship I had with horses probably hadn't changed, but I wasn't so aware of it.

What I was aware of was that I wanted the kid in me to be back!

All of the lessons, all of the pushing, all of the telling and shoving was ruining my relationship with something so beautiful. I don't mean to sound ungrateful, but I wanted what that kid had back. That beautiful ability, the love and acceptance of the horse, all the "Ask don't Tell" and... being present. It was about having fun. It was about smiling. It was about enjoying. It was about... love.

I'm not saying I didn't love my horses over the past 40 years where we have been pushed and shoved and reshaped. I did.

I remember one of my wonderful coaches, Carolyn Lieutenant, answering someone's question: "Why does Sue-Ellen do such and such?" Carolyn's answer - "because she's never been told she can't, so she thinks anything is possible."

I think that is a wonderful way to be, to think anything is possible, to dream. But for heaven's sake, bring back the kid!

Bring back the enjoyment, the fun, the smiles, the spending time brushing your ponies' tail, giving it a bath, putting its tail in plaits, putting some sparkles on it.

For heaven's sake, everyone is so darn serious. Bring back the kid!

Okay I'm probably sounding a little ungrateful, after all during all that push and shove and changes, I got to represent Australia at Sydney Paralympics in 2000, Atlanta 1996 and the World Championships in Denmark in 1999. But none of these were on my horse.

So once again I never got a chance to build a bond with the horse. At those competitions the horse I got to ride was drawn out of a hat, it was random. I only got to ride it for 45 minutes each day for three days! Because these horses were loan horses, once you had ridden them they were taken back to their stable by their groom. Oh how lucky the Paralympic riders are these days, they can take their own horses. That totally rocks! That's what it is all about.

With all my horses I have been so very fortunate. I've had a unique bond and magical feeling inside which can be explained in no other way than pure unadulterated love, while being present and understanding.

I think the past say 20 years and having my horse be drawn out of a hat made me appreciate the bond I have with my horses on a day-to-day basis. It is just so special and so very unique. It is a bond that can't be made in 45 minutes, a day or a week.

Maybe it takes a year of building trust, being present and listening, really listening to what they're saying with their body and/or their behaviour. I suppose I don't just 'Listen' to my horse, because I can't see, I feel what they are saying.

Amanda, a beautiful friend of mine who has sadly passed away, helped me get my flying changes with Desiderata. I was riding him in the arena by myself and oh heavens, I just wasn't getting through to Desi. I wasn't doing something right. I was trying to ask him to do one-time changes, and out of the blue came Amanda's voice in my head.

I started cantering on right lead and counted two strides, then half halted and two strides of walk, then left canter lead. I counted two strides of canter then half halted, then two strides of walk, then take up the right canter lead. This went from right lead to left lead, half halt, walk. Oh my lord, by the next long side Desi was so sharp on his aids and listening. It was all done with 'Ask don't Tell'. It was just a matter of setting him and myself up for a win-win situation.

Okay, by this time perhaps you're thinking I'm absolutely loopy! But I think it's important we listen, really listen. There are so many amazing things out there that the universe is trying to share with us, and tell us. Yet we aren't open to them. We aren't listening.

We need to listen to our horse.

We need to be present.

We need to share, and we need to bring the fun back.

We need to have happy horses again.

Not jammed up, tight, frustrated, pig rooting, kicking out and bucking horses because they're uncomfortable.

We need to listen and feel if their bodies are sore.

Work with your horse, listen to them.

It's not hard, it's not rocket science.

It's about being present, being present, being present, listening, listening, loving and enjoying your time together.

Bring back the kid in you.

It feels good, it makes you smile.

We do this because we love them and we want them to be part of our life.

The time you spend with them is special.

Bring back the kid in you.

It intrigues me all the podcasts and videos out there that talk on and on about being 'present', about 'going down rabbit holes' and about 'being able to feel!'

We have been able to do that for forever. We could do that when we were kids. But, some of us lost our way as we grew up.

Go back and find that kid in you, that person that loves their horse for just loving the horse's sake.

Learn to listen again.

Learn to be present.

Learn to smile again.

This is such a cool journey; we are so privileged to have horses in our life. They are game changers for most people. So, take the time to listen to them. Let them change your life, because they can. They will if you listen, be present and love them.

Okay! I've now shown an underbelly. I am a square peg in a round hole. I have been for most of my life. But you know what? That's okay. There will be people that don't agree with me, and that's okay too. That's the beauty of being an individual, we can have our own point of view and live our life with our horses however we choose.

In the past 20 years the horse that has taught me the most about this, the horse that my wonderful husband Matthew bought for me, was the amazing Johno. Sadly, Johno had a neurological degenerative disease called Equine Shivers. We didn't know this when we bought him as he passed his vet check. If the check was done as it was supposed to have been things would have been very different.

Johno taught me to listen on so many levels, and to be so very present. I picked up everything he put down; I felt his anxiety, his fear, his terror when he couldn't move in the morning because of the Equine Shivers.

I would sit down at his paddock crying of a morning while he worked out with his brain how to connect to his legs so he could walk. How cruel. But at least he had me to share it with.

Johno had so much to say, and he wanted to share it with the world. He wanted to share his journey about his neurological condition Equine Shivers with the world. Why? Firstly, to educate and let people know about Equine Shivers, and secondly to bring understanding, that people should look a little bit further, they're not always being naughty horses.

One day someone suggested Johno have his own Facebook page, so it began. I introduced Johno and from then on it was very hard for me to do a post. Johno did most of the posts about what he was doing, what he was doing with the Blind Chick, how he thought when the Blind Chick got zapped by the electric fence - it was hilarious, he had such a sense of humour. He was also really sensible. He tried so hard to have my back and protect me all the time, but because of his neurological condition this couldn't always happen. He didn't always have control of himself.

Johno took me to a whole new level of listening. When he was going to be euthanised I spent an hour and a half in the paddock with him just walking and talking to him. But he kept taking me back to the gate, leading me down to where the hole in the ground was, where he was to be buried! I couldn't get my head around this, but it was Johno telling me it's time, it's okay.

I still struggle with this to this day, knowing that he knew but he was happy to go! He was sick of how things were and being partially sedated all the time. It was not a life.

My wonderful friend Jackie Cantrall was there with me when Don came out to euthanise Johno. My wonderful husband Matthew was there as Don wouldn't let me hold Johno while he was being euthanised. While Jackie was holding me as Johno went to sleep, something amazing and magical happened to me.

As soon as Johno went to sleep the fog cleared; my heart stopped hurting, my head stopped hurting and Johno was at peace. I could not believe the freedom my body, my heart, and my soul had now Johno was free from pain.

It wasn't my imagination, it was real. Johno is free now. He's by my side every day, I can feel his warmth, his gentleness, the whole 18 3 hands of him. He was meant to be with me for two years and two days. We were meant to be on this journey, as hard and as unpleasant as it was. But he had things to teach me. One of these being - I had to learn to LISTEN MORE, because he channelled through me so he could write every post on our Johno & The Blind Chick Facebook page. I had to go back after I'd posted his words and re-read them. Why? Because I never remembered writing them!

So now I have beautiful Lola and I am taking Lola and I on a different journey.

I'm spending time getting to know Lola. I'm getting to know her body, doing the Myofascial Release Therapy so I can help her body. I've been doing Liberty Work and holy cow that can be interesting with the Blind Chick and a loose horse! I'm teaching her tricks! It's been working so far. Believe me, I'm flying blind. We're a work in progress, but we're having a hell of a lot of fun.

I spend hours like I used to do with Johno, just sitting in the paddock and enjoying her company. We go for walks, and rides. I have all these wonderful things I'd like to do with Lola. I want to go mustering, I want to ride on the beach, I want to just enjoy my horse because I can. I don't want the pressure of competitions. Yes, one day we will get back and maybe compete again, but maybe we won't! It doesn't matter, it's all about being present, loving your horse, listening to your horse and being a kid again.

Have some fun. Make sure you are smiling because that's what it's all about.

Unlock your heart. Dare to Dream Big.

Stop winging it and start flying.

*

REFLECTIONS

The following pages are reflections on a special time, with a special horse called Johno.

WHAT'S IT LIKE?

Feeling Empathy | 23 June 2020

Prada & the Blind Chick

Diary entry by Johno

Well good morning all from Chile Southern Highlands. I have been giving this one a lot of thought and I have questions for the Blind Chick that may interest you because the answer definitely interests me. I'm wondering, what makes her tick?

My first question to the Blind Chick is about how hard it must be, going blind. Where do you get the energy, the strength, the reason to want to get up of a morning and do something? Wouldn't it be easier to just sit and have things done for you?

Wow! I don't think the Blind Chick likes this question.

"Going blind has not been a choice. Living has been a choice, moving forward has been a choice, my attitude is the choice, my love of life is a choice. I choose to live, I choose to enjoy, I choose to make a difference, and I choose to have a hell of a lot of fun while doing it. Everybody has their cross to bear. It just depends on how you choose to carry it.

I could choose to let being blind be a burden. But I have chosen to make it work for me. Because of my blindness, my Guide Dog and my horse, I have raised millions of dollars for charity. By making my so-called blindness work for me, I tend to try and make an opportunity out of everything that comes into my life. Whether it be positive or whether it be negative.

Going blind has been pretty crappy at times, but I tend to think I have had an amazing opportunity and if there isn't an opportunity in front of me, like if there isn't a light at the end of the tunnel, go down and light the bloody thing yourself.

Life is no dress rehearsal. We are here to give it our best go. So, let's make it work, let's make a difference, let's be happy, let's be united and make a positive impact. It's a little bit like the diary entry Johno did the other day about a smile. Smiling really is contagious, so is being happy and sharing joy, sharing goodwill and good thoughts. They're so contagious. I think this is one of the special reasons that Johno and I have chosen to share our journey. It's because it is special, it's about love, it's about kindness, it's about sharing and having so many beautiful people on this journey with us. All that makes it so very special.

To sum up going blind I tend to think it has made me the person I am. We need to be happy with the person we are. I am happy with who I am and what I represent. It's also important to love yourself for who you are and what you represent. This is so very important. Because if you can't love yourself, you can't love anybody else. Hence, I spend my life sharing love, joy and happiness, and hopefully it is contagious, and it can spread like a pandemic. We need more love and joy in the world.

To sum up Johno's question, has it been hard going blind? Yes, sometimes. But if I was given a deck of cards and asked would I like to draw this card all over again, I would take the life I have. It's pretty terrific and I am extremely happy in the skin I'm in".

Wow, holy cow, what an answer! I wasn't sure what to expect. I knew it would be positive but so determined, so courageous. I will give my next question a lot of thought.

I hope you're having a spectacular day.

Loads of love and hugs, Johno and the Blind Chick with attitude.

P.S: Just a thought. If you think someone needs a little bit of a lift, some awesome encouragement, share this diary entry with them. I think the Blind Chick's message is really important. Love Johno.

NO REGRETS

Feeling Nostalgic | 24 June 2020

Diary entry by Johno to the Blind Chick

No regrets Sue Ellen.
No matter how blind, it improved your vision.
No matter how foolish, it made you wiser.
And no matter how generous, it made you more.
I wrote this for my Blind Chick. She's a bit of okay you know. She has the most amazing strength and determination.
I hope you are having a spectacular day. Don't forget those smiles, keep spreading them. We need a pandemic of smiles.
Love always, Johno.

WALK IN MY SHOES, FOR JUST ONE DAY

"Dare to Dream."
Sue-Ellen Lovett

Johno, Matt and I | © 2C Photography

Let me share with you what it's like to walk in my Blind Chick's shoes, for just one day.

I'll describe what a typical day is like. I'll probably add in a few other little things as we go along, but I will try to keep it to what her life is like on a day-to-day basis.

Most mornings start at 6am when the Blind Chickie babe gets up and gets her husband Matthew his breakfast; puts the jug on and makes a cuppa tea. Just this start is an awakener for her, for anyone! Why? For the Blind Chick to pour a cuppa she must put a finger in the top of the cup so when the boiling water meets that finger, she knows to stop pouring, Ouch! Now she's very much awake.

Then she comes down to feed me. That involves walking out the back door, putting her boots on and picking up her trusty white cane. Never ever did she think she'd rely on a white cane.

She had a Guide Dog for 38 years, she never liked using the cane. I remember her telling the story of before she got a Guide Dog, she'd had to do white cane training. She'd called her cane Fred. He's buried it in the backyard somewhere in Victoria. Why? Because as soon on as she got the Guide Dog, no more white cane. But these days it's white cane all the way around the farm.

I will digress in a little while and tell you a couple of white cane stories, but let's continue for now with the morning routine. She heads out to the tack shed, tap, tap, tap, tap with the white cane, I hear her coming. She measures out my supplements, mixes the feed then off to my paddock to feed me. Watching the Blind Chick finding the paddock gate is sometimes really funny for me, not for her. If she isn't holding the cane's rubber handle, she's holding the long metal part, Zappo! My fence has a hot wire running around it. Some mornings I hear her get zapped. Her second ouch for the morning.

Probably not the best way to totally wake up with a zap from the electric fence, but it happens reasonably often. I admit to having a wee chuckle to myself, I know the Blind Chick laughs about it too, later. Right at that time, it's not that funny for her.

I'm always conscious of anytime the Blind Chick goes outside, she's very dependent on the sun shining for her orientation. The morning sun comes up from the east, she can feel the warmth of the sun's rays on her face. This warmth helps her knows where she is. As she walks through the garden to my paddock the white cane finds the trees, but the sun on her face orientates her so she can make her way down to my paddock quite easily. Except for one electric fence shock or two.

After she gives me my hard feed she walks down to the stable block and into the spare stable. There she breaks off a couple of biscuits of hay which she puts outside the gate. Once I finish my hard feed, she gives me these.

Oopsy, I missed sharing a funny thing. Luckily, it only happened once.

The Blind Chick has a favourite pair of lovely blue linen shorts.

They're really comfy so she often pops them on first thing in the morning with a clean shirt and down she comes to feed me. Well, one particular morning she came down, how she looked was hilarious. She'd put her shirt and shorts on inside out! She looked like an elephant! The two pockets of the shorts are quite large, so she had elephant ears. Naughty Matthew didn't bother to tell her that the shorts were inside out, but I sure noticed. I had a quiet chuckle to myself. Thankfully when she cut the string of the hay and went to put the string in her pocket, voila! Right there in the hay shed she quickly fixed her wardrobe malfunction before anyone else saw her.

These little things that you take for granted, like dressing yourself without looking like a weirdo, can have serious hiccups for my Blind Chick. Clothes being inside out, socks not matching. She's clever with what she buys though, like her socks. She's got about six pairs of the same colour and same brand, so she doesn't have to worry about wearing odd socks. Not that that matters most of the time, but it can look pretty funny when you have visitors. She's been known to do it.

Back to finishing up my day-to-day feeding routine. She goes back up and washes out the buckets then heads inside to clean up the kitchen and do her domestic Goddess duties.

Once inside she has a quick breakfast and a coffee, of course. Then she gets her phone to read her a bit of Facebook and catch up with all the comments that people are putting on my page. After that she's off to the bathroom to clean her teeth.

Be warned, teeth cleaning can get a bit precarious!

The first totally hilarious time things went pear shaped was when she was getting ready to go and do a radio interview with a local radio announcer Leo De Kroo at 2DU, the Dubbo Radio Station. After the Blind Chick had a shower, she went to brush her teeth. She put the paste on her toothbrush and put that in her mouth. Oh, my heavens what's on the brush? As well as the toothpaste a Daddy long legs spider had stuck to her toothbrush! Yuck. Yes, there was a lot of spluttering and gagging that followed.

So now, when the Blind Chickie babe cleans her teeth, she puts a bit of toothpaste in her mouth first, then the brush. Voila!

It pays to smell things before you put them in your mouth or on your face! With her new routine of putting some toothpaste in her mouth first, one day she felt in her beauty case, found the toothpaste, didn't think to smell it first then gee whiz! She'd squirted some hair conditioner in her mouth. Again, lots of spluttering and gagging. This not seeing gig can sometimes suck, literally.

My Blind Chick is big on applying sunscreen. Our Aussie sun can be deadly. One day instead of grabbing the sunscreen, she applied her husband's Pinetarsol gel. Man, oh man, definitely not effective sunscreen and holy cow does it stink. Aaagh! Sometimes it's not easy to do simple things when bottles feel the same.

With being totally blind, she also doesn't have the best radar system. So often as she goes down the hall it's a little bit like a pinball hitting one side, then bounces off and hits the other. Generally, it's a crash with the left shoulder then a shuffle to the right. So quite a few bruises can result from a simple walk down the hall.

As a finale to that hall catwalk, she typically walks through the dining room to the kitchen, which often results in a corked thigh! Yes, she walks straight into the corner of the dining table. Ouch!

After finishing cleaning up the kitchen, it's about time for the girls to arrive to come and work me. If the sun is out the Blind Chickie babe will try to have me up at the tack shed, brushed and with fly spray on before they arrive, so they don't have as much to do.

Sometimes when the Blind Chick comes to find me, if I wanted to be naughty, I could hold my breath or stop my feet from moving. She won't know where I was! But being the nice lad that I am, I don't do that. Plus, I know she has a carrot! So, I typically meet her halfway, or she comes to my usual haunt, which is down in the bottom paddock looking out at the river.

Once she finds me, she gives me a carrot. Imagine what it was like the first few times she walked towards me though. A new person in my life waving a white cane, coming at me! Naturally at first, I was very wary of that white cane. Yes, she got me around the legs with it a few times, but now once she hears me, she puts her hand up with the carrot. I then walk to her. We worked out that this is a much less dangerous way for me of getting together, I don't get walloped with that cane.

Then I guide her back up to the gate and up to the tack shed. Sometimes I can get a little distracted, which can be a bit difficult for the Blind Chick. While she's not able to see what I'm looking at or what I'm thinking about shying at, she can feel it through my body that I'm anxious. This can be a little bit hard to orientate, depending on whether it is a sunny day or an overcast day. Sometimes on the overcast days the Blind Chick will wait till the girls get here, they catch me. When it is overcast it's exceedingly difficult for the Blind Chick, as she has no orientation to work by.

The other thing I've noticed about our day-to-day routine is the Blind Chick never works me of an afternoon, it's always mornings. Again, this is to do with the sun. When she goes into the arena to ride me of a morning, she starts on the right rein with the sun is on her left cheek when she rides down the long side. I think it's incredible how she can rely on the sun for her orientation, it rocks. Finding a way to do something you love, when you can't see, helps heighten your other senses, like your feel.

In the tack shed everything has its place and everything goes back in its place. If not, the Blind Chick can't find it. I know she's quite anal about her gear being clean, particularly my beautiful saddle cloths. Everything is clean and washed regularly, including my boots and rugs. I'm especially lucky in summer when I have a clean rug on every day! Ok, I understand that might be unusual, but there's only one of me. I know the Blind Chick spoils me a little, she loves me, a lot.

Now taking my rug off is no big deal for my Blind Chick. Undo the three straps on the neck rug, undo the chest strap, undo the back legs, do the buckles back up and pull the rug off. Voila! But it is a big deal, hilarious in fact, for the Blind Chick to work out which part of the rug she is holding at the time. Once she finds the fury little bit of padding which sits on my wither, she's fine. It's the finding that and positioning it that's fun to watch. Yes, my rugs are massive, I'm 18.3 hands high. It's like putting a tent up. So sometimes she has her leg in the strap, sometimes a foot on the rug, but eventually she gets it on me. I typically stand ever so patiently, except when I pinch the odd leaf off the Paulownia tree. I've got to, to stop the boredom! Because these things do take time. That's one of the things I learnt early on. Nothing with the Blind Chick happens quickly.

Matthew has spent a lot of time trying to get her to slow down, she was running into things because she was moving so quickly. When she goes to fast, the white cane hasn't time to pick things up, so BAM! Another bruise.

Now we're tacked up we go to the dressage arena, the Blind Chick orientating herself with the sun. Jenelle gives her a riding lesson and Jacqueline stands at the letter C. From C Jacq helps orientate the Blind Chick on where the Quarter Lines and Centre Line is. Anytime they do work on the Centre Line Jacq sits and calls out the letter C, C, C, C, C. So instead of the Blind Chick seeing the letter C, she rides towards the sound. Jacq will call out "Drifting to the right" or "Drifting to the left" and the Blind Chick will fix up her Centre Line.

I think out of all the things we do in the dressage arena, the Centre Line is the hardest for the Blind Chick, as she has absolutely nothing to go on. When we're on a long side it's easy and when we do, say a leg yield, Jacq will call out Quarter Line, Centre Line, then Quarter Line and the Blind Chick will turn down the second quarter line and do a quick yield to the left. Easy peasy. But when you're in no mans' land heading for the letter C, it's hard. There's no point to focus on. That voice calling the letter is it. That voice is especially important.

How's this for surprising. The Blind Chick can ride really good circles! Her wonderful coach from years ago, Judy Cubitt, gave her a few tricks to riding a circle and she applies that knowledge well. Her circles are quite symmetrical. This is intriguing considering she can't see. But as long as she has someone calling on either side of the arena, she orientates herself brilliantly.

Guess how we work out where X is when we're coming down the Centre Line, where we need to halt? The Blind Chick counts the strides. It's the technical details of how to do what most people take for granted that we are practising and play with, often. While we may not get to do a dressage test, I'm hopeful that such miracles do happen.

There's a lot more counting when we're doing lateral work. Let me explain. Say we're doing a shoulder-in from F to B, then we do an eight-meter circle, then half pass to the left; this equates to 12 strides shoulder-in, listening for the B to be called, then at B we do our rock star circle. Ok, I admit it, sometimes my circles are a little big, but we're getting better at the eight-meter circles.

Once the living marker calls B we're back on the track, then the H starts calling and we do a half pass to the left. Then it's 12 strides till we get to G. As soon as the Blind Chick leaves B the person standing at H is calling H, H, H, H so the Blind Chick knows the angle to go on to get our half pass exactly right. Then Jacq will start calling the C, C, C, C about two strides before she gets there and then keep calling C, C, C, C to get the Blind Chick on the Centre Line and travelling straight so we can track left and do our extension. Phew! Yes, there's a lot going on in my Blind Chicks brain all at once.

She must listen, count, guide me, be mindful of her own posture and not just correctly riding the movement we're doing, but getting ready to set me up for the movement that comes next. All at the same time! I know my brain would explode with all that going on. Would you cope juggling all that? And if it all gets a bit overwhelming the Blind Chick can't just open her eyes. They're already open. They don't make a difference.

So, as you can see for the Blind Chick to ride, it's incredibly involved. You may wonder why we train so hard to perfect our dressage movements if we can't compete right now? But that's the thing. The Blind Chick's ultimate goal is to get back to competing in Open top-level dressage again. I'm sure we will one day. How can I be sure? Because I see her day-in-day out. She can be incredibly determined and so resilient when she sets her mind on something.

Yes, we will struggle with doing a dressage test if it has backing in it because of my Equine Shivers. Shivers makes me back up like I'm doing a weird goose step. But like I say, miracles do happen. One day there might be a cure.

When the sun goes away and it's overcast, everything changes for the Blind Chick. On such days she isn't nearly as adventurous or as bold. Typically, she doesn't ride at all. Why? Because of the confidence thing. I know that C word it a sensitive topic, but I wanted to share it with you, it's an important thing to talk about.

The last time the Blind Chick competed was in February 2019 at Dressage by the Sea at the beautiful Willinga Park, she rode her previous horse, Desiderata, Desi for short. They competed in the Prix St George, Inter 1, plus they did a Grand Prix demonstration. Pretty impressive, pretty hectic.

Yes, it's been a long time since the Blind Chick has competed. Add to that her losing her confidence from her unceremonious dismount off me and you start to understand why this rebuilding her confidence gig has been a biggie.

I think she feels embarrassed. The fact that she was riding at quite a high level, in the

top 10% of able-bodied riders in Australia, and now she's frightened to ride on an overcast day or if it's really windy!

Sometimes she calls herself a fair-weather rider. I can tell she's extremely hard on herself. She's actually quite relentless on punishing herself, but as one of her lovely coaches said to her years ago, "You have nothing to prove." But I think deep inside all she wants to do is keep proving to herself that she can do it. But her determination, guts, bloody mindedness, and inner strength can sometimes fail her. It's gut wrenching that she can't do something that she loves so much. I know she's determined to get her confidence back, beat the niggling "Itty-Bitty Shitty Committee" in her head that makes her doubt herself. We'll see how things go.

If I could talk, I'd ask her to "Cut yourself some slack", "Give yourself more time", "What's meant to be will be." I know my Equine Shivers hasn't helped the situation. It's made me quite anxious and overreactive and sometimes quite naughty. That hasn't helped either of our confidences, but we're on this journey together, one day at a time. We'll see how things play out.

Ooops, I digressed. Back to our day-to-day routine.

Generally, Jenelle brings Johno in from being worked and Jacqueline guides the Blind Chickie babe back to the tack up area. There, it's like being a Formula 1 car coming into the pits, a veritable pit crew converges on me. Boots off, saddle off, bridal off, I'm washed, rugged and in amongst all this activity the Blind Chickie babe wanders off in the wrong direction, and has to be called back. But that's part of the fun I suppose. Yes, maybe not such fun for the Blind Chick, maybe frustrating, but it is what it is. Like with the diary entries we share with you, this is the reality of life for us; the good, the bad and the ugly.

Then comes the bit I like very much. The girls, Janelle and Jacq, put me in my paddock and I get to relax for the rest of the day. They go and sit together on the veranda; have a drink, discuss the days ride, and work out the program for the next ride two days later. It's such fun listening to them giggling and rehashing what has happened and working out a better way to do things, so it is easier for the Blind Chick. How cool are they! What they're doing is so important for us.

Oh, I've got to tell you a Blind Chick funny. She admits it's funny now, but at the time I'm sure it wasn't so. The dressage arena had been blown down, so the Blind Chick went out with her trusty white cane to find all the arena pieces and run a string from end to end to help ensure the arena sides were straight. Then she got busy finding all the blown away bits strewn across the paddock and reassemble them all. When Matthew and the Blind Chick do this job together, it's 30 minutes tops. When the Blind Chick does it by herself, it's easily 2.5 hours. She and her cane: find everything, find the string, get caught up in the string, trip over the string and trip over the dressage arena pieces. It's hilarious to watch. But onwards she persists, determined. Yes, often the dressage arena edges aren't straight, but the arena is standing, just maybe not quite a rectangle.

But I have to give her 10 out of 10 for having a go.

Another time wasn't quite so funny, it was actually really quite sad. It was getting late; the sun was in the west which didn't help the Blind Chick with any orientation. She was in their garden, 2 acres of lots of big trees. Nothing felt familiar, she felt like she was in no man's land. The Blind Chick had gotten lost, she was in tears. So, what could she do? She had to ring her husband Matthew who was out on the tractor to come and get her.

This really shook her up because she takes great pride in thinking she knows where she is. It was a confronting reality check getting lost in your own garden! Then there has been the odd occasion she has been lost in my paddock. Thank heavens for mobile phones. She rang her father-in-law John; Matthew's parents live in the neighboring property. He came and saved the day.

These days of getting lost typically happen on overcast days, not sunny days. If she's going to get lost it will be of an afternoon when she has no sun to work by. It's those days that the electric fence tends to get her as well, double ouch.

Did you know the Blind Chick is a bit of a snake charmer? In the 20 years she's been married to her wonderful husband Matthew, she's been bitten by them and fallen on them!

Yes, bitten by three brown snakes! Thank heavens their fangs didn't penetrate her boots or her riding breeches. She fell on one whilst leading a horse called Mr Bojangles. Matthew was out the back but heard her screaming over the noise of two loud irrigator machines that were watering the lucerne paddocks. He came and annihilated the Gazania garden looking for the snake. He never found it.

One of the other snake encounters happened when she'd walked next door to talk to Matthew, he was at his Mum and Dad 's place. After she spoke to him, she started down the pathway back home. I tend to think they thought she was a little girl calling wolf, looking for attention, but next thing there was screaming and yelling and more screaming and the Blind Chick impaled across a rosebush in the garden! Matthew came running, "What's wrong" and learnt she'd stepped on a slithering something that hissed loudly. It struck her on the outside of her breeches three times!

Everybody came out of the house to help look for the snake. The Blind Chick was a bit in shock. At first, I think everyone was dubious whether there was a snake or not, until ...... all of a sudden Matthew's Mum Lee spotted it. John and Matthew carefully dispatched it off the property. What was it? A six-foot brown snake, potentially deadly. The Blind Chick was so lucky the fangs didn't penetrate her breeches.

Then there was the time Desiderata had dirtied his stable, so she picked it out with the poo rake, and let the stable dry out, shutting the stable door so he didn't go back in during the day. That evening she went down to make his bed; went in with the bedding fork, opened the door and straight away stepped on ... another brown snake! She didn't realise she was standing on its tail. Mighty annoyed he was swishing and swishing in the bedding making seriously scary sounds. It was only when he flicked back and struck her on the inside of her boot, she realised what she was standing on. Once again lots of screaming and yelling. Again, Matthew came and saved the day, but because there was so much grass around, he couldn't find this one. Again, a rather shaken Blind Chick.

The other time was years ago when the Blind Chick had her beautiful stallion Hecco. She'd finished riding him and was going around the other side of the house to turn a sprinkler off, so she could have more pressure for Hecco's wash. When she was walking back, she heard a noise down at the river, so she stopped. She didn't think twice about the thing under her foot, she assumed it was the hose. No! It was another snake. This one was a three-foot brown snake. Luckily, Matthew was close by to save the day yet again. I think living on the river doesn't help the snake situation.

One particular day was especially funny, all in hindsight of course. It was the day the Blind Chick fell on the snake and Matthew annihilated the garden searching for it. After her heart calmed down enough, she rang her Dad. All she could get out was "I fell on a snake", that's all she kept repeating. "I fell on a snake". All her Dad wanted to know was did it bite her. But all she could get out was, "I fell on a snake". That night when her Dad rang to check on her, he asked Matthew if he could speak to the ...... Snake Charmer. Thank heavens people have a sense of humour.

You can appreciate why I'm quickly coming to the conclusion this blind gig isn't much chop. When you're blind living on a farm comes with serious risks. So many things can go wrong.

But my Blind Chick wouldn't change any of it.

What had the biggest impact on me when I first met the Blind Chick, before they bought me, was how she lives for her horses. It's her reason for breathing and living.

Now I've lived with her a while I understand more this incredible passion she has for horses. We give her freedom; we give her independence. She loves being able to do the things an able-bodied person can do. Okay she might need some help but that's okay, if there's a will there's a way. I know sometimes there are days of great frustration for her. She can't just get in the car and drive into town and pick up some horse feed when it's needed. She's at the mercy of other people, all the time.

When I hear her crying, I'd love to be able to give her my eyes. Maybe not both, but she could have one! I don't blame her for shedding tears. Imagine how frustrating it must be to be sent beautiful photos? Weddings, birthdays, the celebration of new life reflected in amazing baby photos. She can't enjoy them.

I know when she received my baby photos she just sat in the chair and cried. She so wanted to see how I looked. More tears when she was sent a video of my rather magnificent father, Gymnastic Star. She sat and listened to the beautiful man's German accent as he spoke of my Dad being the last horse from hundreds he inspected, with a view to purchasing a Hanoverian stallion worthy of importing to Australia. The background music, the sound of my Dad's hooves as he danced in the arena and his owner, Holger Schmorl's impassioned words narrating Dad's movement, unleashed a flood of happy and sad tears from my Blind Chick. My heart breaks when things like this happen.

It happens so often. People saying beautiful comments about me, saying how lovely I am, how perfect I am. Recently the Blind Chick was saying to a friend how she was so sad she can't really enjoy any of that. Her friend made the comment which I thought was so right – "You lay your hand on that beautiful horse and you feel his beauty."

Yes, the Blind Chick knows this. But sometimes I think she needs to be reminded that she feels so many other things, things most people don't get to feel. See feels them in a very deep and meaningful place deep in her heart. I know when she rides me her smile never leaves her face.

Where does my Blind Chick feel most at home? In the saddle. That's where she belongs. Her smile comes from so deep down inside. Isn't it amazing something like riding a horse can be so special, so precious, and be the thing that makes everything else in one's life, work?

What other things does the Blind Chick love? My list in answer to this is growing with each day we're together. She loves people describing a sunset, a starry night, the swans on the river. All the things that cost you nothing, that you take for granted. It's the little things that count. It's the little things that mean the most, like a smile. As you can tell the Blind Chick is a lover and a hugger. She will always give someone a hug. Until then, she sends her love.

Feel is so important. On so many levels they talk about feel when you're riding. The Blind Chick gets that, but she also gets a feel from people in a handshake, a hug. They tell you so much about a person that we will never know.

But the Blind Chick feels it all.

Does this sometimes get the Blind Chick down and distress her? Yes.

Are there days there are tears? Yes.

Are there days of frustration? Yes.

But very rarely do you see it publicly or is it shared, because I know the Blind Chick wants you to see strength and ability, not a disability.

So, I take my hat off to my Blind Chick. She soldiers on through thick and thin. She makes the best of everything she can. Her philosophy of 'Just one step at a time' totally rocks! Why? Because if you keep doing that, soon enough you may actually find yourself standing at the top of that beautiful mountain having achieved all of the things you wanted to.

I know she's a big dreamer. She believes in dreams. She believes in magic.

I know the Blind Chick and I being on this journey together is total magic and full of dreams. Thank you for coming along with us and sharing in our amazing journey.

And remember - Vision is much more than Seeing.

OOPSY!

Feeling Sorry | 25 June 2020

Diary entry by Johno

I'm feeling pretty bad, I have a very big confession to make. Yesterday when I was feeling so spritely and healthy, I did a couple of big leaps in the arena. Why? For no other reason other than I was feeling good. Yes, maybe the Blind Chick had given me a little extra feed, which she has now taken back off me.

So, the Blind Chick had a fall off me!

I feel so bad. It wasn't done intentionally. I was just feeling good and playing. I suppose when you think of someone 18.3hh playing around, it was a big leap.

Needless to say, I'm feeling really bad about what happened. But after the Blind Chick came off Gwen caught me and the Blind Chicks mother-in-law Lee and father-in-law John came up and got her up off the ground. God love her cotton socks, she got straight back on!

She walked me for a bit then did a bit of a trot on both reins. Just lovely soft swinging trot, all done with confidence. Then when she dismounted, she hobbled over and got the lunging cavesson and took me into the round yard. There she gave me a little bit of a lunge to see if I wanted to play anymore. I admit, I did think of doing some more in the beginning, but I soon settled and worked very nicely.

Since then ... Matthew, her wonderful husband, took her to the doctor yesterday evening. She's now off to get x-rays today. She's still in quite a bit of pain and can't take weight on the leg. It maybe just some big bruising, but hopefully we'll know today after x-rays. If she needs a scan they'll do that later.

I missed the Blind Chick feeding me this morning. Matthew brought my feed down as the Blind Chick couldn't walk.

I feel so guilty and so bad about what happened, but it wasn't me being naughty. I was just exuberant and playing. Yes, I know that is not an excuse. I'll try much harder to be a good boy. We really did some beautiful work in the arena yesterday.

I hope everybody is safe and well. We are coming into another weekend, so take some time to drop somebody a line, give them a ring. Tell somebody you love them and miss them. Take the time to make somebody's day.

Have a spectacular weekend. Loads of love and hugs, Johno.

P.S: I gave it a lot of thought on whether to share the Blind Chicks fall or not. I decided to, because we're all on this journey together. The good, the bad, the ugly, the warts and the happiness. I thought it was important to share this hiccup we'd had.

Onwards and upwards, all good.

Lots of love, Johno.

THE AMAZING ANGEL

Feeling Grateful | 23 December 2020

Diary entry by Johno

This is a really special message about an amazing angel who, out of the blue, contacted the Blind Chick to help me after my second bout of colic.

Grab a cuppa and I'll tell you all about it.

We have a lovely friend on Facebook called Jean. She is a great mate of the Blind Chick and I. She was most disturbed by me having colic, again, so she contacted her beautiful daughter Jade enquiring if Jade knew of anything to help me. Jade is a professional eventer who straight away contacted the amazing Linda.

Jade informed Linda about this Blind Chick and her horse that's frequently getting colic. Jade wondered whether Linda could do anything to help.

This is what happen next.

Out of the blue the day after my bad colic attack, the Blind Chick received a phone call, which she missed. There was a message for her to get in contact with a lady called Linda.

So that afternoon the Blind Chick rang Linda. Oh, my heavens! You know how the Blind Chick is always talking about Angels and Magic, well this beautiful lady came in the guise of the most amazing angel offering help! Linda wanted to make a difference. She and the Blind Chick talked for ages and ages.

The Blind Chick was absolutely hanging onto every word this amazing lady had to say. You'll never guess what the topic was mainly about .... gut health! Until meeting Linda, the Blind Chick didn't know managing stress was so connected with gut health. Linda's approach was all about being holistic and how you treat your horse.

Linda spoke about this amazing paste you could give your horse called Stress Paste. Next thing in the mail the very next day came a box of Stress Paste! I was started on this amazing paste straight away. Plus, we received an absolutely massive tub of a great product called Digestive EQ.

Linda asked the Blind Chick to send her a list of what I had in my diet, so they could make sure I had a balanced diet with no grain in it, but lots of fibre. The Blind Chick was totally chuffed when Linda gave her the results of my diet analysis. The only change needed was to add a little salt, and everything was perfect.

But getting back to the Stress Paste! Oh, my heavens it made such a difference. It reduced my anxiety attacks nearly straight away. With the Blind Chick adding the Digestive EQ to my diet that has been the icing on the cake. Just think about it for a moment. If your tummy is not right, nothing else in your life is quite right. It's so important to get that gut health correct.

Then a few days later another product arrived, Digestive VM. This super charger is a Vitamin and Mineral mix in pellet form. I quite like them. So, wow things have changed a lot. I'm really starting to feel a little different ... better. Okay I still have Shivers, but I honestly think in time this holistic approach with my gut health and these vitamins and miners will make a difference for me.

The other day the Blind Chick was pretty stressed because I'd had that massive anxiety attack, followed by colic, again! If she'd known about Stress Paste before then and been able to give me some as soon as I'd started showing colic symptoms, I'm sure it would have made the world of difference. As you can imagine the Blind Chick was pretty stressed out with walking me, calling the vet, and trying to stop me from rolling. But next time she'll be more on the ball and remember to give me the Stress Paste.

The Stress Paste has also been amazingly helpful for when we travel and on really scorcher day, like when we've been 40°C. It helps my body cope with these extreme conditions.

Watch this space! Things are on the improve. Okay we're not going to be able to stop the Shivers, but through having good gut health we might be able to make a difference to managing the Shivers. That would be totally awesome.

So, don't stop believing in Miracles, Magic, and Angels! They are out there. There are beautiful Angels out there watching over you all the time. Our Angel came in the guise of a beautiful lady called Linda, to whom we are so very very grateful.

The beautiful Linda owns the company Poseidon Equine and the Blind Chick, and I are both so very grateful for her phone call, for her caring and for believing that we can all make a difference in the world. You just need to reach out.

So dearest Linda, from the bottom of our hearts, we are so grateful.

We hope everybody is safe and well. I'm feeling magnificent. Loads of love and hugs, Johno and his Blind Chick.

LIVING WITH EQUINE SHIVERS

Feeling Optimistic | 11 February 2021

Diary entry from the Blind Chick

This is serious from the heart stuff.
Living with the neurological degenerative condition - Equine Shivers!

I've been giving it a lot of thought about writing this diary entry and I think it is an especially important one to share. This journey is not an easy journey for Johno or myself or my amazing support team.

Keep in mind it is Neurological and it is Degenerative. They are probably the two hardest things to be working with .... or .... trying to work with and manage.

The first time I rode Johno there was something magical that clicked inside us both. I had the most wonderful ride. Our journey was meant to be. But when I rode him, I asked him to back up a couple of times and he resisted quite badly, so I left it alone. I thought heavens girl, give him a chance, you've been on him 20 minutes and you ask him to back up! But keep in mind he is a medium advanced dressage horse.

Also keep in mind, Johno passed a vet check with this degenerative neurological condition.

After Matthew had bought Johno for me, Janelle my coach took me down to ride Johno before we brought him home. We also had a wonderful saddle fitting from the amazing Jason to make sure everything was right for when we came home to Dubbo.

On this occasion, again after walking, trotting and cantering and asking for some lateral work, which he obligingly did with no problem at all, I asked for another back up. Once again he resisted and put his head up and said "No, No, No, I can't do this". So once again, I put this down to giving the horse a chance for me to get to know him better.

Then we noticed when he was coming off the float, he stepped backwards in a really weird and awkward way. But again, I had a reason for that. He'd just spent six hours on the float travelling from near Penrith to Dubbo, so he could've been stiff. I'm always giving him the benefit of the doubt.

I had a lovely friend who is a Chiropractor come and have a look at Johno for me, to check him out. He simply asked Johno to square up. Based on Johno's back leg reaction, my friend said he wouldn't touch the horse as "Johno has a patella problem, commonly known as a locking patella."

I noticed how Johno often didn't want to step forward after I caught him in the paddock, or after being saddled, or when he'd stood still for five minutes. He wouldn't walk forward. I just thought he was being a bit stubborn, so I'd just wait for him to oblige. But once again, it's these little issues you don't know about, they meant something. They were all symptoms of Shivers!

I'd never heard of this horrid disease before.

So I continued working Johno, oblivious to everything other than the fact that he couldn't back and that he took ages to walk off after standing and when he did walk off, he had a funny spastic movement with his nearside hind leg.

I had no idea why. All I knew was it didn't affect him when he walked, trotted, or cantered after he walked out of this weird movement.

Then BAM! We went down to have lessons with the beautiful Melanie Schmerglatt and Melanie picks up within five minutes of us arriving, having seen Johno back off the float .... "Your horse has Equine Shivers!!!"

Everything went fast from there. We went and got diagnosis after diagnosis. We learnt that nothing can cure this hideous disease. It keeps degenerating! Johno's brain was not communicating with his hind legs; hence he was finding trouble backing and if he stands for a while, he has trouble moving forward.

The other thing that has happened with time, keeping in mind this is a degenerative disease, is it is affecting his front legs as well? Plus if Johno has a stressful time, like anything new in his life or a change, like going to Lochinvar for lessons, Johno's Shivers is greatly affected.

It affects his movement in his hind legs. His brain doesn't connect to his hind legs, so he has trouble moving forward and once he is moving, he is quite fine. But when I got him home the Shivers had really got worse, it was affecting his front legs as well. He was having trouble moving at all!

First thing in the morning he would stand there, wanting to

come for his carrot and a pat, but he couldn't move because his brain wasn't communicating with his legs. I think it's important I haven't put any videos of this on Facebook, because I think most people would find it very distressing. As do I, having to listen to it every morning.

So all this time I'm hunting, hunting, hunting, for something to help this beautiful animal that does not deserve to have this hideous neurological degenerative disease. He has been on lots of different drugs to try and help him.

Under the supervision of the beautiful Dr Sarah Gough from Hunter Equine, we even tried a human drug. This didn't work well enough for me to ride Johno. Now he takes other medication. This medication doesn't fix the Shivers, it helps him manage the anxiety attacks he has. Hence my unceremonious buster!

He has these moments of explosion. Hence his big leaps in the air and me falling off. Also, out of the blue when lunging him, he can just explode and start bucking or running flat out. As his anxiety attacks in the paddock got worse and worse, he would run frantically for hours. I'd go to catch him, and he'd rear at me. He was really quite dangerous.

We really needed to find something that was going to help this beautiful animal not be stressed out because of the Equine Shivers causing the anxiety.

Hence where the medication has come in. The only way that Johno is quiet in his paddock and for me to ride him, is by medicating him.

Otherwise, the only other option is euthanasia.

And that to me is not an option.

Along with his anxiety attacks, his mass running around, screaming, and carrying on, being so out of control, would come colic! In one of his episodes, he had colic twice in less than 10 days. This is horrific for him to have to go through. All because of this hideous disease.

Sorry, this is not one of my more positive diary entries.

It is an honest sharing of what we go through on a daily basis to keep Johno sound. Okay we cannot stop the Shivers, but we can try and manage the episodes he has with his anxiety.

It's a one day at a time prospect.

Amazing Poseidon Equine products have helped us a lot to get Johno's gut healthy. But they aren't going to stop the Shivers. They help us manage it, but there's nothing that's going to cure this hideous disease.

I suppose the main reason for sharing this with you is so you get an idea of the huge amount of behind-the-scenes work that goes into managing this horrible degenerative condition Johno has. He had a relapse the other day that lasted for five days. It was so heartbreaking hearing him stressed again. Thankfully, with medication, we have this under control, for now.

So THANK YOU for reading this. I think it is important to share the good, the bad, and the ugly.

This is the sad side of things. All the other beautiful things that we do; the riding, the diary entries, rebuilding my confidence in getting back on Johno have all been rather massive.

It wouldn't have happened if he did not have Equine Shivers.

But there's nothing we can do about that.

Hence everything here is one day at a time, trying the best we can to manage Johno's Shivers and giving him the best quality of life we can.

For now, while I can ride him and it is not too dangerous, what a bonus to be riding such a spectacular beautiful horse. When he has his moments, I know it's not Johno being naughty, it's his neurological condition. Which he has no control over.

I will continue to share our amazing journey. I think I'm very blessed to have Johno in my life even with as much stress as it causes me .... we have written a book together!

We have another book to be published hopefully in July, all going well. We will keep sharing our journey.

So here's to one day hoping they find a cure for this horrible neurological degenerative disease - Equine Shivers. Here's to being able to give horses who have it a better life, including my beautiful Johno.

To be honest this would have to be one of the hardest diary entries I've ever written.

I'm so used to writing about all of the beautiful things we do, not about the hard things that make you cry.

A massive thank you to our amazing Team that keep Johno and I on track. Our amazing veterinary surgeons Sarah and Don, Johno's Craniosacral lady the beautiful Tanya, amazing Adam Sutton doing his desensitisation work on Johno and building up my confidence, the beautiful Linda from Poseidon Equine - the Angel that reached out to help us, and to my two beautiful, amazing friends Janelle and Jacqueline for getting me back in the saddle.

I'm now cantering again!

So many good things.

I hope you don't mind me sharing this.

Be safe and well. Loads of love and hugs the Blind Chick.

NO 'I' IN TEAM

Feeling Humble | 27 February 2021

Diary entry by Johno and the Blind Chick

There is no 'I' in Team!

On a massive scale I think the Blind Chick and I have much to be grateful for.

But one of the main things is the amazing Team we are surrounded by and how important that above quote is.

There is no 'I' in Team!

In the Blind Chick's world, in my world, nothing happens without a Team effort.

Whether it be getting the Blind Chick ready to ride and have a lesson, this is accomplished by the wonderful Jenelle Waters and the amazing Jacq Benn. Jenelle is the coach and Jacq is the coordinator and organiser. Together we are a formidable Team.

Everything runs smoothly and everything is well organised, but most of all they have fun doing it, training with the Blind Chick. Always laughter. Always encouragement. We are so very grateful for their assistance.

Our awesome farrier Troy Lomax keeps me sound. He has spent quite a lot of time making sure everything is right when he shoes me, no rushing. His great apprentice Henry is full of empathy and understanding with my Shivers condition. So again, our Team of Troy and Henry.

To the amazing veterinarians in my life. The wonderful Dr Sarah Gough, Hunter Valley Equine Vets, who speaks with the Blind Chick regularly about: how I'm travelling with my condition, whether I'm degenerating, whether we change medication? So grateful to be able to ring Dr Sarah directly and get advice.

Then we have the amazing vets in Dubbo: Dr Don Crosby and his Team who are just a phone call away. The beautiful Wendy makes sure everything is just right for looking after me, especially when I have colic and Wendy has someone here within 10-15 minutes.

So very grateful. Once again there is no 'I' in Team.

Then we have my beautiful Tanya with her magic hands doing her Craniosacral work on me every couple of weeks. Without this I'm sure my condition would be degenerating much quicker and I wouldn't be coping as well. Lucky me Tanya is just a phone call away and she's only 5 km up the road! So she's here in a flash when we need her.

We are so very blessed to be surrounded by so many amazing, beautiful, talented people who make such a difference to the Blind Chick and me.

Then we have beautiful angels that enter our life because they want to help and make a difference to my quality of life.

Enter stage left the beautiful Linda Lord from Poseidon Equine and her amazing products.

Linda has educated the Blind Chick about the importance of gut health. I must say it really has made the world a difference.

I now have absolutely no grain and no extruded food in my diet. Okay it might be a bit bland, but I am healthy, and my gut is very healthy. This will hopefully help slow down the Equine Shivers if we can keep my gut health improving every day.

We are surrounded by the wonderful Linda and her amazing Poseidon Equine Team. The lovely Nerida Richards does my diet and helps look after me.

So very grateful. Again, there is no 'I' in Team.

And where would we be without the amazing Adam Sutton? Adam has invested many hours in helping with my desensitisation, with building up the Blind Chick's confidence and with stretching our benchmark little bit, by little bit.

Definitely he is taking the Blind Chick out of her comfort zone. A couple of times I've certainly been taken out of my comfort zone. But Adam always does this with great confidence, and it's had the most profound effect on me.

A prime example of this was the other day when our lovely friend and Photographer Prue Crichton came to do photos of me. Ooops, no one could get me to put my ears forward. Why? Because nothing they did startled me!!!!

I was just taking everything in my stride, and it took the Blind Chicks husband Matthew rolling across the lawn to get my attention. I must say I looked at him with a peculiar look on my face, I wasn't startled or worried. I did happen to put my ears forward though, and Prue got some lovely photos.

The efforts people go to, to get you to put your ears forward, ha ha.

A special thank you for being a part of our Team must go to the Blind Chick's wonderful mother-in-law Lee for all her love and support.

Then, there is the amazing team from EQUISSAGE. I so

appreciate the back massager, it's totally awesome. Plus .... the handheld massager!!! The Blind Chick generally uses the handheld unit on me while I have the back pad massaging me. Oh my heavens! Isn't EQUISSAGE so good at getting into spots where you are a little bit tight and sore?

The amazing team from EQUISSAGE have Sponsored the Blind Chick for many years. I think I am the fourth horse that has had the privilege of the EQUISSAGE machine being used on them. Boy oh boy is it a great warm up before you start working, or if you have any sore muscles?

Plus the boss, Ian Bellion, is a good mate of the Blind Chick's. The EQUISSAGE Team have backed all the different projects the Blind Chick has done. Even when she did one of her long-distance rides to raise money for the local Oncology Unit here in Dubbo. They donated a beautiful EQUISSAGE machine to be auctioned off for the ride.

So very generous! Once again, it shows the importance of there is no 'I' in Team.

And then there are the behind-the-scenes people like the wonderful Jacqueline Thompson who is always just a phone call away to help the Blind Chick out. She helps her with correspondence and getting our next book ready. The book about the Blind Chick's amazing husband Matthew who brought me for the Blind Chick. I think we can both be very grateful to him for getting the Blind Chick and I on this journey together.

So once again we should be so incredibly grateful for these most amazing people in our life. They help us make our dreams come true. They help us have the best quality of life we can, whilst also living with Equine Shivers.

What an amazing Team!!!

To our beautiful Team THANK YOU, from the bottom of our hearts. We so appreciate all of the things you've done for us in the past and will do in the future.

We want you to know how incredibly grateful we are.

And to our amazing Team on Facebook!!!

What would we do without your interaction, love, support, and encouragement? You have got us through many a sticky situation, we are so grateful.

To all of our friends, we hope you're having a lovely day. Thank you for your support, your friendship, and your encouragement.

We hope you are all safe and well.

Loads of love and hugs, Johno and the Blind Chick.

THE BED THAT LEVITATED!

Feeling Fantastic | 30 June 2020

Diary entry by Johno

Well, a lovely sunny good morning from the Southern Highlands.

I had a spectacular ride with the amazing José this morning, again working on transitions, softness, suppleness, and relaxation.

I'm so loving this Ask – Don't Tell, this invitation to do something, not being shoved and jammed into a position. Why wouldn't you want to be obliging when someone is asking you so nicely? It's such a different way of doing things. I love it.

Only one more sleep till the Blind Chickie babe gets down here. I'm still running the book on whether she will be riding or not. I put odds on she will want to ride.

Oh, my lordy. What a story I heard this morning, I've got to share it with you. Apparently, the Blind Chick and her wonderful husband Matthew went shopping for a new bed. Well Matthew discussed with the nice young sales lady what they were looking for, and she pointed out a bed she thought might be suitable. So here they are, both of them, laying on the bed. Then Matthew gets up and continues talking to the sales lady.

The Blind Chickie babe is still lying on the bed relaxing, saying how comfortable the bed is and so on, when oh my, the bed started to move! The Blind Chick thought she was hallucinating. The bottom of the bed raised up and the top of the bed was moving too. She was moving! Holy cow did it frighten the hell out of her. Apparently, the sales lady, not knowing the Blind Chick could not see at all, had the controls and was making the electronic bed head rise and the foot rise. The Blind Chick thought she was losing her marbles, her balance and everything else.

Well once Matthew, the sales lady and the Blind Chick had re-assembled themselves from being on the ground laughing at the Blind Chick fearing this levitating bed, they ended up buying the bed. Without the extra buttons though!

The new bed will be here in three weeks apparently.

Keep smiling, keep laughing. Lots of love and hugs, Johno.

RIDE WITH ME

Feeling Relaxed | 21 July 2020

Diary entry by Johno and the Blind Chick

Well, a hearty good morning from the Southern Highlands. It's definitely a little bit crisp here today.

Now the Blind Chick had an idea, she'll listen to some lessons that her friend Jenelle videoed of her and I with the wonderful José. She gets lots of information from José's lessons, but she didn't know how to explain it all to you, what she's doing in the video. So, she thought she might try and just do a little explanation on how she rides around the arena.

Morning all, Blind Chick here.

I'll do my best to explain what happens when I first get on Johno, what I'm feeling and doing. I'll probably miss out on many points, and some of the points might not be correct. This isn't a riding lesson, it's just me trying to explain what I'm doing.

After I mount, I'm taken into the arena, there I put Johno into a long rein walk, generally on the buckle. What I'm feeling at this stage is Johno as he drops his neck and comes up through the back. The further we go, the more swing he's getting, he's loosening up. I'm not asking for anything other than for him to walk forward, be relaxed and enjoy the ride.

We do this exercise of long rein walk for approximately five minutes each side, asking for nothing more than for Johno to drop his head, bring his back up, and swing through from behind. The further we go, the looser he gets and the bigger the walk strides we're getting. It feels like magic.

While we're walking, I'm concentrating on the evenness in my seat bones.

I then quietly take the reins up and as we are approaching the corner, it's inside leg into a steady outside rein. I'm not asking for bend, I'm just asking him to go around the corner, the hind legs following the front legs. We go across the short side, past "C" then next corner, inside leg into a steady outside rein. Then down the long side. Each corner and short side requires the same softness, rhythm and regularity of the long sides. That doesn't change.

After the next long side, we come up the Quarter Line, I keep the softness a little to the right, I put my right leg just behind the girth, and gently squeeze and we do a leg yield, keeping the body lovely and straight, forwards and sideways, forwards and sideways, then we walk straight ahead. With this exercise it's so lovely, I feel the softening in Johno's body. After the first leg yield the walk is often even bigger, and with more swing.

We do the same exercise a couple of times, more on the right rein and then change to the left rein across the diagonal. On the diagonal I allow Johno to have all the rein, I'm holding the buckle. This allows him to stretch and use that powerful hindquarters of his. He can get an over track of up to 18 inches after these exercises, which is pretty good.

Personally, I think the walk is one of the most important gaits, we can accomplish so much in the walk like longitudinal flexion and lateral flexion. You can do lovely leg yields, half pass, walk pirouettes, 10 metre circles winding out and then winding back in. It's such an awesome gait to get the horse supple.

While I'm riding I need to be thinking; is Johno straight, do I have too much bend through the neck, which I am guilty of on the left rein, I really need to keep a more consistent right rein when we are on the left rein. Dah, it's totally different when I am on the right rein. I need a little bit of softness on the right rein, and not so much left rein, still have a constant contact but not as much left rein.

I should be concentrating on having an even weight through both seat bones. I can influence Johno's walk with my seat, pushing him out and slowing him down. Often, I'm in trouble for rushing. I need to address this; I'm so used to pushing and asking for more. I need to allow a Johno to offer this, more 'Ask - Don't Tell'.

I need to be conscious of my right shoulder, it wants to keep dropping, I have to keep it up and back and keep an even weight in both seat bones, so I'm not interfering with Johno's balance.

Apart from all these things that I need to be thinking of, I've got to allow my hands to move backwards and forwards with the movement of his big swinging walk, so I don't inhibit his movement. This is one of our biggest things in the walk, allowing the horse to take your hands. José is always reminding me to keep giving with my hands. We often get caught up with overriding and doing too much.

Apart from all these things, I also need to be listening to my wonderful coach José telling me where I am in the arena, his guidance setting me up for each movement and what we are going to do next.

So, this is my explanation of what I'm doing in the walk. I'm probably doing a lot of other things as well, like possibly overriding, but let me know if this doesn't make sense. Another time I'll attempt to explain to you how I ride the trot and a leg yield.

Thank you so much for your friendship and following the Blind Chick and I. This is such a pretty cool journey. Thank you for making your way through these diary entries. We hope you're enjoying sharing in our adventures.

Wishing everybody a wonderful day. Please keep safe and well.

Loads of love and hugs, Johno and the Blind Chick.

TABOO SUBJECTS!

Feeling Thoughtful | 22 August 2020

Diary entry by Johno and the Blind Chick

This is one of those taboo subjects no one wants to talk about! It's something no one wants to admit they may have. But I'm sure, it happens to all of us.

I'm talking about losing confidence, fear and anxiety.

Whether it is going down to catch my horse, whether it be getting on my horse and having a ride, these things are real in everyday people's lives. For one reason or another some people have lost faith, or they've had a scare and they don't know how to rectify it.

I would like to share with you what the Blind Chick is going through. I think it's easier for me to share, being the third party, than for her as it is pretty hard to admit to losing your confidence. But I think this topic is something that needs to come out of the closet. It is okay, and it will be alright, we just need to find a way.

Two things have happened to the Blind Chick which has not helped with her confidence level. One being her coming off me from a great height when I thought I would like to be a gazelle in the dressage arena! Doing a couple of really big leaps she understandably came out of the saddle from my 18.3hh and damaged her knee on landing. I honestly think this is still in the back of her mind, just a little, the nagging question "Can I trust him, will he do it again?"

The other thing that is probably even bigger than the Blind Chick having a buster off me, is the fact that she is not spending consistent time in the saddle. Not having regular saddle time is very disorientating when she does get to ride. As you can imagine, being totally blind and being disorientated, can be more than a little frightening. So, this has not helped the Blind Chick.

So, let's look at the ways we can make a difference and help her get her confidence back. At this stage with her knee, she can only ride me at a walk. Just being in the saddle is critical for her confidence, even if it's just riding at a walk. Doing all those wonderful movements at the walk, being able to concentrate on her position, that her hands are moving backward and forward with my movement and that she's able to breathe and relax are important confidence building sessions.

The breathing part of the exercise is critical. As you know most people when they are a little bit on edge or frightened, they hold their breath! That shade of blue is not a good look when riding a horse.

Fear is not a bad thing, it's okay to be frightened, it's okay to be anxious. We just need to work out a way to make it manageable. To do this we go - One Step at a Time! One manageable step at a time.

The other thing that will help the Blind Chick is for her to ride in the dressage arena in the sunlight. This allows her to orientate herself by where the sun is on her face, or on her back, or in her face. This is so important when you are totally blind, being able to orientate yourself and know where you are.

It makes a massive difference when her wonderful coach José calls out the letters in the arena, this gives the Blind Chick her orientation, and a feel for where she is. Yes, she could count the strides, but doing that with so much else that she has to think about is too much to expect of her.

So, when the Blind Chick comes down on Tuesday, she'll put the pad on knee to protect it and she will train at a walk. She'll do lateral work in the dressage arena and focus on breathing and giving herself the time to adjust, to get back into the rhythm of my movement. She'll take the time that it takes to do this. There is no rush, no hurry, just walking and remembering to keep breathing.

One of the Blind Chick's coaches years ago said to her "You have nothing to prove!" That's just it, to the Blind Chick this isn't about proving anything, it's about her living her dream and getting back in the saddle, doing what she loves which is riding me. That coach, Carolyn Lieutenant, was so right in saying she had nothing to prove, that it's not about proving. It's about a passion, it's about fulfilling a dream, to live that dream - it's about overcoming a fear.

I think it's good to have a plan, a workable plan, don't be too ambitious, do what you know you can do. Now the Blind Chick knows she can ride, she knows she can canter! But for both to occur with joy, she needs three things. She needs to get orientated, get her confidence back and rebuild the bridges of trust with me.

So, watch this space! Next Tuesday we shall see how our plan comes together.

If you know anyone who is going through the same thing as the Blind Chick, please share this with them, it may help. They're welcome to contact my Blind Chickie babe, they could chat and share what they're going through.

I so hope everyone has enjoyed my babble; I hope it makes sense. Let's see what happens - One Step at a Time!

THE ITTY-BITTY SHITTY COMMITTEE

Feeling Grateful | 24 August 2020

Diary entry from the Blind Chick

Well firstly, I would like to thank everybody that sent me a message or comment on Facebook with support and encouragement regarding my lack of confidence. I'm sure with time, this will just be one of the little glitches and hiccups in Johno and my journey.

I've endeavoured to have my phone read me a couple of books that are meant to help you with anxiety, fear and lack of confidence. I must say, these haven't been a massive success! It was a great idea, but I think things need to be put into practice.

I have also been listening to podcasts. I've found the ones by Jane Pike extremely interesting and helpful. I especially love her reference to the Itty-Bitty Shitty Committee! Allowing our bad thoughts to get into our head and direct the way we are thinking isn't ideal. We need to get rid of the Itty-Bitty Shitty Committee. That's the plan.

I've also been busy getting Johno's stable and everything ready for his homecoming. I'll probably change how we get him prepared to ride. Maybe I'll saddle him up down at the stables instead of bringing him up through the garden into the where the tack shed is. I think that would be much safer for all concerned. The change won't be a problem for Johno, I think it just makes it safer for me.

I've been out and had a feel around the dressage arena. Wow, it's blown down with all this wind we've had. I'll pull it apart and maybe see if Matt can drag the arena for me, but we'll need to wait another few day for the water to drain away and it too dry out first.

I'm so looking forward to Johno's homecoming. We're going down tomorrow and putting into practice our plan of One Step at a Time and making everything manageable. I think this will make the world of difference, being able to spend more time with a Johno, creating that lovely bond and relationship we had when I was doing everything with him.

I'm very spoilt with him being down at Fay and José's, he is prepared for me, I just get on and ride. This means I don't get to do any of the preparation work. Maybe I could start doing that this week and see how things go. I think it is very important to have a great relationship on the ground with your horse, this then conveys into the saddle.

As Johno has pointed out, my knee is still not recovered properly, my beautiful friend Neeni has made me a knee guard, but I think between you, me, and the gate post, I truly will only be able to walk, as the pressure on the fracture really does irritate, a lot. So, a walk sounds great to me, it's probably where I need to stay for a bit, while I get orientated

This disorientated stuff is not good, I have no idea where I am in the arena, and it is really quite disconcerting. Not great for the confidence. So, if I can get my orientation skills up and running much better, I'm sure that that my confidence will come back slowly, One Step at a Time.

To give you an idea of what feeling disorientated is like, put on a blindfold and get spun around a couple of times. Then try and find your way from one point of your house to the other. It might be just from the kitchen table to the sink, but it's really difficult that feeling of no direction.

Yippee, just one more sleep! Watch this space and I'll let you know how it feels and what happens. I'm sure Johno will have his version, which might differ a little from mine, but that's what partnerships are all about.

I've been out enjoying the sunshine this morning; I've walked 8 km and will try and do some more walking this afternoon. I need to keep fit.

Hold onto your dreams, love and hugs, the Blind Chick.

Guess Who Is Driving?

Feeling Excited | 4 December 2020

Diary entry by Johno

Welcome to another beautiful morning on the Macquarie River. There are a few clouds sneaking about, but I think that rain will wait until tomorrow.

I had a great day in the arena yesterday. Today is no riding involved, just lunging and a bit of ground work desensitisation. Our session went for 40 minutes and my walk was lovely with a big over tracking swinging through my back. I felt good.

I have to share with you a fun observation yesterday while Matthew and the Blind Chick were in the header, finishing off harvesting the wheat. It really did look like it was going to storm, so they wanted to get the stripping finished and the back of the truck safely closed up after that was done. Matthew and the Blind Chick got back in the header but I saw the Blind Chick get into the .... driver's seat!

Yes. The next thing the Blind Chick is cruising across the paddock driving the header, under Matthews close supervision. She was turning left, she was turning right, she went up the hill, she went round to near the shed, and then she asked Matthew did she have her license to be a header driver? Ha ha. The answer was a definite, NO!

So, all the stripping is finished which is great Matthew will come home this afternoon and move irrigators to put on the lucerne. He is always so very busy

Ooops! I did a ripping job on one of my rugs, so Matthew dropped it off this morning at Horse-Wear Repairs, a friend of the Blind Chicks who does rug repairs. Neeni is going to try and get it done by this afternoon, so we can take it with us on our road trip next week

Watch this spot! We have some exciting things happening next week which we'll share with you. The Blind Chickie babe is getting ready all the things we need and packing up the horse feed to pack into the horse float on Sunday.

Whoohoo and I have the wonderful Tanya Hind coming to do a Craniosacral Treatment on me on Saturday at 8am. I totally love my treatments with Tanya, I can't wait.

I admit that I'm feeling pretty terrific at the moment. Changing my diet has been very effective. The Blind Chick is still soaking my hay and I must say I don't mind it like that. It's like freshly pressed hay, it smells lovely.

I hope everyone has a wonderful weekend. I think we're in for a shower tomorrow, maybe even some storms tonight. Keep safe and well. I can't wait to share our journey next week.

Loads of love and hugs, Johno and my Blind Chick.

Focus On Ability

Did you know that every day is International Day for People with a Disability?

With this in mind, I thought some reflection was needed. I'd like to share with you - What are the things I Celebrate?

I Celebrate my Ability.

I Celebrate how very blessed I am to live in this amazing country, where you can have dreams and make those dreams come true.

I Celebrate being surrounded by beautiful people that believe in me.

I Celebrate friends and friendship.

I Celebrate the feeling of sitting on my beautiful horse Johno and riding across the arena.

I Celebrate these two beautiful brown eyes that guide me around when I ride him.

I Celebrate the amazing things I have experienced in my life:

representing Australia at the Paralympics twice, and riding at the World Championships in Denmark.

I Celebrate the ability to make a difference to sit on a horse and ride 16,000 km for different charities and raise over $3.2 million.

I Celebrate everything I have in my life. I take time to reflect and thank God for this amazing life we have.

I Celebrate my disability. Because it has made me the person I am today.

I Celebrate the fact that Vision is much more than Seeing.

Confidence – One Step at a Time

Feeling Determined | 31 January 2021

Diary entry from the Blind Chick

What a beautiful day here on the Macquarie River.

I started my morning the best way any girl can start, I went down to feed my beautiful Johno. Then it was the domestic Goddess duties. While I was hanging out the clothes, I gave a lot of thought to this confidence issue I have.

I have come to the conclusion that it's a matter of doing the doing. My phone has read me many books on regaining your confidence and people guaranteeing you after you read the book you will have oodles of confidence. I even had a go at hypnotise. Well, that didn't work either. One thing that did work was surrounding myself with very positive people and getting some one I trust to help me move forward.

Hence the steps Johno and I are taking to move forward. Getting the amazing Adam Sutton to help with Johno's desensitising. His help with building up my confidence. Each time we work together he takes us a little out of our comfort zone. Each time he works with Johno, Johno gains more confidence and is less sensitive to noise and what is happening around him. This is making the world a difference for us. But I respect that the confidence journey is very different for everybody.

With confidence, I think there is always going to be two steps forward and maybe one step back. Until you both believe and you both have each other's back. This rebuilding is not going to happen overnight. It is a matter of building a very solid base with your confidence level on the ground first, then looking to get back in the saddle. It's critical you aren't being pushed or shoved; just give it the time it takes - One Step at a Time.

So, moving forward with Johno and I, as you would've read in our last diary entry, we have our amazing coach Jenelle Waters who is a showjumper, a World Cup showjumper and her beautiful friend Jacq Benn.

Personally, I've found surrounding yourself with positive encouraging people makes the world of difference. Also, knowledgeable people. Not someone that's going to bully you and make you feel inferior or rubbish you for not being able to do something. Surround yourself with people who understand and get the fact that you don't need to be taught how to ride, you just need help rebuilding your confidence and believing in yourself and your horse again.

This rebuilding process is rather massive and sometimes quite a struggle, but I am so very grateful for the help I have had from the amazing Adam Sutton and at home, Jenelle and Jacq who work with me two to three times a week. This is just awesome. We will be able to move forward - One Step at a Time. Not great leaps, not great bounds, just One Step at a Time.

It was interesting with my ride the other day on Johno, Jenelle said "Can you feel what is happening? Relax and enjoy the ride, you don't need to override, just relax and enjoy the ride." It was so nice for Johno and I to take away that pressure of how my head is wired, to ride forward more, more, get the horse on the bit, into the bridle, keep that outside rein, more, more. Instead, we just enjoyed the ride!

So hopefully I can rewire my brain to not overthink when I get on Johno. Just enjoy the ride! That's what I'd like to be doing, I want to enjoy riding my pony again, without having the Itty-Bitty Shitty Committee in my head undermining me.

I am resigned to taking the time it takes and I'm surrounding myself with amazing people that believe in our dream of getting me back in the saddle and riding. It will take the time it takes. It will be - One Step at a Time.

So, to everybody out there who is struggling with their confidence, give yourself a break! Take some pressure off. Have another look, surround yourself with people who believe in you and can help you make your dream come true. But please, give yourself the time it takes. This is something I've had to learn.

I can't wait until tomorrow. Jenelle and Jacq we will be out for my lesson tomorrow and it is okay if we only walk and trot. But.... we need to relax and enjoy the ride.

So come along with us and the ups and the downs. We share them all.

Thank you all for your love and support. Have an awesome day. Loads of love, the Blind Chick.

VULNERABLE AND FRIGHTENED

Diary entry by Johno

I think this is something we never consider, being vulnerable and frightened.

We seem to blunder through our lives one step in front of the other and keep moving forward. I know for a fact the Blind Chick puts up this really brave front that everything is okay, she just gets on with it.

But over the past two years it has been really interesting

watching how vulnerable and reliant on other people the Blind Chick has become. She keeps mentioning there is no 'I' in Team because her life does not work without a team. In fact our life does not work without a team.

I think that might be one of the reasons the Blind Chick gave up having a Guide Dog a couple of years ago. Being totally blind she felt quite vulnerable with a Guide Dog in town. There is always that element of what if? I know that's not a good thing because that steps right back into the confidence issue, but I think that was also an issue with a Guide Dog. Having the confidence to go out and brave the world by yourself, sometimes is pretty scary I would think.

I must say I admire the Blind Chicks attitude of Get On With It. But I also see the other side of things, where the wheels fall off the cart. She sits on the veranda crying because she doesn't feel good enough, she feels as if she's let people down, she's gone from riding a lovely horse at Grand Prix level to being frightened to ride at all! Some days my heart breaks for her with this, because she is so passionate. I know it doesn't help with my Equine Shivers that causes me to be a little bit unreliable under saddle.

You know some people think she should just probably retire me, maybe even euthanise me, because without the medication I am really quite dangerous. But she plugs away every day making sure I get my medication, making sure I have the best care possible. If she gets on a thread of information, off she goes hunting it down, seeing if it might be able to help me keep a good quality of life, and maybe help manage this Equine Shivers, which is quite a monster.

I watch the Blind Chick on these very overcast mornings, this is really what prompted me to write this diary entry. With rain forecast and it being very overcast, for the Blind Chick that makes it is as black as the inside of a cow. She relies on the sun for her orientation when she comes down to feed me, or just navigating around the house yard. Without that beautiful sun it really is quite difficult for her to orientate. I often again hear her sobbing as she's hit the electric fence, again! Tears of sheer frustration.

I'm not sure how things go inside, but I often hear some swear words coming from inside the house. Often I think it's because she has run into the kitchen table, again, or the wall in the hall has moved. I know Matthew keeps saying to her "slow down," but I think if she went any slower, she'd feel she was going backwards.

It's interesting how things work out. I've heard Matthew and the Blind Chick talking about her Mum Mary, who is also totally blind, and how she gets disorientated and years and years ago the Blind Chick used to say to her Mum, "just think where you are." Well you know what? It's not that simple for her now, just thinking where you are now.

She is walking in her Mums' shoes being totally blind and getting lost, a lot. Imagine getting lost in your own bedroom! What the heck. How would that make you feel? I know the 'Lost In My Bedroom' occasions are guaranteed to bring on tears.

And you know what, on reflection if I were her, I think it would be really, really easy to give up and not do things. But because of her determination, stubbornness, and bloody mindedness to embrace life and live a full and happy life, she pushes herself every day, to keep a good quality of life. I know she loves cooking. Often there are cremated offerings, but them's the breaks. She keeps her life interesting and has lots of amazing, beautiful friends. I hear her talking with them on the phone each day. But it's the hours between the phone calls, the quiet time, what to do?

How would you fill your day being totally blind? I know the Blind Chick used to love doing craft. Well that's out now. I'm sure the frustration sometimes must be totally ginormous, quite overwhelming. But she keeps soldiering on. Sometimes I'm not sure why, or how.

All these things above I think are frustrations. But I know her biggest fear is, not knowing what to do next. She needs to have a plan, she needs to have a goal, she needs to have a direction. Why? Because it's so important, that - 'One Step at a Time'. By doing this you may arrive at the top of the mountain you quested for, having achieved your goals and perhaps even more! Doing so - One Step at a Time.

I know her wonderful husband Matthew has to step up a lot more, especially when the Blind Chick is having a big dinner party for 12 people, and doing it all herself! It was slow, but she did it all. She copes better with eight people; her wonderful husband Matthew cleans up afterwards. The Blind Chick can work in the kitchen and set the table by herself, but as soon as there are other people there it's difficult. Why? She runs into them a lot! I'd call her dangerous, especially when she has a knife in her hand cutting up vegetables or chicken.

In fact I often think she should count her fingers to make sure they're all still there.

So, even at home there's no 'I' in Team. Matthew and the Blind Chick are a great combination. Both are big stirrers, there's always quite a bit of laughter and cheekiness in the home, which is good fun to listen to.

But I would be stretching the truth if I said it was all a bed of roses. It's not.

I think it must be frustrating for Matthew living with the Blind Chick. Mind you I don't think she has burnt too many holes in his shirts ..... yet. After she's done the washing, he often picks up socks off the ground because they've escaped from the basket when she was getting the washing in. I think with the Blind Chick Matthew needs an extra set of eyes to make up for her sometimes.

Serving dinner out is often rather hilarious. Especially if there's a rice dish with a sauce. Matthew typically serves that out, which is much better on his plate than on the bench. That's where it's ended up quite a bit.

On a daily basis, I think a sense of humour is just so valuable. In fact, I think essential. Otherwise, I don't think the Blind Chick would get through the day. She loves our Facebook which is lots of fun and we have beautiful friends.

I suppose confidence comes in the same basket as the fear and frustration. Often it's the confidence level that is lacking that brings on the fear and the frustration.

Sometimes I don't think it's good for the Blind Chick to have too much time on her hands. If she does, she starts reflecting on what she was able to do quite a few years ago, and what she can't do now. The fact that Matthew lets her drive the tractor, with him by her side, is really cool fun for her. I know she loves going out and doing farm work with him, but often she feels she's more a hindrance than a help.

By the way this isn't a winge, this is fact. The fact that the Blind Chick is always smiling sometimes astounds me, because I don't think life is always that easy for her.

Interestingly I guarantee if you ask the Blind Chick if she had the opportunity to draw the cards again for her life, would she change it, I'm sure the answer would be 'No'. Why? Because going blind and being blind has shaped the amazing person she is today.

Mind you there might be a couple of little decisions she made on her journey that she'd change. But in general, the cards she's been dealt are okay, it's just 'One Step at a Time' and she will get there. Who knows what's around the corner? Time will tell.

I do know her greatest fear is not being able to do 'One Step at a Time'. I think with that attitude; One Step at a Time, One Day at a Time, Make your Goals Manageable and Achievable but Never Stop Driving and Moving Forward, we really can get through anything.

Go the Blind Chick, you rock!

But things change!

SOMETIMES LIFE SUCKS

Feeling sad | 6 April 2021

©2C Photography
Johno
Kinnordy Godolphin
8-11-2010 - 6-4-2021

Not all Angels have Wings.

My beautiful Johno from the moment I stroked your beautiful soft muzzle and I stood and talked to you quietly, you gave me so much.

Right from that first moment, you made something glow so brightly in my heart. I can't even call it Love At First Sight - because I have never seen you! But your image burns so brightly in my heart and my mind. I found it hard to leave after I first rode you. There was something magical about being in your presence.

You brought so very much to our relationship. You brought love and joy and happiness to many.

My wonderful husband Matthew saw it, from the first moment we met. We had something special you and me. So, he brought you for me.

How very privileged I have been to have you in my life for the past two years and two days! The time has flown. They haven't always been easy times. We've been fighting that hideous condition - Equine Shivers. It has caused you so much grief and discomfort, but we both kept soldiering on. I kept looking for something to help you.

We both knew there wasn't a cure. Our aim has been to manage the condition and keep you comfortable. That's all that mattered. The times that I got to ride you, oh heavens! What a privilege and an honour. You are spectacular in every way.

What joy and fun we have had writing your books. The saddest thing is our journey is ending way too soon. We had many more stories to tell, adventures to go on and people to meet.

But this hideous Equine Shivers is degenerative and .... degenerate it has!

Okay we learnt to manage your anxiety attacks in the paddock, which made it safer for you, so you didn't hurt yourself. But the attacks are starting to override the medication. It's now become unsafe to ride you. We know this is not you. It is the Equine Shivers.

Do you know how hard it is to let go of somebody who is so beautiful, so perfect, who brings such magic to your life? Knowing you must do the right thing by them and let them go.

Oh my beautiful amazing Johno, how do you say goodbye and stop fighting for someone so beautiful and perfect in every way!

How do you convince yourself you are doing the right thing by giving the one you love peace, and letting them go?

My beautiful Johno, you have taken my love of horses to another level. Our relationship has been based on Magic and Stardust and Fairies. I am so grateful to all of the beautiful people who have helped keep you going, helped give you a better quality of life. So very grateful.

But my beautiful friend, my heart breaks. How do you move forward after losing something so perfect and beautiful?

But I know in my heart what you would expect of me, so I will endeavour to be strong. I can't promise there will be no tears.

But I will promise to lock all of our beautiful memories deep in my heart, I'll have them with me forever.

I thank God for every moment that I've had to spend with you.

I have lost my best friend and God has just received a beautiful angel. Run free my beautiful friend. Be at peace. I love you forever, I will miss you forever.

Our journey has been way too short, but thank you for the memories and the ride, totally awesome. Thank you from the bottom of my heart for just being …….. Johno.

To our beautiful Facebook friends THANK YOU. You have been part of the journey with Johno and I. We are so privileged and so grateful to have you with us on such a sad day.

It is so hard to say goodbye my beautiful friend.

Rest in peace Johno

PS – This decision has been made with the advice from two of Johno's vets. Please respect I'm devastated, but there was no other choice.

*

THE INNOCENCE OF A CHILD

"Bring back the kid in all of us."
Sue-Ellen Lovett

As a girl I spent a lot of time in trouble, mainly with my mother. I tend to think she was jealous of the relationship my Dad and I had. But I wouldn't have changed anything for the world.

My Mum was very, very good at craft, and used to make things for the local school for their fairs etc. I don't know if you remember the cute little dolls that look like fairies on a cane stick, well that's what Mum used to smack me with. She had a selection of them hidden around the house.

A wonderful friend of ours Tony Jensen used to visit most evenings for a chat with my Dad on how things were going at Kaludabah and just catching up with a mate. Tony would save me from getting the cane! He would find them, break them in half and put them in the open fire, which was so cool. This used to annoy my mother something terrible. I used to sit on Tony's knee and feel quite smug knowing that I was safe from the cane while Tony was there. I hated each evening when he went as I was in trouble again for something I had done.

But when my Dad walked in all was well with the world. We would sit and talk to Cocky, our cockatoo. Dad had taught him to talk. It talked like our local stock and station agent Ted Marskel; it was hilarious! If Ted and the boss, Mr Tim Loneragan, were off buying some new cattle at a sale, Ted's standard line was, "not a penny more, not a penny more." My Dad taught the cockatoo to say it, he sounded just like Ted Marskel. One day Mr Loneragan turned up and he heard Ted talking in the house, but when he kept knocking no one came to the door. That night Tim rang Dad and said "I was knocking at your door, I could hear Ted Marskel in the breakfast room, but I couldn't raise you guys. Where were you?" My Dad had a quiet chuckle to himself, that bird was very clever, it'd chirp away to itself.

We loved that old cockatoo, he lived with us for 15-20 years. Dad also had a wonderful Black Barb dog called Darkie. Black Barb is a dog breed. She used to sit with me when I was a wee little girl, and my bassinet was out in the sun on the grass. Darkie watched over me. One day she was barking incessantly. Mum came out to see what was wrong. There was a big brown snake sneaking up behind me. After dispatching the snake Mum quickly took me inside. But I was safe. I was never in danger while Darkie was there. She also wouldn't let the Station Hands near me.

As soon as I was old enough, I was off on the horse any time of the day. Early morning, afternoon, or evening, I'd be with my Dad's beautiful brown and white, 14.2hh mare Silver, wondering the hills at Kaludabah. One day I went up to check out the station horses. We had 30 station horses in our riding team, but we had breeders out the back as well. They were lovely coloured horses and a beautiful stallion. So, I went out to check them on Silver. Nobody told this kid that probably wasn't very safe. When I got there, I found the stallion with a very nasty injury on his lower leg. It looked like it was half hanging off from what I could see.

So, I promptly rode back to the homestead, went to the stockyards, and opened all the stockyards up to receive the other horses. Then I went to the first aid kit and got a whole heap of Betadine, cottonwool, and warm salty water. You name it, I got it. I put it at the stockyards and went to retrieve the horses. I had to bring them down a couple of miles by myself. No one told me this shouldn't be done alone. No one told me that this would not be possible. So I drove the mob of 30 odd horses down with the stallion very lame on three legs to the stockyard. Once all the horses were in the big holding paddock, I shut the gate.

How was I going to get the stallion in the race so I could treat his leg? This was a horse that had NEVER been touched by a human before. So, I went in and tried drafting him off into a smaller yard. Then I went about trying to draft him off getting closer and closer to the race where I thought I'd be able to secure him so I could treat his foot. Phew, I got him in the race.

God love his cotton socks. What a beautiful natured animal. I placed a halter on him, I have no idea why? (Maybe habit.) But I did it anyway. I kept talking to this beautiful horse all the time. I knelt down and started treating his leg. It was a front hoof. He didn't bite at me, he didn't kick at me, he did not strike at me. He just stood patiently. I was doing really well cleaning up the foot, but the injury was quite nasty. I kept cleaning it as I wasn't about to organise my Dad to have a look. Dad would've probably just said "shoot him, he's not worth the drama as he's so wild and unhandled. No one can catch him."

Well things were going swimmingly until I heard Dad's ute coming from town. It was a Saturday morning; Saturday was shopping day for Dad. He must have noticed the horses in the stockyard. That would have piqued his interest. I can only imagine his reaction at seeing me underneath the stallion, doing something to its leg. He was smart enough not to stop. He drove up the road and just waited until I finished dressing the horse's hoof. While I was cleaning up he came down. Well holy cow! Did all hell break loose! Dad explained to me how dangerous wild horses can be and what wild horses can do to people. He explained that you don't go catching them or putting them in a race and certainly you don't get close enough to treat their leg! Especially untouched stallions.

Well, nobody had told any of that to this Chickadee! And I did just fine.

Thankfully the stallion was very calm. He got a bit stressed when Dad started yelling, but I suggested to my Dad to quieten down a little, that everything was ok, that I'd take them all back to their paddock and keep an eye on the stallion - from a distance.

Dad reluctantly let me put the horses back. He couldn't get over how I could treat a stallion that has never been touched by man before. I told him it was trust, the stallion trusted me, and I trusted him. The innocence of a child. It is amazing what you can do.

Things like this have always happened in my life. Whether it be a horse I was treating, or young heifer, or a myriad of poddy lambs. I've always had many animals in my life. We also had a poddy foal for a while until it ate my Mums evening dress off the line and ate the crutch out of her knickers. She was not impressed! So the poddy foal was moved out of the house yard to another paddock.

On Kaludabah we had up to 14 Station Hands working there at any one time. It was the most amazing childhood. I was out mustering with the Station Hands every chance I could. I was always skylarking with my uncle Ted and my brother. Always up to no good. We would be cantering along, and somebody would fly past and pull the bridle off your horse and throw it in your lap! To think about it now, holy cow, how dangerous, how silly! But no one got hurt, it wasn't malicious, it was just fun.

One day my uncle Ted and I had been taking another mob of sheep back after shearing. We took them out to the paddock they needed to go to and then we had to bring another mob in to put into the shearing shed overnight for shearing the next morning. We were coming over the hill into the Kaludabah Valley when we could both smell smoke. My uncle looked behind him and the hill was in flames.

Well, all hell broke loose! My uncle Ted galloped off down the paddock to Kaludabah to sound the fire alarm. I took the sheep down to the yards where there was shade and water. Then came three days of absolute mayhem and nature at its best. Who'd have thought such a massive fire could be started by a slasher hitting a rock, causing a spark!

For those three days I rode three to five horses a day to rescue stock. Mr Loneragan was up in his plane guiding me to where the cattle or sheep were stuck. My job was to go and get them down off the top of the hill or wherever they were, to safety. The wives and the rest of the families were at home making sandwiches and food for the firefighters. It was a really scary time. The first day it was exhilarating and exciting. The second day I was exhausted, and I was running out of horses! The third day I had had enough. I really didn't want to go out again. But Mr Loneragan needed me, so I went back out again to save more sheep and cattle.

That last time I went out didn't quite go as planned. I got caught on the peak of a hill with fire approaching from all sides! Thank heavens for the Rural Fire Service. Some guys that were fighting the fire saw me stuck with a mob of heifers on the top of the hill. We were surrounded by fire. They came and cut the fence so we could get out another way. I was so grateful. I have never been so scared in my life. I really should have had some pliers with me. But I wasn't expecting to be caught by the fire.

Each evening we'd spend time driving around in the ute, going around putting out anything that was still on fire or smouldering. The job was relentless. We couldn't afford to not keep vigil on the fires, even the smallest smouldering ones. After a week everything was nearly back to normal. The fire had burnt over 10,000 acres, a massive area of land. Because so much land was burnt meant there wasn't enough feed for all the stock. So, we had to ring a drover from Orange to see what we could do to keep feed up to the stock.

My Dad was really good mates with Jack Ash. Jack and his family were our drovers. Jack took quite a few of the stock on the road for about three or four months. This gave the property time to recover. Gosh it felt good when we had a shower of rain and the grass started to grow.

A highlight at Kaludabah was the annual Santa Gertrudis Cattle Sale. It was so much fun and nice to sit and watch my Poppy break the bulls in. He also had a donkey called Elvis that we used to attach the bulls to. Why? It was how we taught them to lead. Well, what a battle of wits. Poppy said it was much better than him being dragged around. But guess what, Elvis always won and on the Sale day, the bulls walked on the lead and were presented beautifully.

Poppy did such a good job with the bulls. He broke them in, and also looked after them. He injured himself quite badly a couple of times trying to break up... fighting bulls! Yes, not such a smart move I must say.

Then one day, and in hindsight it is hilarious, but at the time not so, Dad was having trouble getting one of the bulls out. They had taken a mob of cows that were ready for breeding out of the paddock, and just left the bull behind. Dad wanted the bull put down in the bull paddock, with the rest of the bulls. But he could not get the bull out of that paddock. He was in his ute, so he comes and gets me on the horse and says "okay, can you get the bull out please. I can't budge him from under the tree."

So I ride in there on my horse. Well, the bull started pouring the ground, throwing his head, snorting and being quite aggressive and ugly. I thought "no! This isn't a good position to be in." So I tempted him a couple of times and he chased me. Yes, not ideal but it was having the desired effect, I was getting him closer to the gate! Oops! The third time I let him get a little bit too close and he charged in and got his head under my horse. He pushed us full pelt into the dam, me on Silver, and Silver on the bull's neck! I have never been more scared.

We had a great bath though! Luckily the bull just dumped us in the water and got out. When I gathered my horse and myself back together, luckily Silver wasn't hurt and neither was I, I just went to my Dad and said "he's yours! I'm going home."

Dad and a couple of the guys eventually got him out of that paddock outside and into the stockyards at the end of the laneway. "Well, that's a start" Dad thought. Then the old bull went and laid himself down to rest under the peppercorn tree. How the hell are we going to get him from under there? So Dad went and got the old Bedford truck with a couple of feed bins full of grain on the back. He backed this right up to the bull. He didn't drive in front ways because that bull would've put a hole in the radiator it was that big. So, Dad backed in and then the unexpected happened.

The bull turned around and went under the truck and lifted the truck two feet off the ground! My heavens he was a powerful brute. We did get him moved a little further up the laneway, but still not to the bull paddock.

Then one of the other gentlemen came down, Ross Lowe and he bought his gun with him that was full of salt pellets. Similar to paintballs except instead of pain a fine spray of salt hits the target. So, we sat on the back of the truck and peppered the bulls bum with salt pellets. Well, I tend to think that stung a bit and he went forward, and he made it all the way down to the bull paddock. If he'd only done that right from the get-go, we wouldn't have had to pepper his ass!

To give you an idea of how strong these Santa Gertrudis bulls were, let me tell you about Dictator! This lovely bull was so nice, as a little girl I used to ride him in the yards. He was a beautiful big white bull. Well Acrobat, the bull that we had trouble getting to the bull paddock, lifted Dictator up and threw him over the fence! Yes. Not bad when you consider Dictator weighed over a tonne. Oh my God! Acrobat wasn't just strong, he was scary! The day we sent him to the abattoirs because his progeny was just as nasty, he busted up poor old Jimmy Cook's truck real bad. Jimmy had a lot of things held together by string and gaffa tape after that.

We used to have lots of wonderful picnics on the ponies. My cousins, the Mills family, my Dad's sister, Auntie Nancy and her husband Uncle Bruce, used to bring their family out and their girls, my sister Lizzie and I would go riding. I remember one particular day we were out riding and Judy went to open the gate. She leaned over and whooska! Her saddle slipped, big time! It slipped right around underneath the horse, with her still in the saddle hanging upside down! Everyone nearly wet themselves. Except Judy, she was not impressed. So we rectified the saddle and off we went for a lovely picnic down at Cloudy Bay. We had fun swimming the horses. We had a lovely old horse called Shianne that you could use as a diving board. Someone sat on her, someone stood on her back, then the rider brought their feet back and pushed them into her flank! Oh my goodness. She would pigroot you off into the river. She was a great diving board.

As well as fun with the horses we also got to do lots of fishing and gold panning. Mum loved gold panning. One day my brother and I were off fishing while Mum was gold panning. Peter was only about 5 years young at the time, and he managed to put a hook through his toe! So, Mum and Dad took Peter into the hospital, the worm still attached to the hook! Not surprisingly no nurse would touch it until my Dad got the worm off. Then they cut the end of the hook off and threaded it back through my brother's toe. Pete came home with a bandage and a tetanus needle and went back fishing again. What a tough little lad.

*

Keep on Keeping On

"Don't let your dreams be swallowed by your fears."
Sue-Ellen Lovett

As the wind blows from the west another bank of clouds, rainless clouds rolling in. Hot, dry, dusty, beating wind. But no rain. The sun is going to shine, just not quite yet.

It is seven in the morning and my beautiful Johno and I have made our way to the dressage arena with the aid of our friend Karen. Karen is helping train Johno to walk me to the dressage arena... alone! How cool will that be.

It is a time for reflection, while I wait for the sun to shine. What a wonderful word – 'INDEPENDENCE'. Being your own person. Being able to go and ride whenever you'd like to. Not always having to depend on someone else's time and help. Independence is one of our goals, Johno and I.

Karen is also training Johno to line up on the mounting block so I can get on unaided. Johno is a beautiful brown Warmblood gelding with a small shite star on his forehead. That's the only small thing about him. He is 18.3 hands high, 1.9m. Yes, definitely you wouldn't call Johno 'Shorty'!

Come on sun! I know you're there somewhere. Slowly but surely the sun shines through and I can mount. As I generally only ride when the sun is out, I generally only ride early of a morning. What's so important about the sun for me? The sun is critical, it allows me to orient myself. I know I'm on the right rein when the sun is on my left shoulder. So, all is well with the world as I ride up the long side. Then when I turn and go across the short side, the sun is on my back. The suns warmth for some people may seem like such a little thing, but to me it makes a big difference.

I lift my leg, placing my foot in the stirrup. Gently I swing my leg over Johno's back and settle myself into the saddle. Wow! What a magical feeling. Every day that I get to ride this magnificent horse is a blessing, it makes my heart smile. It's too cool.

For a short time Johno and I stand at the mounting block doing suppling exercises. Johno brings his head around and touches my left toe with his nose. Then he brings his head around and touches my right toe with his nose. All the time he's just softening and softening that beautiful big neck. I then asked Johno to walk on, and with the sun gleaming on my left side we find the long side of the arena and we are off. Our training has started and I pray that the sunshine keeps there for the next 45 minutes.

Now we start counting our strides along the short side, then turning down the long side. Inside leg into that outside rein, keeping softness through the corners. I'm not quite sure how deep to go into the corners. I don't want him to step over the edge of the arena. But one very large stride at a time it all slowly starts to happen.

We do about 20 minutes of walk on both reins, keeping things nice and even. We are coming along the short side, turning early and leg yielding to the edge of the arena. All the time I'm concentrating on keeping him straight through the neck and keeping the rhythm and regularity and being conscious of my heels down, sitting tall, steady hands and using my core muscles. Wow, where are they? I think they've gone missing in action! I probably should think about going to the gym. HAHA! That would last for possibly two sessions if I'm lucky! I should think about doing sit ups inside the house. Yeah, no, I don't think so. I think Johno and I will just work on it together.

All the time while I am riding my wonderful friend Karen is at the side of the arena giving us feedback. At the moment Johno is doing a beautiful big swinging walk. His over track is 18 inches. Wow it feels magnificent! I shorten the reins and I give him a squeeze with my lower leg and up into a trot we go. Oh my heavens, this feels so cool. He gives me a beautiful, big, swinging trot. This is what little girl's dreams are made of. In fact, big girls dreams are made of horses like Johno. I feel so very blessed.

Again, in the trot we're counting those strides, so we know when to prepare to come around the corner, not over shooting and going out over the arena edge. I so don't want to give Johno a bad experience and do the wrong thing. So, I take the corners very cautiously at the moment. I'm not as deep as I should be, but we're getting better each ride. I do a little squeeze with my outside leg, and we are into the canter on the right lead. My heavens, you could ride to London in this canter. He is so beautiful and soft through the back. We do some transitions, canter - trot, canter - half halt, half halt - walk.

Lots more transitions, canter - trot, trot up to canter, canter - half halt, half halt and walk. Sometimes I ask for a different lead, sometimes I ask for a flying change. Every moment of this ride I am... smiling! Oh my God, it doesn't get any better than this. I am so very, very blessed. I said you would hear me signing his praises a lot. I am incredibly smitten with this horse and so passionate about my riding.

Okay, keeping in mind, only eight weeks ago I had quite invasive eye surgery to stop pains in my right eye. The lens and capsule had collapsed in my right eye and were banging around in there near the retina. That movement was creating quite a lot of pain. So, my wonderful surgeon fixed the problem and when we went back for our check-up post operation, it was totally successful. No pain, yay!

That was the good news! I wasn't ready for the bad.

While talking with my surgeon, I asked if after another week of not riding, could I then return to riding? His answer was a resounding NO! "No more riding at all, it will only cause more problems with your left eye, which is also about to collapse. Then you'll have to have eye surgery again. I'm worried about the surgery that we have just done. So No! No riding."

Well holy cow! He certainly knew how to pull a person's life apart and drop it from a great height. I was busted. I was gutted. I could not come to terms with this. I was NEVER to ride again!

As soon as I could I rang my husband Matthew in tears. I told him what my surgeon had said, and he kept saying, "now stop crying, now stop crying and listen, what do you have to lose? You are already totally blind. You can't lose any more sight." So that was the start of me rebuilding. One week later I was back riding my beautiful Johno.

But I did give my eyes one more week of recovery before I went down to ride Johno at my coach Melanie's place. I have to tell you; it was the most amazing thing sitting back in the saddle on top of my beautiful horse. That seat is home, it is where I'm meant to be. Johno and I were meant to meet. It was written in the stars. Karen would often tell me how when we'd be saddling Johno up, he had a smirk or a smile on his face. I think he loves what we do.

He certainly puts a smile on my face every day. I can be sitting out on the front veranda having breakfast and I can hear the gate, a gentle jingle, or a big bang, as Johno is hitting the gate letting me know he is there. He ever so politely asks if I could come down and give him some breckie or go down for a chat and a cuddle. He just loves company, and he is such a clever lad.

Then of an evening when I'm sitting out on the veranda enjoying a glass of wine, Johno is at the gate again. "Come on chickie, come and give us a hug, or maybe a carrot would be good." If I could, I'd have him in the house yard, but that's totally impractical. He has a pretty cool home where he is. He has a lovely stable and breezeway, trees, and green grass. Well as green as we can given the drought doesn't allow much to grow and as we're on water restrictions we aren't allowed to water it.

Whoops, I got a little diverted!

Back to the arena. Johno and I are now warming down after our lovely ride. The sun has managed to stay out for nearly an hour which I greatly appreciate. As we warm down, we are doing more flexing exercises. Johno is a little bit weak in the near hind, so we are always working on strengthening that. To help get it stronger we do a couple of halt exercises. With Karen as my eyes on the ground to tell me if we are square or not.

The other thing Karen is teaching Johno is to go to the mounting block when I finish riding. We say, "mounting block, Johno, mounting block." Karen stands at the mounting block, it's up to him to walk to the mounting block and square himself up next to it so I can dismount. The surgeon said I'm not allowed to have any jars so it's critical I don't just dismount from 18.3 hands high, that's a long way down onto the ground. That'd be a big jar on landing. So, we get off Johno by stepping down onto the mounting block. This makes everything very comfortable indeed.

The next thing is getting Johno trained to guide me back to the tack shed area. Karen and I have been working on this with him for a while. He is getting better each day. What we have to watch is that he doesn't get side tracked by eating a little bit of grass on the way to the tack shed. Yes it may be just a wee morsel of grass, but a wee morsel still puts us off track.

We get to the tack shed area and start untacking. We've already taught Johno to stand once his bridle has come off. He just stands by himself, not tied to anything except the ground. This is called 'Ground Tying.' It is his responsibility to stay where he has been put. Then we remove his boots and saddle, pull out the hose and give him a lovely big bath, which he loves. The whole time this is going on Johno doesn't move. This is extra important for me because if he does, I can't find him! Even though he is 18.3 hands high, I still couldn't find him. It'd be quite a drama.

And even though he is so big his footsteps are so quiet, so he could sneak away without me hearing him go. But after he has had his bath and a scrape down, I put a lovely clean rug on and he guides me back down to his paddock.

Navigating around the property is something Karen has been working on with us. Every day it's our goal to build more independence. Who knows, maybe one day I might be able to go down and catch Johno, get him to take me to the tack shed, saddle him up and have him take me out to the dressage arena and line up perfectly beside the mounting block.

Watch this space! Who knows what might happen?

Once we get inside Johno's paddock he stops and stands patiently while we put his fly mask on. He's also waiting for his carrot! Which he really deserves. Once I've let him loose, we go and get him a lovely big biscuit of lucerne hay. Then he settles in for a pretty relaxed afternoon.

*

CHILDREN

*"Make every minute count.
Take no moment for granted."*
Sue-Ellen Lovett

Nephew Nicholas

Nephew Daniel on Mudgee
at Mudgee Show

Well, this is an interesting subject. From a very young age I was never that enthusiastic about having children, I much preferred my horses. I suppose this sounds selfish but, in a way, it worked out perfectly.

I can remember my mother going crook at me when I was a young girl, saying "you wait till you grow up and you have children! See how they treat you." I quietly thought about that growing up bit, but having kids was never on my run sheet. I have other things to do with my ponies.

I am not like my beautiful sister Lizzie; she is very maternal and has two wonderful children Sarah and Jack. They have grown into the most amazing young adults. We have had so much fun together over the years.

When Jack and Sarah were little Grandpa, my Dad, Sarah, Jack, and I would sit in the sunroom of Mum and Dad's house and play games. The word games were typically played on a great big quilt my Mum had made, it had the alphabet and animals on it and was so cool. We'd play a game like twister and the kids would laugh and frolic about. What special times and beauty children bring to your life.

In a way my not wanting to have children has been a blessing. Having a degenerative hereditary disease, I would not wish to pass this Retinitis Pigmentosa disease on to anybody.   Instead, I've been blessed with the most amazing nieces and nephews.

My brother Pete has three beautiful boys Bradley, Daniel, and Nicholas. When Bradley and Daniel were little, 3 and 4 years old respectively, I spent a lot of time with them, and they spent a lot of time riding on my stallion Hectic having lessons with Judy Cubitt. I can remember Bradley and Daniel in the bath at the cottage washing Eccles for our big trip down for the Sydney Paralympic Games. Oh my heavens what beautiful, beautiful memories. There were soap suds and dog hair everywhere. They even dried Eccles with the hairdryer.

Both Bradley and Daniel went to a Kindy in Mudgee called Squeakers. Grandpa affectionately called it Squawker's when he teased the boys. They'd come home reciting poetry and singing songs. One I remember was about Little Green Frogs. The boys taught us all their songs. It was so much fun. Those years were full of so much laughter. I have been privileged to share so many beautiful moments with these wonderful children. I haven't been able to spend as much time with Nicholas, because he's been away a lot, busy competing in Motocross. He's such a beautiful young man.

I've also had a lovely time with William and Nyssa, my husband Matthew's niece, and nephew. Matthew's brother Anthony and wife Melanie have gorgeous young people. William has this thing about reptiles, he has had a lizard as a pet for years. Now to his Grandma's horror he has a couple of snakes! William is an awesome scholar, such a clever young man. Nyssa loves writing and she gives the most beautiful hugs. Sadly, we don't get to catch up with our Sydney family nearly often enough.

As far as having children goes, my choosing not to have them was a big decision. I am really grateful Matthew had no problem with that. The reality for him is he does have a kid! He has a big kid in me. My Dad said I would never grow up and that I often acted my shoe size, which is only a 7 1/2 by the way!

I am so very grateful for the children in my life, my nieces and nephews bring such joy, such love and so much fun. I can't wait for them to grow into lovely adults, albeit that is happening way too quickly.

My beautiful niece Sarah did the last ride with me, which was wonderful. She helped look after the horses and take footage for social media. She is an all-round gorgeous girl. It was so nice to have her on the ride and have her share that part of my journey.

I have no regrets. We have Thunder Paws, our fur child, Lola and hopefully very soon, a new Guide Dog.

Over the years I've had many children that I've taught to ride. This meant lots of interaction with beautiful young people. Now a couple of those young people, Ebony Howard, and Samantha Hyde, have grown up but we still share more than just our love of horses. Ebony and Sam help me warm me up at a competitions and Sam even drives my horse float to international competitions. In my mind this totally rocks. I taught these beautiful young people when they were so young. I remember saying to Sam when we were driving up to the Brisbane CDI, "Oh my Lord, I can remember teaching you when you were 12, and now you are driving the horse float and ute to an international competition."

I am so grateful for my amazing life and for the beautiful children that I've had the privilege of teaching, and those I've been part of their growing up. We've had such fun.

I really am truly blessed.

*

BUT... YOU'RE BLIND!

"Stand up for what you believe in,
even if it means standing alone..."
Anon

Me painting Woody's kennel

How important is it to enable, not disable?

Personally, I think this is the coolest thing that has ever been said to me - "you can't do that because you're blind!"

This was where I was blessed having such amazing parents.

Mum and Dad never saw those limitations, they never put those limitations on us. They supported, encouraged, and watched us succeed. While we are no scholars, we've all done okay. Why? Because we were taught there are no barriers, only barriers that people make for themselves!

But it's the barriers that other people put on us that are so cruel and limiting. These barriers can slowly undermine you and disable you.

There was an instance not so long ago when we had some fencing that needed be taken down here at home. The fence had to come down before the imposing flood that had been forecast arrived. The fence in question was made up of a series of big steel panels, panels typically used to make a stockyard. We'd used them for Johno. Big fence for a big horse!

But with the flood approaching those panels had to come down and be removed from Lola's paddock.

While Matthew and his mother were preparing temporary paddocks on higher ground in the garden, to move the horses to, I moved all those panels by myself. They were hideously heavy, and the grass was long. I had to drag them about 80 metres up into the garden. Slowly but surely, one step at a time, I moved them. After which I was feeling very relieved.

To be told off the next day that I shouldn't have moved the panels, because I was blind, hurt, a lot. Yet I had just wanted to contribute to the huge amount of preparation that was need for the pending flood. I don't cope with being told what I can and can't do, because I'm blind! I think I'm pretty capable as a Blind Chick. Those words hurt, a lot. Those words were disabling, not enabling.

I think it is critical to work with people, to work out what their skill levels are and to encourage them and help them be part of the Team that's making things happen. Whether it be building a fence or pulling a fence down, teamwork is important.

With removing the fence mind you, I did have some moral support. From Lola! Every step of the way she followed me as

I hauled each panel. God love her. She could've helped! I did suggest that, many times. I could have hooked a rope around her and asked her to pull the panels for me, but I thought maybe not, ha ha.

People think it's amazing I do the washing, the ironing, the cooking, and the cleaning. Okay sometimes when I'm serving dinner, some of it doesn't make it onto the plate, but the bench is clean! Use it or lose it is my motto. So keep those skills, keep being stubborn and keep doing your best.

I realise working with someone who is blind can be a little extra hard, but it's doable. All it takes is patience and including that person in the Team.

Don't think I don't realise it is hard for some people to work with me. They spend all their time thinking "you can't do that because you're blind." How about giving me a go! Give me a chance to prove what I can and can't do. Give me some credit, I will tell you if I can't do something. Mind you I don't like admitting defeat very often, hence pulling all the panels out by myself. I must admit though that night of my big panel moving gig, my poor body was so sore that night I could hardly move.

It's important never to underestimate the capabilities of anyone. Give them a chance. Include them, even if it is a little harder to have someone blind or with a disability helping out. Be patient. Be kind.

The other thing, which is always a good idea, is to give the person that's not as fast or efficient at doing whatever you need them to do, some time! It's like Lola and I, we are building our relationship. My confidence with her keeps improving. Everything is going amazingly well on the ground. We have so much fun together and I know she loves my company. When I ride her now, I haven't got that Itty-Bitty Shitty Committee in my head undermining me with all the What If's.

But I also know that Itty-Bitty Shitty Committee could be just around the corner! So I remind myself, One Step At A Time and Take the Time it Takes.

Okay. compared to some people I don't consider myself the sharpest knife in the drawer. But... I will give whatever I do a go, I will do my best and try my hardest. I will not use my blindness as an excuse. I don't want anyone to do that. That's all I ask.

So, bring on the challenges! They are there EVERY day. Whether it be walking down the hallway at home where I'm like a virtual pinball banging into the walls, from left to right. Don't laugh - I often get lost in the bedroom! Yes, I get found again. Routinely I get lost in the garden. Sometimes with getting lost there are tears. Sometimes I can laugh about it later, but it's all about ability not the disability. I focus on what I can do, not what I can't do.

*

WE LOVE LOLA

"Not all Angels have wings"
Sue-Ellen Lovett

After 'trialling her' for about three months we made the decision to buy her. But I knew from that first ride at Jacinta's that this beautiful mare was a keeper.

Losing our wonderful Johno was more than just heartbreaking, his passing caused me to struggle emotionally. I'm not ashamed to admit it, I don't cope very well not having a horse in my life. To me they are and have always been, someone to talk to, a partner to share my secrets with, and a magnificent spirit to love unconditionally. They are not and have never been just 'a horse'.

The grieving over the ongoing loss of his health in the months and months prior to having to make the decision to euthanise Johno, was massive. Yet I still felt I had let him down, I questioned if I could have done more, should have done more. But I am also a realist, I knew there was no more that we could have done.

As part of the brilliant Team helping care for Johno, we had two amazing vets looking after him.

Moving forward there was a lot of beautiful memories, there was a lot of sorrow, there was a lot of learning. I knew Johno would want me to move on, one step at a time. I have done so with his memories locked deep in my heart.

So, I contacted my wonderful friend Jacqueline Thompson and together we composed an advertisement seeking my NEW DANCE PARTNER. I desperately needed to move forward otherwise I was going to get consumed by the darkness. I needed to show the love and the joy of what it is like to be as one with a beautiful horse.

The reaction and support on Facebook was amazing. The plight of my looking for a new dance partner, my next forever horse, got shared everywhere. I felt my beautiful Johno by my side in spirit. He was helping in our search.

We had responses from all over Australia, from the top of Queensland to the bottom of Victoria and everywhere in between. I was offered Grand Prix horses, I was offered horses that had done endurance, I was offered elementary horses. There was such an assortment, but everyone wanted to help me. It was so touching and yet quite overwhelming.

And then out of the blue I had a message from a beautiful lady called Jacinta Ledlan.

Jacinta owns a beautiful property called Araluen Park near the lovely little village of Sandy Hollow in the Hunter Valley. It was just 2.5 hours down the road.

Jacinta told me about this beautiful little mare she had called Lola. Lola is truly a black beauty. This versatile and courageous lady is 16.1 hh, who has twice won in hacking at the Grand National and won at the Sydney Royal Agricultural Show. She has evented, show jumped and done dressage.

When I first started talking with Jacinta, we were still scheduled to go to Equitana in a few months, to do a riding display. Yet I no longer had a horse. Jacinta offered to loan me Lola to take to

Equitana, so I had a horse to do the presentation on and consider buying.

This beautiful lady, this amazing angel, offered me her precious Lola on trial for as long as we needed her. Really! Who does this? Where did this amazing lady and her generosity and kindness come from?

I can never ever thank Jacinta enough for her kindness, for her love in offering me her beautiful Lola on such a long trial. She even gave me the loan of Lola's bridle and saddle so I could get used to Lola in her own gear. To this day I still cannot get my head around someone being so kind to someone they didn't know. The trust that Jacinta put in me, allowing me to take her beautiful Lola was quite overwhelming. There were tears when we picked Lola up.

But I'm jumping the gun. Once we got down to Araluen Park, we meet the beautiful Lola. I spent time patting her and talking to her. Jacinta tacked her up and we went across the road where we started riding. First Jacinta rode Lola, then it was my turn. I walked, trotted, and cantered around Matthew, he was calling to me as I rode, so I could orientate. I felt quite comfortable. Lola was very forward, much more forward than I was used to with Johno. But she was an absolute treasure and such a good girl for me.

It was a very easy decision to bring Lola home. We packed all the gear up and popped Lola on the float. Lola loaded herself on the float, which was so cool.

It was quite lovely when we went down to Sandy Hollow to meet Lola, Matthew, my wonderful mother-in-law Lee and me. Lee is always my eyes. She has such a wonderful eye for a good horse. She instantly fell in love with Lola, as did everyone else.

When Lola arrived at her new home, what she didn't know about me was because of my fall from Johno and subsequent lack of consistent riding due to his Equine Shivers, I struggled a little bit with my confidence. No, let me correct that, I struggled a lot with my confidence!

Consequently I spent a lot of time working with Lola on the ground. We did liberty work, we did getting her to step up onto a step, all of the cool things I'd learnt with the wonderful Adam Sutton that we'd done with Johno. Now I was doing all of these amazing desensitising and confidence building exercises with Lola.

All of our groundwork slowly paid off. However, I was still not quite confident in the saddle, and I was still quite wary of Lola's forwardness.

Interestingly, Lola was quite a tense little possum. I've had a big job just getting her to relax and not trying to rush everywhere. At first when I asked for a transition it was as if I had given her an electric shock. I just wanted her to relax so we could both enjoy the ride.

I contacted my wonderful coach Jenelle Waters to help me train Lola to relax and be my eyes on the ground. Jenelle is a professional showjumper and has helped me out quite a lot with quite a few of my horses. She has also been to many international competitions with me as coach and living marker. I also got her best mate Jacqueline Benn to come and help as well.

Jacq makes sure I've saddled the horse correctly, that boots aren't on upside down then she helps orientate me in the arena. She does this by calling out the markers when I'm riding, so I know where I am which takes away a lot of pressure from Jenelle. She can focus on coaching me rather than telling me to turn right, left or where I am.

We've done loads and loads of work on transitions, keeping it simple and relaxed, no pressure. I also had Jenelle ride Lola for a little bit as Lola was doing these funny mini pig roots when she went across the middle of the arena. Although she has been highly schooled, with me being a new rider for her, she'd often get a little confused with what was being asked of her. All I might have wanted her to do was trot on, or canter, but she has lots of buttons and she's so keen to please. Being so confused meant she'd sometimes pig root, jack up or suck back behind the movement. None of which were at all what I'd asked her to do. She just needed to learn to relax.

In addition to Lola's little pig roots, which were caused from tension, she had another party trick. When she was in the trot, every time she felt under pressure, she'd start doing Passage! It's been a process of teaching her to relax, unwinding this little elastic band, she was wound up so incredibly tight.

This process was only done by just taking one step at a time and taking the time it takes. There is no instant cure to getting a horse to relax or for me to build my confidence back up. They take the time it takes. If you want to train correctly, there are no short cuts.

My goal is to ride Lola by myself in the arena, which includes me tacking her up on my own, no one else there to help or supervise. Okay, I get it, you think this is unsafe - Blind Chick riding a horse on her own! But it is possible, I know it's possible, I've ridden on my own with all my previous horses, including Johno. I want that trust and independence again. So, I'm working to make it happen.

Having Janelle ride Lola first, warming her up, getting her on the path to relaxing, then me riding the rest of that session, has helped be an important building block in regain my confidence.

At this stage I have had Lola for about six months. I have mainly been focusing on doing basic stuff. Just walk, trot, canter, loads of transitions, leg yield, shoulder-in, and the odd walk pirouette. But mainly I'm keeping it very basic.

I haven't attempted any flying changes because they are what Lola wants to do at the drop of a hat! So we do simple changes; we walk through or trot through the change, keeping everything very low-key.

I was feeling quite rusty! It had been a while since I'd had a dressage lesson. Now that Lola was able to relax more, I started looking for a new instructor.

Enter the amazing Lisa Martin, five hours down south in the Hunter Valley at her beautiful property. So far I've gone down for a couple of blocks of three lessons with the amazing Lisa. The first block was like 'oh my God!' Did she push me out of my comfort zone, did she believe in me? Holy cow ... YES! Did I come home with extra tools in my toolbox, feeling good about riding Lola and being able to cope with those little moments where Lola would like to pig root ... ABSOLUTELY! Lisa gave me new tools, so now I can ride in the arena by myself. I'm starting to fulfil my goals.

With my lessons with Lisa, we had many mini lightbulb moments. Like how important it is having a Living Marker calling directions to me, so I have a place to ride to. Being totally blind I have no idea what a straight line is unless someone is calling me towards them. Like when I was trying to set up a shoulder-in and Lisa was talking, and she happened to be in front of me. We both had a lightbulb moment. I was riding my horse on three tracks towards her because I had a direction to follow, her voice. I started being able to ride straight to Lisa's voice on three tracks. It was so cool, it was so much fun, and Lisa is so, so very patient, and passionate.

Lisa got Anita, who drives me down for lessons, to be my Living Marker. This freed up Lisa to concentrate on giving me lessons, instead of giving me directions as well. Anita would call to me, so I rode to her. It didn't really matter what she calls out, where her voice is coming from gives me direction, something to orientate from. It could've been as simple as now, now, now, on every stride and it help me set up a movement and ride straight.

When we returned home, I gave Lola the next day off, then the next day I was ready. I went and caught her, gave her a brush, saddled up and went out to the dressage arena helmet on. It was on my head and I was determined to ride on my own.

And guess what? I didn't have any butterflies with my Blundstone boots on. With my white cane guiding Lola and I, we went out to the dressage arena and lined up beside the mounting block. I mounted, rode forward three strides and we were in the dressage arena. We did it all by ourselves! Oh my heavens. I was a tad pleased with myself.

So, since that day I've had many rides by myself with the

beautiful Lola. Plus, we don't have any of her jack ups or pig rooting! I'm not going to say they'll never happen again if she is feeling over faced though. Likewise, I'm not going to say the Itty-Bitty Shitty Committee isn't going to get back in my head and undermine my confidence again. That would be unrealistic. But as our beautiful Johno used to say – "one step at a time and you never know where you'll end up."

I had organised to go back down for another block of lessons with the wonderful Lisa but we had pretty massive rain. My dressage arena was in flood and so was Lisa's. So we've put the training off till next week.

So watch this space! I can't wait to get back doing dressage. I'm loving the journey. Maybe we'll do some competitions and demonstrations, time will tell.

I have a couple of things on my Bucket List that I'd love to do with the beautiful Lola. One is a desensitisation session with the amazing Adam Sutton, over obstacles and things. I did this with Johno, and we had a blast, it was so much fun going over bridges and see-saws. It certainly took me right out of my comfort zone. It was such a great learning experience.

The other thing we are going to do with Adam is go for a ride with Lola on the beach. This is going to happen in the next few weeks. I'm so excited. I was hoping to have my new Guide Dog by then, but that's not happening until next year. So, we'll go for another beach ride then.

Guess who is going mustering? Yes, me. It's not fully finalised yet, it's in the pipeline. I can't wait to get behind a mob of cattle with Lola. I'm sure she will truly enjoy the experience.

Just digressing a little bit on the mustering topic, when I was first speaking with Jacinta, before we'd even gone down and looked at Lola, I asked her "when was the last time you rode Lola?" Her reply nailed it for me, I knew then that Lola and I would be perfect for each other. She said, "Two days ago, I rode her to get the bulls in." Any horse that can do stock work, dressage, show jumping, hacking, and eventing ticked my boxes.

What are my plans, goals and dreams with Lola? Who knows what's around the corner! Yes, I would love to get back doing dressage competitions but if it doesn't happen that's okay too. Keep a look out for Lola's book, Lola & The Blind Chick, it will be out next year. She'll tell you all about what she's been up to.

Once again, I am so grateful to my wonderful husband Matthew for buying me Lola, who is such a magnificent horse. He is so insightful. He knows exactly how special horses are in my life. He is so supportive and has always helped make my dreams come true. I am so blessed.

But to the beautiful angel Jacinta Ledlan, THANK YOU for trusting me with your beautiful Lola, and giving me the amazing honour of owning her. I am so grateful.

Our black beauty's official name is 'We Love Lola'. We certainly do indeed.

Who said angels don't have wings?

*

MATTHEW

"Love makes the world go around."
Sue-Ellen Lovett

Credit: Debra Lovett (Wedding Pic)

Okey-dokey, you'll never guess where I met a lovely young man called Matthew.

Matthew's Mum kept saying to him – "You will never meet anybody in the lounge room." Well it wasn't quite in the lounge room that we met, it was on the lawn at the farm on Macquarie River in Dubbo, New South Wales. He was quiet, he was shy, but very polite.

I think my wonderful coach Judy Cubitt would like to think she had a hand in this match making endeavour. Judy was absolutely chuffed when Matthew and I started dating. She laid claim to being the matchmaker, which was just beautiful.

Matt's Mum and Dad, Lee and John, hosted Judy and I while I was in Dubbo training on various horses in preparation for the Paralympics in 2000. I was working to get on the Team and as you know our horses were drawn out of a hat. So, this meant I had to ride as many horses as possible.

While we were there training, I was also organising a fundraiser in Mudgee, my hometown, for the Sydney Paralympics, a Paralympic Ball. Chairman of the Australian Paralympic Board Dr Grant and his beautiful wife, as was the Honourable Michael Knight, Minister for the Sydney Olympics, and Paralympics were invited. It was a big deal for the town of Mudgee. I asked Matt's mother Lee if she would organise a table, which she did.

As I was leaving the farm after my training session on the horses in Dubbo, in passing I asked Matthew if he would come to the Ball. He said, "Probably not, I'll probably be sitting at home watching the rugby." "No problems" I replied.

I already had a date for the ball. He was one of the pilots with Hazleton Airlines who used to fly me backwards and forwards to Sydney for Board meetings with the Paralympic Committee. But as fate would have it, he got called away to do another trip shortly before the ball. Voila! I was now dateless, which was fine.

Soon enough, the night of the Ball rolled around. After all the speeches and formalities were taken care of the rest of the night was left to our amazing entertainment - the brilliant James Blundell. Wow, such great music to dance to, but I didn't have a dance partner.

So I decided to go and catch up with Judy Cubitt, Lee and John. They were all seated at the same table. My Guide Dog Eccles guided me over there and while I was sitting talking to Jude and Lee, I asked Lee if Matthew did end up coming to the ball. She said "Yes, he is sitting at the end of this table." This is where it all started.

I'm sure you know by now that I'm not backward in coming forward. So off I went and asked Matthew, "Would you like to dance?" We danced the night away. We had such a lovely time.

Then he escorted me back to my room and we sat and talked for hours. When he left to drive home to Dubbo, he promised to ring me. Hmm, five days went by, a week, 10 days … still no phone call. Okay, C'est la vie says I.

Then about two weeks later Matthew did ring and we started chatting on the phone whenever we could. He visited Mudgee and met my Mum and Dad. On his visits we'd go swimming in the pool at Mum and Dad's each afternoon. Dad would give us a mouthful of cheek. It was always lots of fun visiting my parents. Dad was such a character.

Matthew even helped me train the horses for the long-distance fundraising ride for the Paralympics. He rode a lovely big horse called Jed. What was particularly hilarious was teaching him how to do rising trot for the first time. He used to do Pony Club, but he professed to not enjoying it very much. Yet he was quite a good rider all the same.

Time passed really quickly. The year 2000 was a massive year for us. Not only did Matthew and I get married, it was also the year of the Sydney 2000 Paralympic Games.

Matthew had an absolute ball at the Paralympic Games. He was a VIP because I was on the Board of the Sydney Paralympic Games. His VIP pass took him more places than the Premier of New South Wales, so he had an awesome time. I competed and what an honour it was to compete for your country.

Just before Matthew and I were married we started building a cottage on his Mum and Dad's property on the Macquarie River in Dubbo. The cottage has three bedrooms, but it isn't a large home, which suits us down to the ground.

Yes, some people said it wouldn't last and some questioned why he'd want to marry a Blind Chick who is 11 years older than him! I was called a Cougar. Yes, we had lots of ups and downs early in our marriage, but who the hell doesn't? That's life and getting to know each other really, really well. But if you truly love somebody, you learn to work together, there's a lot of compromise.

I am so very grateful for what Matthew has brought to my

life. He's given me so much love, caring and generosity. He has taken me to many International competitions, he's been a Living Marker, a groom, he's driven thousands of kilometres for me. Not everybody would do that for their wife, let alone all the extra things he does because yes .... I'm blind.

But that's the thing, I'm his Blind Chick.

While we've been to Canada and have been on a few holidays over our 20+ years together, we are both pretty much homebodies. Mind you I do love travelling, but I am happiest when I am at home, with Matthew.

Matthew has two jobs! One is as a Head Teacher at Distance Education in Dubbo, teaching Agriculture and Primary Industries, which he is very, very dedicated to. His second job is working the family farm. He loves his farm and works very hard growing lucerne hay, wheat, barley and for a short time the odd crop of canola. Sadly, the canola made everybody sick from hay fever, so he hasn't grown it again.

Dad gave Matthew a lovely old tractor called Farmall H. Matthew has diligently done up this beautiful tractor. I tell everybody that this tractor was my dowry! Matthew has spent hundreds of hours doing it up, it's been worth it. It's in mint condition now.

Some of the amazing things Matthew has done with me over the years include letting me drive the ute. He does this by being in the tractor behind me and guiding me with instructions as we talk on our phones. I've even had a go at driving the Header. Oops, I put my foot on the wrong pedal, the brake instead of the accelerator. Matthew face planted like a dead mozzie into the windscreen! Hence no more Header driving for the Blind Chick. But it was hilarious and such awesome fun having a go at driving the Header.

It's like, who would let the Blind Chick do this stuff? I've even had a go at driving the forklift. Matthew won't let me use the chainsaw for some reason. Heaven knows why not.

And over the years various horses have come and gone. Yet Matthew is always there, supporting me. When Desiderata retired, I went seeking a new horse, a special horse because at 60 years young I knew this horse may be my last competition horse. I wanted one that I could have for 10+ years. I sent photos and adverts of potential horses to my wonderful mother-in-law Lee, and she'd go through them and say which horse she liked and which horse moved well. On a whim Matthew and I went down to Sydney to look at a horse called ... Johno.

Right away Matthew could see there was something magical between Johno and I. God love him, he bought this amazing horse for me. It's tragic that we only had him in our lives for two years and two days. Johno had a neurological degenerative condition called Equine Shivers. And degenerate it did, over a very short time. But the time we had with Johno was magical and Matthew and I both learnt so much.

This meant I was horse-less again. It may sound very selfish, talking about me at such a time, but this is what this beautiful man has brought to my life. We were offered a lovely horse called Lola who lived near Sandy Hollow in the Hunter Valley, only 2.5 hours away. We went down and picked Lola up. Jacinta Ledlan, the beautiful lady who owned her offered her to me to trial for three or four months, whatever timeframe I'd like.

So we came home with Lola. And once again Matthew bought me this amazing horse, who we all love.

How very lucky I am I to have met this beautiful man. His love, his ability to understand how special horses are in my life is perfect for me. And on a daily basis he keeps helping make my dreams come true. Whether it is out helping me with coaching, bringing hay over for my horse, he just keeps giving and makes my life so very special.

I had a dream about the man I would meet and marry. This man drove a white ute, he wore a blue chambray shirt and moleskins. The day Matthew turned up at my cottage, guess what he was wearing? Who said dreams don't come true!

We can be out doing a service on the irrigator, we can be down watering our pumpkins, always my hand in Matthews. I am so grateful to this beautiful man for his strength of character, for loving me, for who I am. And... I can tell you I'm probably not the easiest person to love! I'm strong willed, I'm independent and I can be pigheaded. He would agree with all these things, but he loves me for who I am.

Thank you, Matthew, for being in my life, for loving me for who I am. You truly are an amazing gentleman. I am so proud of you.

Matthew is also the Captain of our Local Bushfire Brigade. He is so dedicated. He loves the training, and he loves the people he works with. The Local Brigade have been such a wonderful part of Matthew's life, and such a wonderful thing to be involved in.

He is a giver, he makes a difference to lots of people's lives, I am so grateful he is in my life. Thank you for being the beautiful person you are. You totally rock. I'm sure Judy Cubitt would be very, very, happy with her matchmaking.

I will love you for ever.

*

WHAT'S NEXT?

"I choose to see the beauty, the love
and the magic in the world."
Sue-Ellen Lovett

Lola & I

Credit: Jacqueline Benn

Well, it's a wrap!
For this book at least.
So more many journeys to go on, so many new adventures to be had. So many goals. So many dreams... to come true.

One of the extra special things I'm looking forward to in the very near future, I'm getting a new Guide Dog! But first a dog that is suitable for me, needs to be found.

I truly thought I was doing the right thing by retiring Amani, my last Guide Dog. I wasn't totally confident using her in town, which was not her fault. The issue was people deliberately distracting her while she was trying to work. They would whistle to her, try to pat her, try and feed her treats – all the while she is supposed to be guiding me! I found this level of people's ignorance very disconcerting. Hence Amani and I stopped going into town on our own anymore.

Around this time the NDIS launched in Australia. The NDIS provided me with the ability to pay people to take me shopping or do the essential things a Guide Dog had previously done for me, for 38 years. So, it seemed a much easier option at that time to retire Amani and work with the NDIS.

Interestingly, I had never thought of making use of my Guide Dog as a form of independence here at home on the farm. Primarily this was because of our snake situation! Living next to the Macquarie River there are quite a lot of brown snakes and as you would've read already, I have been struck by three brown snakes. Such occurrences are certainly not my favourite past time.

While I use my white cane to get around at home, it does not provide me with the independence and mobility a Guide Dog would.

Plus, having a Guide Dog means I won't get lost anymore! I've been lost in our garden so many times that I've lost count. Each time I have to ring Matthew, Lee or John, to come and find me. While I feel quite humiliated at the time, we can laugh about it later. But I could do without the excitement of being lost in the garden. Hopefully a Guide Dog will remedy this problem.

Bring on a new Guide Dog! Independence and mobility sound good to me.

On reflection there are so many things and so many people I

have not mentioned. My life has been full of amazing adventures and more than amazing people. The friendships I have made I will treasure for ever. The awesome experiences I have had will live on in my heart for ever. I shall treasure them. It is quite amazing how many things you do forget. Sometimes it takes a friend to remind you of some of these beautiful times in your life.

One of these reminders happened a year ago. I received a message from Robbie Aikin, Robbie was one of the sighted guides on the ride we did for the Paralympics - from Melbourne to Sydney. As we were chatting backward and forward, Robbie said "remember the day you did the interview with Doug Mulray." Well, he certainly did, he was so excited about it. But I'd forgotten! There had been so many interviews, so many amazing people.

The loyalty of some of my friends over the years has been more than extraordinary. One of these amazing friends, okay yes, I do use this word a lot, but he is amazing and loyal, and beautiful. His name is Steve Cumberland. Steve has been part of nine of my 10 rides. He is always there with a shining smile, a mouthful of cheek, and a whole heap of love and caring. Steve always makes sure everything flows smoothly. Whenever Steve is around, I don't have to worry about anything. He is one of those amazing people that effortlessly gets on with the job. He either drove the horse truck or was one of my sighted guides. Times with Steve are never dull. He leaves you laughing.

Here's a bit of trivia for you. I'm not an alcoholic however you may think otherwise when you know I've visited the inside of over 600 Australian pubs! Why? Such fun visits were all part of the 10 long distance rides fundraising adventures.

Another amazing person that has come into my life, is a wonderful gentleman called Bobby Cooper. While we lost wonderful Bob a couple of years ago, oh my heavens the memories of this lovely man live strong in my heart. He had lived with aborigines, he had flown helicopters, he had lived up in the Gulf. He was a true adventurer, Opal Miner and... the list goes on.

He was this Blind Chicks best mate. He also had the ability to write the most amazing poetry. He came with us on one of the rides, the one from Mudgee to Mudgee, 1800km through Central Western New South Wales that we did raising funds for Camperdown Children's Hospital, Sydney, New South Wales. He was flown in by light plane in true Bobby style. He slept under the truck in his swag and as he snored through the night, the truck lifted and came down! Typically, he slept a good hundred metres away from everyone else, his snoring was legendary.

But Bobby's generosity and kindness were relentless. I remember a particular time together, we had just had a big night in Cobar where we'd gone around the five pubs fundraising, then we'd gone to the RSL Club. At this time, I'd acquired a little kangaroo called Roo-Ted, kindly named by Bob. Because it's Mum had died, roadkill, this little fella would have died had I not taken him in. Roo-Ted accompanied us to all the pubs and to the RSL Club where he thought to pop his head out from my backpack. The Manager of the RSL Club wasn't that impressed, but it caused a great laugh.

The next day I had a cracker of a migraine, we'd been doing very long days. This ride was 1,800 km and okay, I had had a couple of wines that night. It was probably just a stress headache. Bob was so kind. He had a lovely old aboriginal remedy which had my migraine cured in about half an hour. He found the right leaves from a particular tree, crushed them up and I had to breathe in the vapours from the leaves. My heavens! Bobby Cooper was a true gentleman and a true friend. I miss him.

This amazing gentleman was able to make magic with his words, his poetry. He could paint a picture just with words. It was not unusual for hm to be jotting down his next masterpiece on the back of a serviette or a cardboard coaster at a pub.

THE CHILDREN, THE FUTURE & YOU
By Bob Cooper

They will find when the ride is over,
when the dust settles down once again,

In the mould of the High Plain's Drover,
that they've beaten the heat and the rain.

For they ride with a singular purpose,
with a natural deep stubborn pride.

To raise the funds to Fight Cancer and
Halt its far-reaching stride.

Small children, the cream of the nation,
the future and hope of this land,

Lay wasted with pain by the ravages,
wrought by its far-reaching hand.

Your son, my daughter, a grandchild, a nephew,
or niece here and there,

These cancers are not that selective,
they strike anytime, anywhere.

Sue-Ellen is riding to save them, with blind
courage, you know the score.

Her eyes see just darkness, but her heart
sees the hope and much more.

She rides through the small townships,
through cities and trails seldom crossed.

She rides through the hearts of those parents,
whose child has been stricken or lost.

These words yes are meant to inspire you,
they are meant to compel you to give.

For the children require your donation,
for we need those children to live.

Take this chance to show your opinion,
your abhorrence to death and despair.

Put your strength into beating the monster,
put your heart into showing you care.

When the dust of this long ride settles,
and the echoes of hoof beats have passed,

You can say that you rode with Sue-Ellen and
have joined in the battle at last.

For she carries the burden of caring,
she pines for the children that have died,

And you good souls who helped in the sharing,
are all locked in her heart on this ride.

In October 2018 sadly my wonderful friend Bob Cooper suddenly passed away. RIP Bobby Cooper. Thank you for the beautiful words and friendship. I shall miss you, always.

Imagine the enormous confidence you get when you know you have a business that supports your every hope and dream. Imagine the delight when that feeling isn't just business, its personal as well. That's how Ian Bellion, Head of EQUISSAGE Australia, and his wonderful Sales Representative Katie Classon, make me feel. We've all worked together for 14+ years and I don't imagine my life without Ian, Katie or the EQUISSAGE Team in it. I love the EQUISSAGE products, I know first hand that they work. But what works better, is the friendship and support I receive from

Ian, Katie and the Team. It is lovely being part of the EQUISSAGE family.

I worry I haven't mentioned everyone who has touched my heart or made a positive difference to my life. To all the beautiful people I have met and who have helped on the rides, helped being Living Markers, taken me to competitions or guided me around, I am so very grateful and blessed having you in my life.

Well, this is just the end of this particular book. I am 61 years young, so there's still a hell of a lot of living to do. I am not sure if there will be any more long-distance rides, but I did hear there was a 100 km walk on the horizon this year, 2022. A fundraising walk for the Western Cancer Council Oncology Unit. We will see how it plays out.

It is one thing putting the miles in on a fit horse each day, and knocking out 60 – 70, up to 100 kilometres a day. Easy pesi! But no horse and walking 100 kilometres will be quite different. This walk will be done over a few days and require getting people involved and lots of fundraising in each town we walk through. These are plans for the future, these are dreams that we will make come true. We will help make a difference to people's lives.

I'm sure things here on the home front will continue with Matthew farming and doing what he loves. Our wonderful cat Thunder Paws will continue as our contraceptive cat and lying between Matthew and I each night. Which is quite hilarious. I'm sure he knows exactly what he's doing.

I look forward to many adventures, including getting back into the dressage arena. Whether I end up just doing riding demonstrations I'm not sure. In my heart I would love to get back to competing at Pre St-George and Inter One level. I know these tests really well and find comfort in them. So, this is my goal, and I will go one step at a time to making it come true.

It will take the time it takes. I have been with the beautiful Lola seven months now, and it has taken me awhile to regain my confidence and shake the monkey off my back. My lack of confidence was from the buster off Johno. So onwards and upwards. Let's see where this one goes. I'm excited for the future for Lola and me. I can't wait to go swimming at the beach, that will be magical. Maybe I'll have some photos of that before this book gets printed. Who knows? But again, every day is an adventure for me.

For me some days the task of simply walking down the hall isn't quite so simple. I resemble a pin ball! I bounce from one wall to the other. And when I make it into the bedroom... I can get lost! Just navigating my way around my home, is an adventure! Getting lost happens to me quite a bit. I can remember giving my Mum a hard time about her lack of direction. I used to have the most wonderful sense of direction. Well guess what? Now there is none. I'm just like my Mum. Hence getting lost in the bedroom and get disorientated quite quickly happens quite regularly. But... I always find myself. There is always the door out of the bedroom. I've just got to find it first.

I want to thank the beautiful people who have helped me through some of the truly hard times in my life. Going blind has not been an easy journey. I would be lying if I said it was.

The importance of being able to ask for help when the dark times are there was reinforced to me by a wonderful gentleman called Ben Schwarz. Ben held my hand through many a hard day as my sight diminished. At that time, I didn't know until many years later, that Ben had the same disease as me! He was living the same journey. What an amazing gentleman and what generosity and kindness he showed me.

When we would have our phone calls, when I'd rung him to ask for help because even though I'd tried to be tough all the time, to be strong and make out I didn't need help, sometimes I did! He would always take the Mickey out of me, "brave Sue-Ellen Lovett needs help!" he'd laugh. How he treated me, was perfect. He always started things off with us laughing. He helped take the weight off me. He helped me learn that the best thing you can do if you aren't coping is... ask for help! And surround yourself with people who give a dam.

Oh, heavens! I think this chapter could go on for a very, very, long time. I keep thinking of amazing people that would pick me up when I've been down. I keep thinking of the amazing experiences that I've shared with so many beautiful people that have come and gone in my life.

One of the things that I really struggled with for a long, long, time was... accepting that sometimes people come into your life at the right time, and they also leave at the right time! I am a very loyal friend, so I found it hard when people had spent their time and they move on. I didn't always understand why this happened. But that's okay, I know now. People come into your life for a reason and then they go. They generally come into your life when you need them the most. Sometimes we just don't realise their importance at the time.

To all the beautiful people who have come into my life and made a difference, whether it be for a day, a year, or five years, thank you from the bottom of my heart for being part of my journey, for making my life richer and for teaching me. I think that the lessons we learn from people is one of the most important things people can do for each other. To receive this gift of learning though, we need to be open, to listen and be kind. (This includes being kind to yourself!)

Thank you to everyone for their kindness and for listening to me. I hope I have been able to do this for my friends, to be there for you and be a good friend, a loyal friend.

By now you would have picked up that my life is about trying to make a difference, to spread kindness and love. Why? Because that's the key to everything. There is not enough love in the world. If people took time to share more love and kindness, the world would be a much better place. I'm sure you've heard that before but that's the easy part, 'hearing it'. The harder part that people aren't as good at, is actually doing it! Making a difference. Did you know you can make someone's day with just a smile or saying "good morning." Let's start smiling more. Let's spread the love more.

Thank you for taking the time to pick this book and taking the time to read it. I hope you enjoyed the journey. There are so many more stories I could share with you. I think there is more that I have forgotten than I remember. My journey has been amazing. I wouldn't swap my life for all the tea in China.

Every day has been blessed with magic, beauty, love, and kindness. Yes there have been shitty days, but you know what? Every cloud does indeed have a silver lining - you just need to look for it.

So keep smiling. Keep spreading the love and thank you from the bottom of my heart for being part of my life and making it totally magical. I feel so very blessed.

*

SURPRISE - WOODY!

"Independence and mobility – totally rocks!"
Sue-Ellen Lovett

I dared to dream.
Then my dream came true.

I really didn't think I'd be excited about getting a new Guide Dog. Over a period of 38 years, I'd had six Guide Dogs, it was a way of life for me, they were always there. I retired beautiful Amani two years ago, because I thought I really didn't need the assistance of a Guide Dog any more. Boy oh boy, was I wrong!

With my trusty white cane, I navigate my way around the farm. Most of the time I'm okay. I'm not so okay if the day is overcast, or if the sun goes behind a cloud. Guess what happens then? Without the ability to use the sun for my orientation, I get totally lost!

Getting lost in my own backyard these last two years has totally sucked!

So, I contacted my wonderful friend Michael Ponting at Guide Dogs and asked him if he thought it would be possible to put my name on a list for a Guide Dog again. His answer was a swift yes! So after doing the necessary interviews, videos and other things for Guide Dogs to decide if I met their Assessment criteria - I passed! This was very cool. So, then it became a waiting game.

As I write this, it is mid-January. Just before Christmas I had a phone call from a lovely girl called Hayley. She told me about a wonderful Guide Dog called... Woody! They thought Woody and I might be a good match. He is a caramel coloured two-year-old Labrador. It has been really interesting finding out that he was the class clown. Since then, I've put up some posts on Facebook about getting a new Guide Dog. How amazing, quite a few people know Woody!

I discovered that he has had an interesting upbringing. Perhaps the most suitable description for him is an extrovert, a troubled child who gets into strife a bit too often. Although he has been through a few homes while he was growing up and being puppy walked, I think he'll settle in here mighty fine. Why do I have such confidence in him? Because I'm a bit of a square peg in a round hole. I'm also quite cheeky. While I'm not the class clown, I'm definitely one of our families' clowns.

To say I was a little excited when Hayley said she and Woody would be up to visit with me the week before Christmas is an understatement. They travelled up to Dubbo on the Monday and come visit me on the Tuesday, arriving at 9.30am. Woody wasn't full of bounce and vigour, he was such a man about town, so very cool and laid-back. Hayley and I sat under the Paulownia tree out near my tack shed where Woody sat at my feet. He was quite contented. After he did a little bit of sniffing, he was happy to just hang with us while the girls had a chat. While we talked, I took the time to get to know Woody.

The thing I couldn't get over though was oh my heavens, he is ginormous! He has the longest legs and a very solid body. He is easily the biggest Guide Dog I have ever had. Yet, he is so laid-back, just so happy to hang with me.

Matthew then came out and we all chatted about what we would do next. Matthew went and got Lola and we all went for a walk up the road, the five of us. Hayley had Woody and Matthew had Lola and I. Woody took no notice of Lola when they met, not even when we walked down to the gate and Matthew caught her. Woody was so laid-back. I think Lola and Woody will get on okay. I don't see any dramas there at all.

After we'd walked about 400 meters down the road, we went to turn back. But before we did, I asked Hayley if I could work Woody in harness. I put Woody's harness on, and we proceeded to lead everyone back home and into the garden. When we got close to where the chair in the garden was, Hayley quickly walked in front of us. I said to Woody "follow Hayley," then I gave him the second command - "to the chair". When I get to the chair I said, "good boy" and give him lots of pats. As soon as I sat down, I gave him the command to turn around and sit between my legs. That command is me tapping my hand against the inside of my knee. Woody settled in between my legs and sat quietly. This felt so very cool. He was lovely in harness. He wasn't as strong as most of the Guide Dogs I have had, but he still felt very nice in my hand and he worked really well, no sniffing.

He showed great leadership and gave me a lot of confidence.

Matthew put Lola away and we did a few walks out to the dressage arena with Matthew walking in front of Woody and I. I would just say to Woody, "Woody follow" and he would follow behind Matthew. He was really good at cornering, and he did great destination work.

We used the mounting block as a destination. While Matthew walked to the mounting block my first command was "Woody follow". As Matthew got closer to the Mounting Block my command changed to "Woody, to the mounting block." He was a legend. He went straight to the mounting block.

We stood out there and talked for a little while, then went back to the house. He did a great job navigating across the lawn and through the garden where I get lost all the time. Whoohoo, it was totally awesome.

We all sat and talked together for a little while longer. Woody sat quietly at my feet the entire time. Which was lovely. Hayley then put Woody on a long lead, and we practised getting Woody to come to me when I called him. This was very cool. He was quick coming to me when I called him. This made me feel quite confident that we would work well together.

He was already starting to bond with me. When he was with me, he wasn't looking to Hayley for direction. This was really awesome.

We then went inside and had a cup of tea, Woody again sat at my feet. Oh my heavens! He took up nearly all of the dining area. He really is one very, very, big dog. But once again, he was super relaxed, so chilled in fact, he fell asleep while Hayley, Matthew and I chatted.

Now keep in mind this was a test run and it all took only about 2.5 hours. But it was lovely. I look forward to the day Woody comes back and we get to start our training together.

So grab a cuppa while we wait for Woody to arrive.

Have you got that cuppa handy?
Drum roll... Woody is here! Our training is about to start.

Read all about our exciting adventures in our next book titled:
Guide Dog Woody, Lola & The Blind Chick.

*

THE END

Wow, haven't we discovered so much joy, love, and hope. Sometimes all we hear about in the news is hate. But there is so much love in the world.

This book is so much more than a biography of my life. At its core it is about friendship and the amazing things we can achieve when we work together. I couldn't have created these pages for you without my friends. Thank you beautiful people: Jacqueline Thompson, Emily Blackburn, Lee Manny (Mother-In-Law Extraordinaire), Belinda Crawford, Katie Classon and Bill Classon, my beautiful family, Noni McCarthy, Prue Crichton, ... to name but a few whose conversations and love are the fabric of these pages.

No one comes into our life without making a difference in some way, shape or form. Thanks to all those who have reached out to me and shared their heart, their love, their dreams, their aspirations with me. Thank you for the difference you have made to my life. This book is for you.

To my wonderful friends on social media thank you, thank you. Your encouragement empowers me.

Thank you to my wonderful husband Matthew for believing in my dreams, for your love and endless support. A special thankyou to our contraceptive cat, Thunder Paws. He curls up for cuddles between Matthew and I in bed each night! Thank you to my beautiful horse Lola and Angel Johno and all the four-legged friends I've shared precious time with.

Some may be gone, but all are never forgotten.

Right about now I'm reminded of words that came to me in an advert - for Johno! "Don't be put off by my size" it said, which I totally get given he wasn't a Shetland. How many people didn't bother to enquire about him as soon as they saw those few numbers, 18 3hh? How many people forgot that their good horsemanship skills apply to ALL horses, regardless of the horses' size?

I learnt so many life lessons from Johno. So much of what he gifted me had nothing to do with the size of his body, but everything to do with the size of his heart.

This is what I hope for you. That my autobiography helps you embrace being more open to someone or something, even if that first impression, like Johno's size, seems a bit overwhelming at first.

I am still working through Johno's passing. To do this I celebrate him by remembering our good times. Like you I know how it feels when something really horrible happens. But time really does heal.

So please pop back into these chapters whenever you'd like. Revisit the adventures that made your heart swell. Secure these passages into your long-term memory, so they're there anytime you need them.

And all the while you are doing that, I'll be there, sending you love and a big hug from wherever I am.

Loads of love and hugs to you.

*

Sometimes you look back and realize

that a very special person

passed through your life

and that person was

you!

It's never too late to

find that person again.

"Just one step at a time, is all it takes"
Mudgee, Eccles & I

"You never know what's around the corner.
It could be everything. Or it could be nothing.
You keep putting one foot in front of the other,
and then one day you look back,
and you've climbed a mountain."
Tom Hiddleston

Front & Back Cover Design:

Belinda Crawford,

www.DesignedByBoots.com

Front Cover Image:

Guide Dog Eccles, Sue-Ellen Lovett & mare Mudgee

Back Cover Image:

Cascador, Sue-Ellen Lovett & Guide Dog Amani,

©Noni McCarthy,

www.SixtyByTwenty.com.au

Various Images:

©Prue Crichton,

www.2CPhotography.com.au

Edited by:

Jacqueline Thompson,

www.EQUUS101.com

Emily Blackburn

Proofread by:

Lee Manny